Degrees of Grace

To Mayfonen & Nellie
Thank you for your
support. In all things,
may God bless you abun-
dantly.

Marcelle Day Payne
_M_

Degrees of Grace

Marcelle Morgan Payne

Vine &
Branch
Publishing

Biblical references and scriptures are taken from The King James Version of the Holy Bible.

Published by:

Vine &
Branch
Publishing
P. O. Box 713
Marietta, GA 30061

Cover illustration and design by:
Lydell A. Jackson, Jaxon Communications, LLC

ISBN 0-9755004-5-7
Library of Congress Control Number: 2004108588

ACKNOWLEDGEMENTS

This book is dedicated to God who performs miracles in my life everyday. You are and will always be the source and substance of my existence. It is through this book that I honor You. I pray that You are pleased with what I have done for I love You with all my heart, my soul, my mind, and my possessions. For all that You have given me; this is my gift to You.

To my mother for loving me enough to give me roots and loving me even more to give me wings. Your legacy continues to live in me and I know you are setting new heights in Heaven. I love you with the all that is in me. I miss you desperately.

To my son, Matthew who left this Earth far too soon. You are the grandson my mother can now love in Heaven. I did not have you long, but I loved you a lifetime in only eight hours. You and your grandmother are the angels that watch over me.

To my son, Julian who is the light of my heart and the center of my life. You taught me how to play and laugh at myself. Thank you for allowing me to love you. I am proud to be your mom. You are a beautiful, intelligent, loving and happy child. You are my greatest gift!

And last, but not least, to my husband, Anthony who has inspired, encouraged, and loved me through all of my complex moods. He is the epitome of a man who is strong yet sensitive, loving, and patient. Thanks for walking this journey with me. I promise to give you paradise.

Many people are responsible for motivating me along this journey and ensuring a successful and safe arrival at my destination. I would like to thank the following parts of me who are also my friends. They are listed in no respective order. Tee C. Royal, Jamise L. Dames, AngelaMichelle Smith, Rena Finney, Linda Dominique Grosvenor, T. C. Matthews, Carla Curtis, Peggy Eldridge-Love, Cherlyn Michaels, Evelyn Palfrey, Tina Brooks McKinney, Candace Cottrell, Shunda Leigh, and Lydell Jackson. To Jonita Haynes and Marjorie Bryant, two marvelously mature women who have guided me with their years of wisdom and love. To the Payne family, I am indebted to your unwavering support—Amos, Doris, Allen, Clay, Jackie, Tim, Alexis, Brook, Jordan, Terrell, Karla, Zharia, Zakia, and Dexter. To the Hanson family, Rollie, Donnie, Michael, Lisa, Michael Jr., and Kyle. To my sisters in the spirit who are the best friends anyone could ask for Theresa Morgan Walser, Donna Freeman, Jacque Ross and Carolyn Johnson. If I have forgotten anyone, please know that it was not intentional for I am a better person because you have touched my life.

To My Readers

This book is fiction as are some of the best parts of life. Our lives are scripts, which are written and rewritten, some true, some not so true in an effort to discover what works for us. That which is "not true" is not always a lie, quite often; it is the script that we have written for ourselves through the erroneous perceptions and opinions of others as they are reflected upon us. This script is rehearsed until it is manifested in our lives. We memorize these behaviors until the reflection that others see becomes our truth. But by then, we find ourselves locked in a box that is easier to get into than out of. The key to escape is recognizing when it is time to bury that which no longer gives life and when it is time to resurrect it.

This journey of exploration is one we must travel if we are to have any substantial significance in life. Sometimes we are willing drivers and other times we are just along for the ride. If we continue the search, we find the hidden reservoir within that has been and will always be there, if we choose to tap into its power. The fundamental nature of our being—spirit, truth and inherent wisdom should prevent us from settling for anything less than what we are destined to have or who we are purposed to be. Unfortunately, we realize this only when all else has failed. We are then forced to look inward after we have exhausted all other avenues. When we take an introspective look, we uncover the exquisite treasures living deep within the recesses of us all. What we do with our inner treasures is up to us. We can either polish them to brilliant perfection or let them continue to be covered and subsequently, decay.

When perseverance and determination are combined with God's omnipotent power, an impenetrable force is created which protects, uplifts, prospers, and inspires.

May you always move from one degree of grace to another and may God bless you on your journey. Thank you for your support.

PROLOGUE

Satan sat on his dilapidated, charred stool surrounded by the lake of fire. Not long ago, he had a choice of willing souls to do his bidding, but lately, there were not many from which to choose. Of course, there were the brutally special ones like Jeffrey Dahmer, snipers, or mothers who killed their young as the small voices begged for life, but these were becoming scarce, and the thought disturbed Satan. Sighing heavily, he placed his chin into cupped hands while drumming fingers against his cheeks. His idle mind became his own workshop, and he did not like playing against himself.

It was amazing to him that people were so vainly ignorant of the active role he played in their lives, and of his existence. He thought it absurd that people believed there would be an actual war between good and evil. Little did they know, the battleground was their mind and that is where he would engrave his mark, the mark of the beast. Unknowingly, their disbelief gave him absolute access to infiltrate their lives and gain complete control. But he also observed more people creating an intimate relationship with The Almighty God and he could hear their incessant prayers regarding the chaos in the world. They had grown tired of the senseless violence, hatred, and evil that ran rampant in the streets. It seemed these believers felt society had reached the end of its moral rope, and there was nowhere to go except to the beginning, which started with God.

Satan snickered and shook his head. He found the weakness of humans amusing and the ease of manipulating them laughable. Knowing the end of his reign was imminent, immediate action was needed to maintain control of the world and give him a much needed reprieve from his boredom.

He gazed upward seeing scenes of people's lives passing before him, but he caught a glimpse of one that made him retract his steps and take a second look. An older woman was lying in bed, apparently in the last stage of her life. Her face grimaced intermittently with pain, but there was a peace that resonated from her. She was ready for the next phase, and as she accepted her fate, a slight smile appeared on her face.

A beautiful young lady sat beside her with an open Bible on her lap, gently stroking the hand of the sick woman as she spoke to her. Reaching slowly toward the ill woman's face, her hands lovingly caressed the soft, dewy cheek, while her fingers quivered slightly and lingered, content to spend the night.

A tear slid down the face of the bedridden matron as though she could sense the other's sorrow. Trying to offer comfort to the young woman sitting beside her, another tear silently escaped just as she discovered her voice had. Knowing he could not claim the one near death, his excitement was not abated, but gained momentum as he was moved by the intensity of the young lady's blue-gray eyes. What Satan forgot is that God keeps a few secrets to Himself.

Chapter One

"Love is like a garden—if it is not cultivated, it cannot be harvested."
African Proverb

𝕸ontana St. Claire jumped from her sleep not sure what day it was. Turning her head toward the nightstand, she glanced at the clock and saw that it was 7:30 in the morning. Her eyes enlarged and she sat up like a tightly wound spring.

"Oh, man, I can't believe I overslept again!"

Realizing it was too late to panic, she fell back onto the bed with a thud. A few minutes later, she stretched wiggling her toes, and dragged herself out of bed. Hurriedly, Montana ran to awaken Chesne, her daughter. Their Shih Tzu, Scottie, was lying on the bed next to her.

"Chesne, it's time to get up," Montana said, shaking her gently.

"Not yet, Mommy."

"Yes, now. We've only got an hour. You know how many times you change clothes." Montana watched Chesne drifting back to sleep and started tickling her. Chesne wiggled in response and reluctantly sat up.

"Let's roll."

"I'm up." Chesne raised her arms pulling them taut over her head. Dropping them, she slowly stood moving with nailed feet to the bathroom.

Montana returned to her room and took a long look in the mirror, gazing into affectionate blue-gray eyes on a warm vanilla canvas faintly dotted with freckles.

I am thirty-five years old. When will I learn that I will never conform to this world including punching somebody else's clock? Why I don't just start my own business is beyond me. But even as the thought crossed her mind, she already knew the answer. It was the security of a paycheck that kept her in the rat race. At some point, she had to take responsibility for the decisions she had made that placed her on this path and she decided today would be her moment of change.

From this day forward with God's guidance, I will direct my life according to His plan for me and will not accept anything less.

Montana turned on the TV and walked into the bathroom, as she reached into the shower, she heard Camille Davis on Action News.

"And this just in. On Thursday night, Raymond Kirkpatrick walked into The Morning Star Baptist Church where his estranged wife, Beverly, was attending Bible study class. Kirkpatrick shot and killed his wife; their six-year old son, and another church member. A few hours earlier, he had also shot and killed his mother-in-law, Gertrude Finley."

"Oh great. Nothing like violent news about people killing one another to start my day. Have people always been like this or is this a new form of crazy?" Montana wondered aloud, shaking her head sadly. She thanked God she had never been in a relationship like that, though she was close once. Hearing this story brought back memories.

Before she left San Diego a few years ago, Montana worked as a manager in retail banking at Premier Bank and became close friends with Diane Stephens, Nadine Moore, and Vanessa Harrison. One hot Santa Ana day, they decided to go to Magic Mountain. After Diane pulled into a parking space that seemed to be an eternity away, they caught the shuttle to the entrance of the amusement park. Nadine was the first to notice the man already seated on the bus whose head nearly touched the roof. His cinnamon-colored skin was warm like the sun and black wavy hair graced his head. He had hypnotic mink-brown eyes that actively sought to captivate its object's soul. Bearing broad shoulders and protruding pectoral muscles that were the result of obvious dedication to a fit body, he sat with four young boys who were dwarfed by his presence. The guy nodded as the ladies walked by, sitting a few rows behind him.

"Girl, he is fine," Nadine said in a hushed tone, ready to pounce.

Montana looked at the man and the boys with him. "Yeah, he might be, but he's got four kids with him and that's too much of a package for me." The shuttle came to a stop at the front of the park. The women got off and headed toward the entrance.

Just as Montana turned to say something to Diane, she bumped into the guy on the bus.

"Oh, excuse me." *My goodness this man is really tall,* she thought.

"No problem. I'm glad I got a chance to introduce myself. Hello, I'm Tony Delacroix, and these are my nephews." He extended his hand.

She noticed his voice possessed a slight Louisiana timbre. "Hi, nice to meet you guys," Montana said to the four boys.

"Hi," they chorused as they stared making her blush.

Tony pointed to a tree near the ticket booth. "You guys can wait over there."

The boys reluctantly walked to the tree, dragging their feet as though they were bolted to balls of lead.

"Man, did you see her? She is tight." She overhead the eldest say.

"Naw, man she is phat. You see her eyes? You think they hers?" Another one asked. Montana smiled, embarrassed.

"You'll have to excuse them, sometimes they . . . " Tony hesitated, searching for the words.

"Act like boys," Montana said, finishing the sentence for him. They both laughed.

"You've got a beautiful smile," Tony said. "I don't mean to be so forward, but I caught a glimpse of you as you boarded the bus and wanted to meet you. Do you think I might have a chance to get to know you?"

"I appreciate the offer, but I'm spending the day with my friends. It was nice to meet you though. I hope you and your nephews have a good time. This is a great place."

Montana ran to catch up with her friends, almost frightened of what would happen if she did not leave. Her heart pumped hard as if she were racing toward the finish line of a triathlon. Tony was not easily discouraged and loosely followed her through the park until she conceded and gave him her work number.

Tony's appearance often caught the attention of female admirers, but the only admirer he was interested in was Montana. Her beliefs about her body and her behavior impressed him and he was even more enchanted with her indifference to how she looked. Their relationship moved like a rolling river and she often found herself breathless. Three months later, he proposed. It was too soon, but she loved him and more than anything wanted to start a family. Tony seemed to possess everything she could ever need or want in a man and he was honest, faithful, and adoring.

A few weeks after their engagement, they met for dinner. His eyes sought hers desperately to plead their case before he spoke. "Baby, I need to be with you. I want to make love to you so badly. Our relationship is great but it's missing that connection. I need to touch your body as you lay next to mine. We are almost married. I can please you, but you've got to give me a chance. I promise to search every crevice of your body until I discover its secret to complete satisfaction."

Montana had to admit that his last statement ignited a flame within her, but she could control the temptation. Thanks to the table separating them and the smile she envisioned on Satan's face if she surrendered. "I can understand your body has needs, but as much as I love you, I love God even more, and I will not jeopardize my relationship with Him for anyone. I am touched and I feel what you feel, but I can't. I won't give in."

Tony reached across the table and caressed her hands. "I can't force you to be intimate with me and if that is what you want," he sighed heavily, "I'll wait. I love you more than I have loved anyone in my life."

"I know you do, baby. I also know that it is because of your respect and love for me that you are waiting."

"No. See you still don't understand. I *really* love you, and if I ever saw you with another man, even if you were just giving him directions, I would kill him *and* I would kill you, too."

His words iced Montana's blood, and she shivered from the chill. Tiptoeing around him for the remainder of the evening was difficult, but she did not want him to know she was frightened. The next week, she moved to another apartment, changed her number, and quit her job. It was the last time she ever saw him and she was thankful for her escape.

She heard the remainder of the news and was moved by the death of Beverly Kirkpatrick including the torment that everyone in this woman's life had to endure. Montana shuddered to think how close she had come to living the same nightmare.

"Thank You, God, for protecting me." She thought of Satan's influence in the world and the evil that it produced. "And as for *you*, you slug, your day is coming."

"My day is already here," he responded. "Just look around you. People concentrate on bunnies and eggs instead of remembering the reason for Easter. What do these things have to do with the resurrection of their Savior? They don't challenge tradition or acknowledge responsibility, leaving it to the modern day Pharisees and Sadducees to speak for them. They just accept it as truth since society has also given it a stamp of approval. People don't reverence Him anymore. Their Savior comes in the form of a new outfit or a pair of shoes. Look at the way they celebrate Christmas. Spending enormous amounts of money and getting more wrapped in the gift than the giver." He looked at Montana admiring her beauty recalling another he had tried to possess and lost. "That won't happen this time."

Realizing time was slipping by as quickly as ice melts in the sun; she hurriedly jumped in the shower. The memories and tragic story had dampened her mood. As the water flowed down her curvaceous five-two frame, it soothed her weary spirit.

Montana languidly lathered the lavender gel on her ample breasts, and gently rolled the loofah across her semi-flat stomach. Warm vapors enveloped her, and as she relaxed, she thought of Garrett Rivers, her first love and the man of her dreams—or at least he used to be.

How ironic that after all these years, I would run into him. Just when I had finally gotten him out of my system, she thought. Past emotions welled up inside of her. Surprisingly, she was glad to see him, but as she began to reminisce, anger seared the edges of her thoughts.

How could he not respond to my letter or calls? We have a child together and yet he ignored Chesne and me as if we never existed. Would he accept his child now that they had met again? What excuse would he give for not being a part of their daughter's life? Forgiven, yes, but forgotten, no way. A dull ache started to form at the base of her neck. *Don't expect too much. A leopard's spots never change into stripes,* she cautioned herself.

Finishing up in the shower, she recognized that her heart had hardened against Garrett. *Who are you to judge someone? Are you without sin?* She wondered thoughtfully. *If you see him, ask him. Don't assume the worse even though it's probably true. Now, snap out of this! You've got to get to work.* She shampooed her chestnut brown hair quickly and toweled herself dry. Her waist length hair was much easier to style and blow-dry with her new layered cut.

"Chesne, are you dressed?"

"Yes, Mommy. I'm waiting on you."

"I'll be ready in a few minutes. Honey, take Scottie out for a walk. I know he's about to burst."

"Alright. Do I have time to eat breakfast?"

"If you hurry."

"Okay."

Montana looked through her closet and decided on the navy suit with the asymmetrical slit on the left side of the skirt. She applied Jean Paul Gaultier cream to her body and spritzed on the cologne. The smell was indescribable and renewed her senses. The longer she wore it, the more wonderful the fragrance became.

Dressing quickly, she applied lipstick, and walked downstairs to the kitchen where Chesne was rinsing out her cereal bowl.

"You look pretty, Mommy."

"Thanks, baby. So do you." Montana turned on the house alarm, and they dashed out the door. Suddenly, she remembered that she had not gotten any coffee. Looking at her watch, she realized she did not have time and started the car. Coffee would have to wait until she got to her office.

Quickly merging onto I-20 east, she headed for Woodlawn, Chesne's school. The Atlanta skyline displayed the sun's radiant reflection as it illuminated the buildings making them look like bright golden nuggets before her. The light lifted her spirit and she felt a release of anxiety. The edges of tension still remained and she turned the radio to Jazz Flavors 107.5 to soften those that remained.

Chesne sighed loudly and Montana started laughing. She knew Chesne thought jazz was boring and something that only really old people like her mother enjoyed. "One day, you'll appreciate it."

"I don't think that day will ever come."

"We'll see."

Montana pulled up to the entrance of Woodlawn Preparatory.

"Good-bye, Mommy. Have a good day. I love you."

"I love you, too, baby. Have a great day at school. I'll see you this evening."

Chesne opened the door, placing her foot on the pavement when she was stopped by Montana's touch.

"Hey, where's my kiss?" Montana protested.

Chesne kissed her quickly and got out. She walked toward the door and turned to wave good-bye before she entered.

Once Montana was sure Chesne was safely inside, she pulled off. *I've got to do better about getting to work. If I weren't such a great worker, they would have probably fired me by now.*

Montana had worked at Lafayette Drake for a little over three years. Becoming the director of operations was not what she wanted even when they offered her a salary of $165,000 with a ten-percent annual bonus of the company's profits. To ensure her acceptance, they also promised a 15% contribution of her salary by the company to her 401(k). She was an exemplary employee and though it was an attractive package, she still felt her employer was getting a bargain.

During her six-month review, her boss, Paul Blackburn, promised her a senior vice president position if she continued her outstanding performance, but she was not sure if he would live up to that promise. It had been a while since they discussed the position, and it was time to talk about it again. She inhaled deeply in an effort to release the apprehension she felt about bringing up the subject. Silently she said, *"The Lord is the strength of my life, of whom shall I be afraid?"*

God put me here and when it's time for me to leave, He'll place me somewhere else. What is it people say? 'Don't sweat the small stuff'. Well, honey, consider me on ice 'cause I'm chilling. She thought about what she said and it was so corny, it made her laugh. "Girl, you are definitely losing your mind."

Montana scanned the radio stations, stopping when she heard a discussion about black men dating white women on the *Tom Joyner Morning Show*. They were telling jokes about interracial dating and the ensuing issues that can arise. They talked about O.J. Simpson and the upcoming Kobe Bryant trial. Montana inadvertently slipped off the armor of God and in an instant, Satan planted a seed. *That's what happens when you have crackers in your bed and I'm not talking about Keeblers,* she thought. As soon as she realized what she was thinking, she reprimanded herself. "Where did that come from? I'm not a bigot. If someone made a remark like that about me, I would be angry. Why would I say something like that about someone else?"

Satan was thrilled with his success and snickered wickedly. Racism, among many others was one of his most dependable devices.

Montana looked toward the sky and silently prayed. *Lord, forgive me, I was out of line and out of order. There is no excuse for such vicious hatred. I can never be unprotected. Satan sits waiting for an opportunity.* She shook her head and continued, *Please tame my tongue today and allow it to speak Your truth, not mine. Let me be a blessing to someone and allow someone to be a blessing to me. I sure could use it.*

Montana pulled into the parking deck looking for a space. Hearing a car start, she drove in that direction. It took the driver so long to move that Montana wondered if she was reading an instruction manual on how to back up.

"I don't have time for this today." She quickly pulled into the space as the lady finally backed out. "God bless you, molasses."

She walked to the elevator and got on. Thankfully, no one was on it and she did not have to make unimportant small talk. Patience and tolerance were not her strengths, but she was learning.

She stepped onto the plaza level of the office building and greeted Everett Dixon, the morning security guard. "Hi, Everett. How are you?"

"Fine, Ms. St. Claire." His voice contradicted the words.

"Are you sure? You don't sound fine."

"There is a lot to learn as a new Christian. Habits die hard, but it'll be okay."

"It *will* work out. As long as you have breath in your body, there is always hope and a chance for change. Don't let a problem overwhelm you so much that you can't think about a solution. God has faith in you, and you should have it in yourself. It will be just fine. You'll see. Everything you will ever need is already within you by His grace."

"Thanks, Ms. St. Claire. You are a real inspiration."

"Please call me Montana. I'm not the inspiration, but thanks. Just be strong and seek His wisdom. He'll show you the way."

Montana smiled. She heard the elevator chime and walked toward it. "Have a good day and remember, trust Him," she said as she stepped inside.

She was grateful her mood had changed. It always uplifted her when she could help someone else instead of pitying herself which was a skill she thankfully had not refined. Suddenly, she felt this was going to be a great day.

Satan was exceedingly disgusted. "How can anyone be that caring? It's unnatural. But if she's that committed to Him, I can only imagine what she will do for me. She and I will make a magnificent team. My destiny is becoming clearer. We will conquer the world under the guise of bringing people to God. Oh, the thought of it just thrills me. All those lost souls—wanting, begging to come to me.

"I need to plan this carefully. She is not easily deceived, but I'll think of something, I always do. I can't scare her away before she knows how wonderful I am. She doesn't know what she's missing. I can put some fire into her," he said, laughing at the irony.

CHAPTER TWO

She exited the elevator and turned toward her office. As she entered the lobby, the décor never failed to abbreviate her breath. The furnishings were opulent, but not overwhelming. She smiled when she saw Stephanie Braxton, the receptionist, organizing her area. "Good morning, Steph."

"Hey, Montana! Ooh girl, you looking sharp today! You know you need to give me that suit."

Montana laughed moving to the side of Stephanie's desk who continued to admire her outfit until she saw her shoes. "And give me those 'gators while you're at it."

"As much as these things cost, I ought to have lifetime adoption rights to their offspring."

Stephanie laughed. "You are so crazy, but I feel you. When I grow up, I'm gonna be just like you."

Montana looked at her. "No, you'll be better than me. You never stop improving yourself, and that's the secret."

Stephanie looked at Montana, grateful she had noticed. "Thanks, girl. You're always in my corner."

"And I always will be. Sistas got to stick together. I gotta go now, but I'll talk to you later."

Montana turned on her lamps as she walked into her office. She thought of Stephanie and remembered when she had interviewed her for the receptionist position. During the interview, Montana learned that though Stephanie grew up in an impoverished neighborhood of Atlanta, she managed to maintain a 4.0 grade point average while working a full-time job to help her family. These days that area would be called the "hood" and it seemed Stephanie constantly fought back to keep the hood from hoodwinking her.

Stephanie was a tall, slender woman with high cheekbones and a flawless complexion, which housed chocolate brown eyes. Her chic short hairstyle framed her face and complimented every facial feature.

Montana was impressed with Stephanie's appearance, determination, and drive to succeed. She could not resist the opportunity to reach out especially when she saw Stephanie making an effort to help herself. Firmly believing it was her obligation to reach back and help pull someone else up; Montana frequently mentored to Stephanie and provided her with opportunities for financial gain. Not that she was rich, she was a long way from that, but she embraced what her grandfather used to say, "With what measure you give, it is given unto you."

After watering her plants, Montana plopped down in her chair, settling in for the day. She owned a PDA, but found that writing in her planner painted a mental picture she could remember. Scanning her calendar for the day, she yawned and felt the need for coffee increase.

"Oh man, I forgot about the weekly status meeting! I'm supposed to give my presentation today." In an exasperated breath she said, "This is going to be a long day."

She stood and walked to the break room to get a cup of coffee. As she entered the room, she saw her coworker, Heather Maitland. "Oh, I see you *finally* made it in," Heather said in her usual offensive tone.

Do I really need this crap today? Montana thought. "And good morning to you, Ms. Sunshine."

Heather waited for her to strike back, but Montana controlled her tongue resisting the temptation to flog it on Heather. Confident that she could rile her, Heather said, "Wonder what keeps you up so late at night?"

Montana could almost hear Heather salivating like a rabid dog trying to obtain any information that could be used against her. Not that there was any to get. Her life was mundane, but Heather didn't need to know that and as far as Montana was concerned, the less Heather knew about her the better.

"Well, I hate to break up all this sistahood and everything, but I need to get to work. Have a good day." Montana exited the room gracefully. She had run into people like Heather before, and the only way to handle them was to remain emotionless and non-defensive.

I swear that girl is going to catch me on the wrong day at the wrong time and I will have to kick her into another world. Lord, please help her find peace and keep her out of my way, Montana silently prayed.

Heather was born into a family that struggled financially and emotionally. She was not the smartest or the most popular student in her school and it took a valiant effort for her to maintain a C average. The youngest of seven children, she grew up poor in Union Point, a small rural community in eastern Georgia. Things were always tight not to mention the horribly cramped space of housing nine people in a three-bedroom house.

They, along with other poor white families, lived in a predominately black section of town where housing was cheaper. Heather became friends with the black children in her neighborhood and grew close to them. However, during the seventies, the economic status of blacks rose at an unprecedented rate and due to this newly found success, many of her black friends moved away. Heather was a misfit among the other whites at school and now the blacks were doing better than her own family, which caused Heather to grow bitter, resenting blacks and any progress they achieved.

Shortly after she graduated from high school, Heather worked as a waitress at Waffle House and became friends with Carol Miller who also worked there. Although Carol and Heather never discussed it, their opinions and views of the world confirmed that they grew up in the same environment, which created an immediate bond. They pretended their childhood was great, but it's hard to fool a hillbilly when she's standing on the same hill.

One day at work, Carol saw an issue of *InStyle* that a customer left and called Heather over. Looking through it, they envied the possessions the people pictured seemed to have. Heather grabbed it from her and began flipping through the pages until she saw an article entitled *Jumpstarting Your Career*. There was a picture of a woman with flawless ivory skin and shoulder-length blond hair wearing a navy suit and pearl jewelry. Heather squealed with excitement. "I want to look just like that, but I can't afford the hair salons they have in Atlanta."

"Well, I know this girl at Betty's House of Style. She might be able to cut your hair like that. I don't know how good she is with cutting hair like yours though."

Heather looked deflated. Her curly espresso-brown hair and olive complexion made her look a little different, which added to her insecurity. "Carol, do you think Betty could dye my hair blond, too?"

After working at Waffle House for a year and a half, Heather decided to leave the restaurant, her hometown of Union Point, and her past behind. She moved to Atlanta and created a new identity. To improve herself, she enrolled in secretarial courses and took classes in English and public speaking, but even with that, it was hard for her to stop saying "fixin' to" and "reckon".

Heather had been hired as a secretary with Lafayette Drake four years earlier, and she was still a secretary. She applied for higher positions, but was never selected. There was always someone more qualified, and in more than a few cases, the more qualified candidate turned out to be a black woman.

Realizing, she still held bitter feelings toward the childhood friends that she felt deserted her, she vowed to never allow anyone to outdo her again, especially someone black.

Montana reread her presentation for the tenth time before going into the meeting. She knew she had to cover every possible scenario for the Board to accept her proposal and initiate an internship program she titled BASES (Building Aptitude and Skills for Economic Success). It would give at-risk youths a chance to gain experience in the consulting industry. With Lafayette Drake being Atlanta's leading consulting firm, Montana wanted the experience to open doors and provide these teens with a way to get out of the hood mentally and physically. It was heartbreaking to see what hopelessness did to a person's spirit.

Emphasizing how this internship would greatly improve the company's image within the community and increase the level of pride employees felt, she was confident it would be approved. Of course, she had the numbers to show how much it would save the company in benefits, training, and compensation. With the horrible dragging incident and subsequent death of James Byrd in Jasper, Texas, racial profiling, and wrongful incarceration of innocent blacks; healing needed to take place, and it had to start with white America taking the lead.

Montana swallowed hard to keep the bile that was rising to her throat down as she thought of the unjust suffering of her people. She shook her head, trying to clear it and headed for the conference room.

When the meeting was over, Paul approached Montana to congratulate her. "As usual, you have outdone yourself. I have to present this to the Board, but I have every confidence it will be approved."

"Thank you, Paul. By the way, I would like to meet with you to discuss the executive position we spoke about during my six-month review."

"Uh, of course, Montana. I would as well, but I'm on my way to a Board meeting. Can we talk about it later?"

"Sure, Paul. It shouldn't take more than a few minutes to iron out the monetary details since you promised me the position. I really appreciate how you consistently live up to your word. That is such an admirable quality."

Paul narrowed his eyes, smiling nervously. He admired and detested Montana's ability to elicit a moral response by virtuous inquiry. "Well, I've got to go. We'll talk later."

"Okay, Paul."

Montana thanked everyone as they came to commend her on the job she had done. She saw Paul shake hands with the CFO who stood about six feet in front of her.

Seeing Heather approach her, Montana readied herself, well aware that any wish for goodwill was more out of political protocol or deadly entrapment than sincerity.

"Congratulations, Montana. It seems you have succeeded again."

"Why, thank you, Heather."

"I wish a program like that was around for me when I needed it."

"I would be glad to help you any way I can, Heather," Montana sincerely offered.

Satan cupped Heather's chin in his hand and smiled. Heather's spirit responded in devotion.

"I doubt that someone like *you* could *ever* help me."

Montana was taken aback, but not for long. Looking at Heather with embers of fire burning in her eyes, she whispered, "Look, Heather, I was offering my help not out of pity, but because I have a genuine concern for you as a human being. Obviously, I was greatly mistaken about your being human. You are a bitter, pathetic, empty shell who has no joy in her life except to destroy the lives of others. You are a vessel with a hole in it, you carry nothing. Try to plug up that hole that is supposed to encompass your brain, will you? Air is seeping out everywhere, and the stench is unbearable."

Heather looked at Montana angrily. "Well, I never . . ."

But before she could finish, Montana interrupted. "Well, honey it shows." She swirled around like a tornado destroying everything in its path and walked away leaving Heather too dumbfounded to speak.

Heather was about to leave when Paul walked up to her. "I overhead your comments, Heather. That kind of attitude will not be tolerated if you want to continue to work here. Do you understand?" He didn't wait for a response, but left for his meeting.

Heather felt madder and sadder than ever. She tried to bore holes into Montana's back as she saw her walk into the break room with Stephanie following close behind.

Stephanie took one look at the change in Montana's eyes and knew something was awry. "What is wrong with you?"

"I had to straighten Heather out."

"Well, it's about time. She rakes you over the coals every chance she gets."

"Yeah, I know. I have tried to be nice to her, but I've reached my limit. The next time she tries to pull something like that in front of Paul, I am going to kick her behind straight into hell. No roundtrip available."

"Girl, no she didn't try to do something with Paul there?" Stephanie shook her head. "That girl's got more balls than I thought."

"And the next time she does that, she'll be choking on them."

"Wait. Before you go postal, this guy with a deep, sexy voice called for you. He didn't leave his name, but said he would call back. He sounded so disappointed, I almost told him that I could ease his pain . . . um, um, um."

Montana laughed, "Girl, get your mind out of that man's pants."

"Is he as fine as he sounds?"

"No. Finer."

"Then why are you standing here talking to me? Go get that man, 'cause, honey, somebody will." Stephanie shooed her away.

"I'm going, I'm going." Montana knew who it was since she rarely received personal calls at work.

Returning to her office, Montana remembered the day she bumped into Garrett. She had been stranded on I-285 inspecting her flattened tire when she heard a car pull up behind her. On instinct, she quickly stood and got in her car, giving her some degree of safety. Hearing the car's engine silenced, she looked in her side view mirror and saw the door open, shocked to see Garrett stepping out. Her heart started beating frantically making her hands shake as she tried unsuccessfully to steady them on the steering wheel. *Of all the people in the world to stop. What am I going to say? Calm down. Act like he's a stranger. After all these years, he basically is.* She rolled down the window as he approached her car.

She turned toward him. "Hello, Garrett."

"I thought that was you. I don't believe it! What are you doing here?"

"Held against my will."

"Still have that sharp tongue I see."

"And the mind that goes with it."

"Looks like you have a flat tire. Do you have a spare?"

Montana fought hard to guard her tongue. "Yes, it's in the trunk." She opened the door and walked with him to the rear of her car. Turning around to tell him something, she noticed he was gone. She looked in the direction of his car and saw him place his jacket inside. Walking toward her, he rolled up his sleeves and she saw his muscles flex in response. *Have mercy.* She restrained the emotional tug she felt pull on her heart. *Sometimes dead things are better off buried.*

Garrett intently looked at her. "So how have you been doing?"

"Fine and you."

"Better now. You would not believe it."

"I'm sure I wouldn't."

"Still got a thorn up your butt I see."

"Better than being a butt." She stopped and took a deep breath. "Look, I appreciate you stopping to help me, but I'm sure you've got a lot of things to do. I'll change it myself. You can go."

"Okay, fine. I understand, but I'm not going to leave you like this. We don't have to talk and it's probably better that we don't."

After he changed the tire, she thanked him and they chatted briefly. Anger and need gripped her intermittently. She did not believe in such things as coincidences and knew there was a reason he had unexpectedly entered her life again. She gave him her number the third time he asked, partly because she never stopped loving him, but mainly because of her responsibility to her daughter. She hoped in time, they could be cordial enough to each other so that Chesne could finally get to know her father. Montana would not admit it, but she wondered if she and Garrett could ever have the kind of love that they had in the beginning. She did not know, but she had to swallow her pride and find out. Pride could never fulfill her destiny or her bed. She owed it to Chesne and herself.

Montana picked up the phone to call Garrett. Anne Weitz, Garrett's secretary answered.

"Mr. Rivers' office, this is Anne."

"Hello, Anne, this is Montana St. Claire."

"How are you, Montana? Garrett has told me so much about you."

Montana smiled glad to know that he had spoken about her. For Garrett, that meant a lot because as she remembered, there was a rigid line he drew between his professional and personal lives and to her knowledge, they rarely crossed.

"I'm fine and you?"

"I'm fine, but I'm glad it's Friday. I'm a little tired," Anne said.

"I know the feeling. I haven't left work on time in weeks, but I can't give up just because I'm tired. I do my work unto God who thankfully, never gets tired of working for me."

"You're right. Let me get Garrett for you. It was great talking to you. Have a good day."

"Thank you. You have a great day, too."

Anne pressed the intercom button pleased to find that Montana sounded as warm as Garrett had described her.

In the silence, Montana's heart started to beat a little more rapidly with anticipation.

"Hello there!" Garrett said a few minutes later. He was ecstatic that she had returned his call. For months, he had tried to show her that he had changed. He could not buy her forgiveness and was becoming anxious, fully aware that only time eased the pain of betrayal—time and prayer. His most important concern was trying to ascertain if Montana would give him an opportunity to love her again.

"Well, there's a familiar voice."

"How are you?" he asked.

"I'm fine. I understand you called."

"I was calling to make sure you weren't going to stand me up like you usually do."

"Now, Garrett, would I do that?" Montana was still apprehensive. It was taking more effort than she imagined to rebuild the trust that was so prematurely and abruptly blown away.

"Not only would you, but you have. We've talked off and on for the past few months and I haven't seen you since you had the flat tire."

"I'm sorry, but I've had some things I've had to resolve in my life. You say you've changed and so far, you have given me no reason to doubt you, but it's still early and sometimes it pays to take the slow ride home."

"I understand. I can't excuse what I've done, there is no excuse, but I've tried to prove myself. So when do I get a chance to state my case?"

"Tonight and just for dinner."

"Okay, but did you have to dash my hopes so quickly? You know how to spoil it."

"I didn't think I was spoiling anything, unless *you* were cooking dinner."

"Oh, that was a cheap shot."

"Sorry, but you opened the door." Montana laughed, leaning back in her chair.

"And you just had to walk in."

"I've learned never to refuse a door when a man opens it."

"Very funny. I'll pick you up at eight. Is that okay?"

"That's fine."

Glancing at old pictures of the two of them that were placed around his office, he remembered when they were good. "I'll look forward to tonight then."

Montana was excited about seeing Garrett and was curious to see how things were between them. She had refused his offers of companionship long enough and thoughts of what might have been had haunted her since their breakup. Yes she was over the pain, the past, and even the scars had begun to heal, but her longing for him never dissipated. It was time to put this ghost to rest. She picked up the phone. "Steph, I'm outta here."

"What? It's only three-thirty. What's gotten into you?"

"I'm going to see a man about a mule." Mischief covered Montana's face.

"Or maybe, the man is hung like a mule," Stephanie said, laughing.

"Girl, you are so bad. I'll see you Monday."

CHAPTER THREE

"The path leads toward loved ones not thorns."
Duala Proverb

$\mathfrak{M}$ontana turned left on Lenox Road and merged onto Georgia 400 when she saw that the expressway had become an enormous parking lot.

"Ah, no, come on, not today. I can't believe the traffic in Atlanta. Rush hour is twenty-four hours a day." She brought her black vintage Porsche 356 convertible to a stop. Though she had owned it for five years, the car still looked and performed like it came off the showroom floor. She loved driving it as the wind caressed and tickled her face. It made her feel free to be touched by something so much larger than herself.

The previous owner had restored the car completely even reupholstering it in soft, buttery leather. When Montana sat in the driver's seat, it enveloped her like a warm embrace and she settled in comfortably. She looked over and saw a sparkling new Bentley convertible. *Owning one would be wonderful,* she thought, *but I'm too practical for something that could be destroyed in an instant. That's the problem with mobile homes.* She chuckled to herself until she realized that a Bentley could buy several houses for people in need. *When I make it,* she thought, *I will do my part to care for those who cannot take care of themselves by teaching them about my loving Shepherd.*

Montana's cell phone rang, jolting her from her thoughts.

"Hello."

"Hi, Mommy."

"Hey, Chesne. How are you?"

"I'm fine."

"How was school?"

"It was fun. Guess what? I was voted president of the whole school!"

"That's great! You will be fantastic! Are you at Olivia's?"

"Yes."

"Okay, I'm on my way home. I'll see you in a few minutes. I love you, baby."

"Love you, too."

Montana ended the call and placed the phone on the passenger's seat. She was grateful that Olivia was such a wonderful neighbor.

Olivia Doucette lived next door and was the best neighbor anyone could have. The two women quickly became friends finding common interests and opinions that bonded them. Olivia had been a wonderful comforter when Montana's mother died and was always there for her and Chesne. Olivia needed someone to love, and she and Chesne needed to be loved. Montana recalled Olivia telling her that she had always wanted children, but when she discovered she was unable to, her husband left her. It broke her heart and she had not wanted to marry again, but it left a gaping hole in her heart that needed to love.

Montana turned on the radio and "My First Love" was playing. *How appropriate,* she thought. Garrett was her first love, and after all that had happened between them, still she loved him. She had not locked her feelings away safely as she thought, nor had she successfully extinguished the fire that still burned in her heart for him. Shaking off the emotions like an unwanted chill, she did not need to concentrate on the past. It was the present and what it held that she was most concerned with.

Traffic finally started to move with tortoise speed. A song dedicated to mothers played next and made her think of her mother, Grace. There was an uncommon bond between them. Grace was her best friend and they did everything together. Montana took her mother on surprise trips for her birthday—Hawaii, Acapulco, and San Francisco. They enjoyed listening to jazz, attending the theater, and, of course, shopping. She missed her mother, especially their talks. Grace was such a phenomenal woman who possessed rich wisdom and compassion. It had been two years since her mother passed, but the pain of her loss was still sharp. What was even sharper than missing her mother was that Montana felt so alone in this world. If it were not for Chesne, there would be no one to whom Montana belonged. As badly as her relationship with Garrett ended, Chesne was the gift that was born of her heartache that did not seem so painful in comparison.

Montana marveled at how much of her parents and maternal grandparents comprised her personality. Her paternal grandparents died before she was ten and her father passed during her sophomore year at North Carolina A&T, but they left their mark on her life. Her memories of them were becoming harder to visualize and many times, she found herself making them up. A part of each of them was in her, and Montana was most proud of that. It was an honor and an obligation to respect her heritage by the way she lived.

She inherited the appreciation of fine things and the ability to bargain from her grandmother, and she got the loving, funny, spiritual, compassionate, eloquent, take-charge personality of her mother. From her father, she received the care and maintenance of her body, hair, and skin; and the love of truth and wisdom came from her grandfather.

Montana pulled into the driveway of her house in Historic West End. When she initially moved to Atlanta, she remembered seeing the beautiful old houses and knew this was where she wanted to live. It had a "welcome home" feeling that made her comfortable.

One Sunday, seeing an ad for a fixer-upper in the "Homes for Sale" section of the *Atlanta Journal Constitution,* she called to find out about it and was delighted to learn that it was in the West End area. She tried to maintain her composure as the Realtor described the house. It sounded perfect. The Realtor met her the next day and as soon as she walked through the door, Montana knew she was home.

Montana turned off the ignition and saw Olivia working in the garden. "Hello there," she called out as she walked toward her friend.

Olivia looked up. "Oh, hi, suga'."

"I was wondering, if you would mind watching Chesne tonight? I hate to spring this on you at the last minute, but I have a date."

"A date? You mean you know what a date is? Come on, let's go in." Montana reached out to help her. "Oh, leave me alone. I know it's been a while."

Olivia laughed as she stood, brushing off her knees. "A while? Child, you must be kidding? The last time you went out on a date, dirt had just been discovered." Olivia laughed while Montana pretended to be perturbed with her. "No, I don't mind at all. Chesne is a sweetie. In fact, it'll be my pleasure just to see you have some fun. Someone as young as you shouldn't be so serious." Olivia closed the door behind them.

"I have a lot of responsibilities, you know."

"Yes, I know, but don't forget you are responsible to yourself as well."

"You sound just like my mama. Well, I better hurry up if I don't want anymore cobwebs to grow ..."

"Honey, even *I* don't have that many cobwebs."

Montana gave her a menacing look then waved her away as she walked into the family room to check on Chesne. "Hi, baby. How are you?"

"Hi, Mommy. I'm fine." Chesne looked up from reading a biography about Langston Hughes.

"I need to talk to you. I have a date so I'm going to need you to stay with Olivia tonight. Are you okay with that?"

"Yes. You never go anywhere because you're always with me. You need to be happy, too."

Thanks, baby. I'm glad you understand. I love you."

"I love you, too."

"I'll bring some clothes over for you before I leave."

"Okay."

"Sure you're okay with this?"

Chesne nodded.

"You don't need anything?"

"No, I'm fine. Go and have some fun, Mommy." Chesne saw Olivia join them as she stood next to her mother.

"Come on, girl. Can't you see she's trying to get rid of you," Olivia said, gently pulling Montana's arm.

"I should be back in a few hours or so, Olivia."

"No problem. We'll be fine."

Montana looked at Chesne who was almost her height. *That girl grows faster by the minute.* She was glad Chesne had Garrett's stature.

Her honey complexion was dotted with faint freckles on cheekbones that were like small mountains. Her curly sandy brown hair was pulled into a ponytail framing a face adorned by sage green eyes with flecks of golden brown. A cleft discreetly divided her chin. Montana took one last look at Chesne, and for the first time saw a perfect blend of her and Garrett.

"I'll see you in a few minutes, Chesne. Okay?"

"Okay."

Olivia and Montana walked to the door. Montana looked at her friend, "Thanks so much for taking such good care of us."

"It's a job I love," Olivia said affectionately.

Montana kissed her on the cheek and walked out.

As she stepped up to her Greek Revival home, she marveled at the craftsmanship. She was glad she used the dove gray paint on the outside. It complemented the leaded glass door and transoms with intricate silver etchings. As she opened the door, the warmth of the foyer gave her gentle comfort. The hardwood floors gleamed as the light from the 1934 rock-crystal chandelier softly reflected off the banister of the spiral staircase. It made her feel as though she had stepped back in time to a grander era.

Montana's house was an outward expression of herself—unique and beautiful. There was a Louis XVI commode made of mahogany with a brown- and gold-veined marble top. Along the sides were intricate gold flourishes and burl mahogany veneer on the doors and sides. Hanging above that was a Rococo gold mirror.

Walking through the kitchen, she opened the door to the office/laundry room, placing her briefcase and purse on the desk. It had originally been such a massive room that Montana divided it into two. The side with the sink was kept as the laundry room and the other side was transformed into an office.

Just as she turned to go back into the kitchen, Scottie came pouncing around the corner.

"Where have you been and what have you been doing?"

Scottie stretched and yawned as if he was trying to answer her question.

"Aren't you supposed to greet me at the door?" He jumped up on her legs, wagging his tail.

"Well, hello," she said picking him up. "How was your day? You just don't know how easy you've got it." Scottie stopped trying to lick her face and his big brown eyes looked at her as if he understood.

Montana and her mother redesigned the kitchen with leaded glass maple cabinets that contrasted nicely with the hardwood floors. Appliance garages, a butler's pantry, and a sunroom were added. Grace had chosen the pale lavender granite countertops with pewter markings, which was a perfect complement to the kitchen.

The microwave and oven were installed in the wall. A Dacor grill and stovetop were placed in the island with an eating area on one side. There were wrought-iron barstools upholstered in lavender tapestry with eggplant and moss green tassels. Montana hand-painted ivy, purple, and green grapes on the soft ecru walls which framed the picture window above the sink.

"Mama's got to hurry up and get dressed, okay. Garrett's coming over." She hooked the leash to his collar and quickly took him out for a walk. Scottie sniffed around the yard and relieved himself. When he was done and they were back inside, Montana rushed upstairs to her bedroom with Scottie in tow. He plopped himself on the rug in the bathroom as she undressed. Standing and shaking her head in amazement, "Sometimes, I believe that dog can understand me," she chuckled to herself.

The phone rang and her heart skipped half a beat. *Could it be Garrett canceling the date after all this time?* She could not blame him since she had not fully accepted his proclamation of change.

"Hello."

"Hey," Noelle Nichols, her best friend, answered.

"What's up?" Montana asked.

"Aren't we being a little short today? Oh, I forgot that's *every* day for you," Noelle teased.

"Oh, you're funny. I can't talk right now. I've got to get dressed."

"Where are you going?"

"Where am I going? Since when did you become my mother? Wait a minute, my mother wouldn't even ask me that!"

"Anyway. I was calling to see if you wanted to go to the Black History Celebration at the High Museum."

"I'm sorry, I forgot all about that, Noelle. I really wanted to go, too. I can't do it tomorrow, but how about Sunday? It's the last weekend, isn't it?"

"Yeah, but I'm busy Sunday. I've got to work on my deposition for Monday. But, like I said, where are you going?"

"I don't know."

"Well, who are you going with?"

"I'm going out with, um, with Garrett."

"Oh, I see."

"Well, he kept asking and uh, I did kind of want to see him."

"Girl, you do not have to explain to me. If I had a man like that, I wouldn't be going to see some art on the wall, either. I would be the art on the wall." Noelle laughed.

"He's *not* my man."

"He may as well be. That man can sniff you out a hundred miles away. Anyway, it's not like you don't love him."

"That's not . . . I mean I don't . . ."

"Save that for somebody else. I know you. You have never had a problem saying anything that was on your mind, and now all of a sudden, your tongue keeps tripping over itself. Well, you think you might be able to pull yourself away long enough to go shopping with me tomorrow? I've got to go to this thing for the mayor tomorrow night and . . ."

"I don't have a thing to wear," they said in unison and laughed.

"Noelle, all you have to say is shop, and I'm ready. Chesne and I had planned to hang out tomorrow, but we can hang out at the mall with you. I remember the last time I went out with you, I thought I would have to punch that guy out." Montana laughed, thinking back. "What time did you want to go?"

"Oh, I thought we could go about ten or eleven, have lunch, and maybe you could go with me tomorrow night. Wait, what guy?"

"Oh, you know, what was his name? He was the one who was going bald and had some kind of black acrylic sheepskin rug on his head."

Noelle started laughing. "Oh, you mean Herb Slaton."

"Yeah, girl, that's him. His hair was so nappy it looked like little peppercorns. I thought I would never get rid of him."

"You didn't. He still asks about you."

"Next time you see him, tell him I'm married with five kids. Oh, and I'll let you know about tomorrow night."

She heard Scottie bark. "Girl, I've got to go. Garrett's going to be here soon and I need all the time I can get. I'm a wreck."

"As long as I have known you, you have never been a wreck. I'll talk to you later and, uh, Montana . . ."

"Yeah?"

"Don't do anything I wouldn't do."

"That doesn't leave much, now does it?"

"Funny. I'll see you tomorrow. Give that fine piece of chocolate a piece for me."

"Girl, you are so nasty. Bye."

Noelle and Montana met seventeen years ago when Montana first lived in Atlanta. They were in the dressing room of Neiman Marcus when they walked out wearing the same dress in different colors. They laughed, complimenting each other's wonderful taste. Later that evening, they met again at a private art showing. Montana was apprising a canvas piece that caught her attention and overheard someone giving her opinion about the rendering. Montana spoke up to correct the woman. When the lady turned around, they recognized each other from the dressing room and began to laugh. They instantly became best friends, counseling, consoling, and supporting each other trying not to impose personal judgment or opinion. Over time, they became more like sisters than friends.

Montana walked to her closet. "Maybe I'll wear that little black dress," she said aloud. *Naw, I don't want to give him that kind of idea. I'm not sleeping with him or any other man for that matter. I am a virtuous woman now.* "All men ever want is sex, and if you ever give in, they come back begging and whimpering for more like a lovesick puppy, don't they, Scottie?" On cue, Scottie walked into the closet and whined for Montana to pick him up. "See what I mean." She bent down and rubbed his head.

Numerous selections later, Montana decided to wear her chocolate suede dress, which was fitting looser now.

"Hey, it's not hugging my butt like it used to. Working out with those weights is finally paying off, but I really hate to exercise."

After dressing, she packed a few things for Chesne and walked into the kitchen to pour a glass of wine. She heard Scottie barking and saw him run toward the door just as the doorbell rang.

"Good boy, Scottie. Just a minute," she called out, taking a look at herself in the mirror and sighed. "Scottie, sit." Montana walked to the door, "Who is it?"

"Garrett."

She tried to look through the peephole, but couldn't reach it. "One day, I'm going to have to grow a few inches," she mumbled as she opened the door.

"You've always been the right height in my eyes." Garrett said, standing in his magnificent glory.

"Thanks, Garrett. It's good to see you. How have you been? Come on in."

He stepped into the foyer. "I'm fine, better now."

You sure are, Montana thought. "This man looks good enough to eat," she said louder than she meant to.

"Excuse me, what did you say?"

"I said, it's good we were able to meet," Montana recovered and smiled. *Lord, please forgive me for that lie.* "Won't you come in?" Montana gestured toward the living room.

"I'll be right back. Make yourself comfortable." Garrett sat down and looked around the room. He nodded his head approvingly.

Montana retrieved Chesne's bag and placed it at the foot of the stairs. She was so nervous she felt that she was standing on a high wire desperately trying to balance.

"I see your taste has only gotten better over the years." The eclectic yet exquisite mix of traditional and antique furniture was refined and elegant. He looked at her collection of Thomas Blackshear sculptures that were housed in a mahogany chocolate cabinet. He recognized *The Comforter, The Guardian,* and *The Prayer.* Knowing Montana's heart as he did, he could easily understand the connection she felt to these pieces.

Her art collection was one that even the most avid connoisseur would envy. There were paintings by Paul Goodnight, Charles Bibbs, and other notable African American artists.

"Would you like some wine?"

"Sure."

Montana poured two glasses of wine, marveling at how natural it seemed to have Garrett in her life. *How could I have been so stupid?* She reprimanded herself. *Slow down, girl. Don't jump before you know you have a safety net.* Exhaling deeply, she looked at him again. *But what a beautiful way to fall.*

Montana returned to the living room with the glasses and handed one to Garrett. She noticed how little he had changed over the years. He wore a gray cashmere sport coat, a cream silk sweater, and charcoal gray wool pants. He was a man's man and one who represented the species well. A foot and a two inches taller than she with muscles that seemed to never end, she could see that his chest beneath the sweater was paradise waiting to be discovered. His features were lovingly chiseled by an artisan's skilled hands and resembled those of ancient Egyptian ancestors. His thick eyebrows, sensuous lips, intoxicating sable eyes, and perfectly trimmed mustache would make any woman swoon. The cleft in his chin stood proudly as a mark of distinction. His hair was cut short and its natural wave swirled softly on his head, curling slightly on the ends. Yes, he was the same, but better, much better than she could have ever imagined.

"You look fantastic," Garrett said.

"Thanks. So do you."

"I'm glad you finally decided to go out with me."

"I wanted to see you."

"You did? Well, you sure have a funny way of showing it."

"Just making sure you were sincere."

Garrett did not respond but looked at her with an intense desire in his eyes that made Montana nervous.

"Well, I guess we better get going." Clearing her throat, she grabbed Chesne's overnight bag.

"You going to spend the night with me?" he asked, smiling.

"No," Montana said sweetly. "I just need to drop this off."

She walked to the door and Garrett gestured for her to go first.

"Age before beauty," he said.

"Well, if age is supposed to go first, you should have *been* gone."

"Ha, ha."

Montana turned on the security alarm as they walked out. When they were almost at the car, she said, "Wait for me. I'll be right back." She walked over to Olivia's house and rang the bell.

"Hey, cher. You leaving?" Olivia asked, letting her in.

"Yeah."

"What's wrong?"

"Just a little nervous. Haven't done this in a while."

"You'll be fine. Relax and enjoy yourself."

Montana smiled slightly.

Chesne heard the bell and ran to the door when she recognized her mother's voice. "Hey, Mommy," she said, hugging her.

"Hi, baby. I came by to let you know I was leaving. Be a good girl for Olivia, okay?"

"Okay, Mommy."

"I'll be back soon."

Chesne smiled. "I love you."

Montana bent down to kiss her. "I love you too. I shouldn't be late, okay?"

"Okay. I meant to tell you, you look really pretty."

"Thanks, baby." She kissed Chesne again.

"We've got a special young lady here," Olivia said.

"Yeah, I know and the thought of her just melts my heart sometimes." Montana squeezed Olivia's arm and quickly walked out.

"Is everything okay?" Garrett asked, seeing the moistness in Montana's eyes.

"Yes, everything is fine. I'm ready when you are." Montana looked at her house mentally checking to ensure she had turned everything off, and saw Scottie peeping out of the plantation shutters that he had opened with his paw. She could hear him whining. "He hates to see me go."

"I can understand his pain."

Garrett opened the passenger side and helped Montana into the car. They drove off into the night as the stars lit their path, holding the promise of magical moments.

CHAPTER FOUR

"You cannot handle fire with your hands."
Kanuri Proverb

$\mathcal{L}$earning of a Kirk Whalum concert, Montana decided to treat herself, by herself to a night out and that is where she met Garrett sixteen years ago. Wearing a copper pantsuit that hugged her body suggestively, she entered the room garnering the attention of everyone as she walked—or more aptly, glided by. Her walk was a slow, graceful movement and though it was sexy, it was not intended to be that way. Full hips and a small waist caused her to naturally sway from side to side with the rhythm of a hypnotic Caribbean melody.

Since Montana was extremely self-conscious, she habitually arrived early at social activities, especially when she was alone so attention would not be directed toward her, but it never seemed to halt onlookers. Finding a table in the corner that was close enough to see, but far enough that the speakers would not blow her away, she comfortably settled in admiring her surroundings.

The club had twenty table rounds covered with burgundy cloths and amber candleholders centered on each. The amber walls were painted with burgundy fleur-de-lis borders. Antique bronze torchieres and topaz-colored chandeliers provided the club with light. Beautiful pieces of Venetian glass were housed inside the arches on the walls. A miniature model of Venice complete with water and moving gondolas was placed diagonally from her. It was one of the most interesting pieces she had ever seen. Mirrors were placed strategically along the walls and reflected the light casting the club in a golden glow. The air was cool and mildly fragrant. Quality reproductions of thick Persian carpet along the walkways buffered the sounds coming from the tables and the kitchen.

A server walked toward her. "Good evening. My name is Austin. Would you like something to drink?"

Montana looked in his direction. "Rum and coke, please. Captain Morgan's if you've got it."

"Certainly. I'll be back with your drink shortly."

She heard someone approaching behind her and was astonished by the waiter's promptness. Moving aside to allow Austin room to place her drink on the table, she waited. After a few seconds with no response, she turned around and gasped when she found someone else standing behind her.

"Excuse me. I'm sorry, I didn't mean to scare you. There aren't any more tables or empty seats, and I was wondering if my friend and I could join you."

Montana looked at the speaker, amazed that he could not see the annoyance on her face. "Well, that depends."

"On what?"

"If you include me, myself, and I."

Montana heard him grunt under his breath. She could only imagine what he was thinking and hoped he was aggravated enough to leave her alone, but he continued to stand there.

"It's your choice," she said resignedly. She knew they were going to join her anyway.

Garrett motioned to another man to come over whose name was Marc. When he arrived at the table, he introduced himself and Garrett. There was something about Garrett that Montana did not like, but Marc seemed to be pleasant.

Austin returned with her drink and took the orders of the men who joined her. An uncomfortable silence anchored itself over the table and the apprehension Montana felt about Garrett was as thick as night fog after a hard rain. Montana found relief in Marc who was relaxed, friendly, and had a great sense of humor. They talked passionately about race, religion, politics, and the rapid decline of mankind.

Montana ignored Garrett as much as she could, even though she could feel him watching her. She and Marc talked, laughed, and danced most of the evening while Garrett remained virtually silent.

He was attracted to Montana, but ignored her as he had done to so many other women in his past. In an attempt to remain ambiguous, he honed his talent for equally disregarding those ladies who mattered and those who didn't. *Women sometimes made it hard on themselves*, he thought.

Montana considered Garrett to be arrogant and sexist. His polite disregard made her feel that he expected her to fall on her knees in gratitude just to be in his presence. She felt compassion for the women in his life and all the other women who allowed men to treat them badly simply to avoid being alone, or had such low self-esteem that they did not believe they could do better.

Montana was not looking for a man so Garrett's presence had no effect on her, at least not one that she would acknowledge. Men seemed too inconsequential for her at this point in her life. The majority of the ones she met were either too controlling, wanted only sex or what they could get from her, but none seemed to want to delve beneath the surface to discover her.

Every now and then during the conversation, Garrett would make a comment about their discussion, but Marc and Montana had gotten so heated in the intellectual debate that they barely replied. When they were on the subject of interracial dating, Garrett interrupted.

"I don't see anything wrong with dating a white woman. White women have always wanted black men. Back in the day, they would sneak out to get busy with the new buck that massa had just bought."

Montana looked at him incredulously. "You must be kidding?" she asked, appalled. "How can you sit there on that high horse of yours and say something that ludicrous as justification for dating white women? Our existence was bought with the blood of our ancestors. It is because they fought, struggled, and died that we can enjoy some of the basic freedoms we have today."

Garrett sat back and folded his arms. He was not here to listen to her idealistic babbling. *She is what is wrong with the race,* he thought.

"Yes, our ancestors fought and died so that we could have basic freedoms, but it wasn't to lock us into dating one race exclusively," he said.

Montana looked at him, oblivious to his apparent lack of relevant knowledge or concern. Whether he wanted to hear it or not, she was going to say what was on her mind. Maybe something she said would be absorbed.

"I'm not saying you have to date one race exclusively. What I *am* saying is there is nothing stronger or more beautiful than the love between a black man and a black woman."

Garrett sighed wearily. "Love doesn't dictate the skin color of who I can and cannot be with. It is simply what it is. It does not discriminate nor does it oppress. My attractions are varied and I'm not going to lock myself into a box just because sistas like you have a problem."

"My only problem is black men like you who forgot their heritage as strong African patriarchs because of the indignities and degradation brought upon him when he became the proverbial stepping stone of the white man. Never stopping to fight back when able, to prevent his entrapments from lulling you into a state of complacency where you willingly become the weakest link in our chain."

Garrett leaned in toward Montana. "Look, we can sit here all night going back and forth. You're not going to convince me and I won't convince you. I guess we wear what we are."

"That we do. Do you see me? I have blue-gray eyes and light skin. I don't need to use a relaxer to straighten my hair. How do you think that happened? To show you the evil of the white man, he has made us believe that being fair is an advantage and we have allowed something he created to cause rifts among us forgetting that our rainbow is what makes us beautiful. Being fair simply reminds me of the fact that some white man violated my ancestor against her will. Do you think he approached my great-great-grandmother and asked her out on a date, courted her for a respectable time, and then asked her to marry him? Or did his cattle mean more as he repeatedly debased her by rape? Do you think he thought of her as human then?"

"Some women gave it up willingly. They were begging to give it to Massa Charlie. They thought he might be a little easier on them.

Women are still gullible. All that man wanted was a cheap piece," Garrett argued.

Montana cleared the lump in her throat as she swallowed hard. "But was it really cheap? Look at the price those women ultimately paid for that piece. If you feared for your life, would you not use extraordinary means? If I tell you not to look at a white woman, that is exactly what you will do even if that is not what you, well not you, but any *other* black man would ordinarily do.

"It is so incredible that you have no compelling interest to dig deeper than the surface. Skimming the surface as an approach to life is more akin to dying and being unaware of your own death. Either this is way over your head or you have never stopped to think. I don't know which one is more of a pity," Montana said.

"If I *were* looking for a strong black man, *you* would not be a candidate. No offense taken, none given."

Montana heard Garrett cough and looked at him wondering if his meal of crow was caught in his throat. Her heart was beating wildly against her chest as she futilely tried to calm it down.

Garrett was mad, but he had to admit part of what she said was true. He had not stopped to explore or expound any issue that required investigation or revolutionary thought. He just looked for what brought him pleasure with the least amount of effort.

Marc started to laugh. "Well, my brotha, I guess the next time you jump into the saddle, you'll make sure you have a horse."

Realizing she had probably come off a little too harsh, she knew she needed to apologize to Garrett. After all, he was just stating his opinion, no matter how ignorant it was.

"Look, Garrett, I'm sorry. I didn't mean to attack you like that. You are entitled to your opinion, just like everyone else, no matter how stup . . . uh, how unpopular it may be."

Garrett looked at Montana. *If she weren't so fine, I'd tell her to go to hell.* Garrett had not even shared with Marc that he had dated a few white women. Now, for the first time, he wondered why. He felt like Judas Escariot who had just been given thirty pieces of silver as payment for his betrayal?

Montana was not interested in taking anyone home so it did not matter if he liked what she said, he could just move on—nothing ventured, nothing gained. This mode of thinking gave her freedom since she did not have to concentrate on impressing someone or making sure she said the right thing. She forgot that sometimes what is achieved, often backfires.

By the time the evening was over, Garrett was determined to get Montana's phone number. He was impressed that someone so beautiful was not only equally intelligent, but said what she felt and meant it. It was obvious that Montana did not pull any punches. What you saw was what you got and he wanted to get everything he saw. There was something so attractive about a confident, assertive woman. Most women Garrett met were either pretending to be something they were not or were all over him. Montana was a lady, and he had not met a real lady in a very long time. Though this attracted him, he also saw it as a challenge. Being accustomed to women who lived to please him, he had an uneasy feeling that this time he would live to please her. Garrett used every ounce of charm and persuasion he possessed until Montana surrendered and gave him her number.

"Boy, you're just not going to let it go, are you?"

"I'm just a determined man. I always get what I want."

"But the real trick is wanting what you get. It's kind of like the snake and the charmer. Sometimes you can't tell the difference between the two."

Garrett looked at her and frowned as if he suddenly realized what he had gotten himself into.

She could not help herself and smiled. That smile turned into laughter and that laughter lit up the whole room.

"Oh, so you're a philosopher, too? Maybe we can expound on more philosophical rhetoric a little later," Garrett said.

"You think there'll be a later?"

"I'm betting on it."

Montana had called Noelle later to discuss this new man she had met. "I'm serious, Noelle."

"I know you are, but you're taking it too seriously."

"I don't think so. Yes, I'm attracted to him and he is *fine*. Lord knows he is, but he is so sure of himself, so . . ."

"Sounds like someone else I know."

"No, it's something else. I just can't put my finger on it. Haven't you ever met someone and had the feeling you knew them, but there was something about them that made you uneasy? Does that sound crazy?"

"Look, I don't care if you met him twenty times before, what counts is now. If you don't pursue it, you'll wonder about it your whole life. You can't go back and relive it because you've lost your chance to capture the moment. You don't want regrets. Go out with him, and if you feel the same way, then at least you'll know. And besides it's a free dinner."

"Nothing is free, Noelle."

"Well, what have you got to lose?"

My heart, Montana answered silently.

Montana reluctantly accepted Garrett's invitation when he called. Even though she was not sure if she was doing the right thing, she did not want to question what could have happened if she did not. There was nothing more disheartening than having regrets about the "what ifs" at the end of your life. She had enough of those to write a book.

The joy of a loving relationship seemed to escape her as each one always ended horribly. As a result, she built an impenetrable wall around her. This safe haven kept her heart protected, but more importantly, it prevented her from living and being loved, which was the most unfortunate regret anyone could have.

Garrett and Montana lived with each other for five of the six years they were together. Things between them were wonderful most of the time, but like every couple, they had their moments. Montana wanted to believe the best about him. She wanted to know that he was a man of honor, but as time passed, she noticed that he was not worthy of honor. He intentionally said and did callous things to hurt her and she could not understand his behavior. Slowly, it was getting the best of her.

She should have known something was amiss the first time he came over. There were warning signs all over especially when Garrett automatically assumed that because Montana had asked him to come over, it was an open invitation for sex. When she told him no, he was astounded. Seeing that she was unwavering in her decision, he told her that if they did not have sex, she would never see him again. Her response probably shocked him even more.

She promptly stood and opened the door. Turning around, she looked at him with one hand on her hip and the other motioning toward the doorway. There were no words to say and she did not care if she ever saw him again. Once he understood she meant it, he told her, "One day, you're going to regret this." Montana remembered telling him that she already had and closed him out of her life she thought forever. Two weeks later, he called and apologized.

Their relationship was a hot, steamy, stormy, sunny, mostly happy romance. When it was sweet, it was extremely sweet, but when it was bitter, it left a bad taste in her mouth that nothing could remove.

It was not long before she learned that he didn't just lie sometimes, he lied all the time about things that were unimportant or inconsequential. It was impossible to believe that anyone had that much to hide, but as she uncovered things about him, she discovered things about herself. No matter how much she loved him, she could not handle giving someone the right to determine if she was capable of handling the truth. She had tried on numerous occasions to end the relationship, but Garrett used his innate charm to talk her out it.

Things between them became unstable and Montana was not sure where they stood or even if she stood with him at all. The only thing Montana was certain of was that she had an angel watching over her, and after every dream she had of Garrett's infidelity, the angel would appear. The third time, Montana knew Garrett was unfaithful even though she had no concrete proof.

A week later, a woman called and asked to speak to him. Initially, Montana did not give it a second thought, but something about this woman kept nagging her. She did not want to think the worst about him, but everything inside of her screamed betrayal. When the woman called again, Montana asked, "Exactly what is your relationship with Garrett?"

"We are, uh, friends," she said nervously.

"And what type of friends would that be?"

"Look, I don't want to be in the middle of this."

"Too late, honey, you already are." The woman hung up on her.

After that, the phone calls started rolling in. It took every ounce of strength Montana could muster not to say something to Garrett, but she wanted to get irrefutable evidence so he could not lie about his relationship with the women who called.

Montana came home early one day to decorate the house and surprise him for his birthday. Her arms were overloaded with gifts and decorations so she had a hard time with the lock.

Finally pushing the door open, she discovered the alarm did not go off. Fear and panic attacked her heart ferociously. She quietly put the packages down and reached for the gun in her purse. She was opposed to carrying one, but as crazy as people were, she did not want to be unprotected. Moving through the house as silent as a cat, she heard sounds of passion coming from the bedroom. She opened the door quietly, her heart pounding so hard she thought she was going to faint and saw Garrett with another woman in the midst of having sex. Montana stood shocked, trying to speak, but clumsily incapable of forcing sound from her throat. She heard Garrett ask, "Whose is this?" Montana felt an unfamiliar switch turn on inside her head as she teetered on the brink of insanity. The words began to pour out of her mouth.

"I believe you're supposed to say 'Garrett's,' " Montana said still holding the gun. "I'm glad to know you enjoy him so much. You and he can have each other. You can screw until you die 'cause that's exactly what's going to happen. Now, I want you to continue."

Garrett and the woman looked at each other as if they had not heard her quite right.

"I said go ahead, do it."

"But Montana, this is crazy," Garrett said.

"Your point being," she snarled. "And what's your problem, Ball Park Skank? You're awfully quiet now. Garrett, I believe you were asking her whose it was. Never mind, I am not wasting my time with this anymore."

Montana became so still every creak, pop, and click played a concerto for the deaf. She looked at them with glazed over eyes and calmly said, "To everything there is a season. A time to live and a time to die."

She pointed the gun, aiming it at Garrett's heart.

CHAPTER FIVE

"Until the snake is dead, do not drop the stick."
Ivorian Proverb

arrett was not sure what to do. He did not think Montana would pull the trigger, but he could not be sure. As peculiar as it seemed, Montana was the only woman Garrett had ever truly loved. Caught between the happiness of a lifetime and the image he felt he had to have as a man, he sacrificed her heart for his insecurity.

Garrett, visibly shaken, attempted to recover. "Baby, what are you doing home?"

"What am I doing home? I live here! I came home to surprise you for your stupid birthday, but I see you got your present early. I hope you get every disease man has ever been afflicted with and once that's over I want you to get them all over again! I want you and this *thing* to get out of my house now!" She started towards them and slapped Garrett so hard his head reverberated from the impact.

"Garrett, why couldn't you just leave me if you were going to do this? Was it really necessary to hurt me this way? What have I done to you to make you strike with such harm?"

"I know it's hard to believe, but I *do* love you, baby," he pleaded.

"You wouldn't know love if it bit you on your butt. And as for you, you witch, where did you crawl up from?"

"I'm from Idaho."

"No, kidding." Montana laughed. "You certainly are da ho. Did you know he had a lady?"

The girl nervously nodded.

"And it didn't bother you that you were taking another sister's man? That's what's wrong with black women. Nothing is respected. Instead of being an inspiration and lifting one another up, we become an abomination and an insult to all that is beautiful about us. Things like you set us back twenty years. We don't respect one another, how can we respect ourselves?

"You can have him. He wasn't that good to begin with." Seconds turned into minutes, minutes into more minutes as Montana stared wildly at them. Garrett and the woman were deathly silent as they trembled like insects caught in a web.

"Baby, now, you don't want to do anything you'll regret," Garrett said nervously.

"I told you the first time you came over, I already have. I regret meeting you. I regret the day you were born. If I could put you back in your mother's womb, I would. I regret making love to you. But most of all, I regret loving you. I curse every time I ever told you I loved you or made a loving gesture toward you. And to think I wanted to have your babies. I thank heaven for Ortho Novum."

The woman, sensing Garrett was having no success, decided to try to calm Montana down.

"Look, I didn't mean to hurt you," she said shakily. "I came on to him. He's not responsible."

"And that's supposed to make everything alright? So then tell me, if he's not responsible who is so that I may end my despair?"

The woman could not think of anything to say.

"Come on, baby, now calm down," Garrett begged.

"Calm down. You calm down! Did you catch me screwing my brains out? No. Because I believe in a thing called fidelity, in giving all of me when I'm involved. I believe in loving unconditionally until death do us part." She laughed at the irony.

Montana grabbed the girl's short-cropped hair so tightly she pulled some hairs out. Instinctively, the woman grabbed Montana's hand to prevent further pain. Montana hit her hand with the butt of the gun and pulled her hair even tighter daring her to move again.

"Look at her, couldn't you have picked someone better looking? If ugly were bricks, she would be a project. I don't blame her, but you knew you were wrong and still you did it. What could you possibly have been thinking? Never mind, you were using the head *without* a brain. Did you think I would never find out? I don't know what kind of dick you think you have, but you might want to reconsider that thought. Nothing you have is *that* good."

Satan sat in the midst of the chaos grinning. "I knew I would get her. Money and ego motivate most people, but she values truth, honor, and loyalty. All the things I want with a minor adjustment or two. Come on, pull the trigger already. Your feelings are important and they carelessly tossed them and you to the side. You have every right to defend your honor. Go on and end their lives as they so carelessly ended yours. Revenge is sweetest when served cold. Once you drink of its fruit, you will never be the same. The taste for blood is in all of us. The first time is always the hardest," he whispered.

Satan moved in closer and continued. "That's right, make them sweat. Let them know you mean what you say. He betrayed and humiliated you, and he did it with someone like her. He desired her. He released himself into her and became a part of her. You know how good he is. You heard her. You've heard yourself. No one but you should ever know the sounds of his pleasure. That was your man. You can't let him get away with that! Look at who you are. They can't do this to you," Satan taunted.

Montana fell silent again as she shook her head.

"It's all lost now anyway." Holding out her arm, she pulled the trigger back slightly. "God, and to think ..." She was stopped abruptly. The arms of God reached down and embraced her lovingly. He whispered, *"This is not your destiny, my child. This is not what I created you to be. Remember, I love you, daughter. You have only to call on me. I am with you always."*

She released her grip on the gun. Removing the clip and extra bullet, Montana placed the empty gun on the nightstand and started toward the door. Before leaving, she turned around to face Garrett with tears spilling over onto her cheeks.

"No need to waste bullets on something that's already dead. The two of you can rot in hell. Satan is the king of fools and the two of you will be welcomed company. I'll be back in an hour. I want you and all your stuff gone."

"Montana, wait, baby. I can't lose you. I won't lose you. You can't end it like this!"

"You already have."

Though she was hurt beyond belief, Montana sealed the door to the life she knew with Garrett. She would not allow herself to be abused, misused, or betrayed by anyone. God did not create her to be anyone's footstool.

She closed her heart a little more that day in order to maintain the sanity she needed to go on. She was a survivor by any means and at all costs.

The end of her relationship with Garrett placed Montana in the midst of a storm. She had reached a fork in the road that would define the remainder of her life. This was the beginning of her journey in the wilderness, her personal exodus from Egypt.

Montana wandered for more than a year and though the journey involved hardship, she gained wisdom, faith, and patience. The end of her relationship with Garrett became the beginning of her life. Montana had to literally die before God could mold her into what He had purposed for her. She had allowed others to create her world, and in creating it, they made it too small.

When she approached a crossroad in her walk of life, she would look to God for direction. He was the author and finisher of her faith. God was just, loving, and free. It was only through His grace and mercy that she possessed any goodness at all. When she was lonely and needed companionship, He became her comforter and when she was weak, He gave her the strength to continue. Nothing had power over her, but God and that was how she intended to keep it. Armed with discerning wisdom, she knew that she was in first position on Satan's Most Wanted list and he desired her alive, but if there were no choice, dead would do.

It was revealed to her that there would come a time when she would have to put on the whole armor of God, physically and literally. There was an ongoing battle between Satan and God, and she was an important piece in the victory. Just as Job endured suffering, so, too, would she. Her losses would not be the same, that much she knew, but how the battle would come and in what form was still undetermined, but Heaven was clearly at stake.

Montana prayed for strength, faith, and the wisdom she needed to fulfill God's will and her destiny. She shuddered to think what would happen if she did not.

CHAPTER SIX

"You think of water when the well is empty."
Ethiopian Proverb

"So how have you been, Montana?" Garrett asked as he backed out of her driveway.

Montana was suddenly snapped out of her nostalgic trance into the present. "I've been fine."

"How long has it been since we last saw each other?"

"I don't know. I haven't really kept count." Actually, Montana knew exactly how long it had been—nine years and eight months. *Another lie. Before I ran into Garrett, I never lied and now it's becoming a habit. I never knew how easy it was to lie or how hard it is to stop once you start because you have to tell another lie to cover up the first. Oh, what a tangled web we weave when first we practice to deceive. Please forgive me, Father. I know I can't keep this a secret forever, but I'm just not ready yet.*

"It must have been at least ten years."

"How did you know it was me when I had the flat tire?"

"Are you kidding? I would recognize that walk blind. I'm just glad it was me who stopped to help you and not some nut out here roaming the streets. You are something. You have never changed a tire in your life, to my knowledge, but there you were looking at the tire and reading the manual."

"And just what was I supposed to do? Sit idly by while I waited for a man to stop and rescue me? I am acutely self-sufficient and sometimes that means taking crash courses in things that are necessary. What do you think I've been doing all this time, Garrett? Waiting for you?"

"No, that's not what I meant. I just think men should rescue the damsel."

"Who said the damsel wanted to be rescued? I don't need rescuing." She stopped then continued. "I forgot my manners. Why, thank you, sir. I don't know what I would do without the kindness of strangers. These hands have never known hard work," she said in a genteel Southern accent using her hand as a fan. "You think women are totally helpless unless and until you come to our aid. To be honest, black men can be more of a hindrance. All they do is escape responsibility. Garrett, you are *still* incredibly obtuse sometimes!" Montana tried to douse the embers in her veins before they ignited, but her blood was already boiling.

"Look, you know I didn't mean it like that. I was just happy to run into you, that's all. I see you're still opinionated, stubborn, idealistic, headstrong, and independent." He laughed easily.

His laughter irritated Montana, but she tried to control it. "Why would I change how I am? It works for me."

"I'm just making sure we start on the same page."

Readying herself for battle, she turned to look at him. "Maybe the same book, but the same page is definitely stretching it."

Garrett sighed. "Montana, I don't want to get into an argument. I'm really glad to see you. I was thinking about you the other day and then two days later I run into you. It must be destiny, don't you think?"

"Garrett, I don't know if it's destiny or not, but I really don't plan to start reading a whole lot into this. I'm not as naïve or trusting as I used to be, and I sure don't plan on walking down memory lane with you."

"I knew it was simply a matter of time. It's hard to forget when you've been hurt."

"And *you* would know? If memory serves me correctly, *I* was the one who was hurt and betrayed. You know this wasn't a good idea after all. Please pull over and let me out."

"I expected to have darts thrown at me, but would you hold off a minute?"

Astonished, Montana looked at Garrett. "You are giving yourself too much credit. You're assuming that I care enough about you to hurt you. Sorry to disappoint your ego."

"Despite the attitude, I know there is a part of you that wants us back as much as I do. It's obvious we need to talk about what happened and reach a place where we can live in peace."

"I am already at peace."

"Let's not get started on the wrong foot, okay? Montana, I know I hurt you. I know I betrayed you. We never could talk about what happened then, but I hope we can now. We need to put some closure to this. There are things I need to tell you and things you need to hear. That is, if you can stop with the sarcastic remarks until I'm done. All I ask is that you remain quiet and just listen. Please."

Montana fumed. Between clenched teeth, she said, "Alright. You've got the floor." Breathing deeply, she tried to steady herself. Many times in the past, she had practiced what she would say to Garrett if she ever saw him, but never once had she rehearsed his words to her. She thought back to the night he came over to reconcile with her after she threw him out.

Drinking to the point of intoxication, she started to cry. Garrett held her and consoled her the only way he knew.

Holding her face gently in his hands, probing her eyes for a hint of love and forgiveness, he kissed her hungrily. One kiss led to another until their bodies were immersed in waves of passion that rhythmically ebbed and flowed to the beat of the moment.

Montana always knew Garrett was the only man she would ever truly love. She had missed him and from the moment he entered her, all longing ceased. The feel of him inside her lit fireworks and created her personal Fourth of July. They still fit together like a hand in glove.

The dance they performed was, as always, timed and choreographed with expert precision. They could anticipate each other's movements before they were made. In her drunken, vulnerable state, she told Garrett she loved him and he had said the same. He begged for forgiveness and asked her to take him back. Her only answer had been to fall sound asleep in his arms as they surrendered to each other in the midst of the erotic storm they had created.

For the next few months, Montana was so depressed and on edge that she felt she was going to have a nervous breakdown. The stress from the end of her relationship with Garrett was overwhelming. She got dizzy if she moved too quickly. She tried to eat, but could not keep anything on her stomach because she was nauseated constantly and tired just as much. Her menstrual cycles had become erratic.

At Noelle's urging, she went to see the doctor. A few weeks later, Noelle called to check on her. "Did you see the doctor?"

"Yeah, I saw him and he saw me."

"Well what did he say?"

"Something I didn't want to hear."

"Don't do this to me," Noelle said.

"Look, I really can't talk about it now, Noelle."

"All right, but are you okay?"

"I will be."

"If and when you're ready to talk, I'm here."

"Thanks, you're my bestest buddy."

"Just remember that."

"I'll talk to you later."

"If you need me, I'm only a phone call away."

"Okay." Montana hung up.

◇ ◇ ◇ ◇ ◇

"Did you hear me?" Garrett asked as Montana was swept back to the present.

"I'm sorry, Garrett, my mind must have wandered off. Please go on," she said sincerely.

"Montana, I know that things between us ended badly. I did things to you that I shouldn't have and that you didn't deserve. This is no excuse, but I was scared and yet at the same time, you were so perfect that I didn't feel I was worthy of you. I think subconsciously I did anything I could to prove to you and myself that I didn't deserve you, but all I did was hurt you."

"Yes, you did. It took me concerted effort to forgive you, but when I finally did, I couldn't forget. I reached the point where the anger I felt was tearing me apart and I had to find some kind of peace. Holding on to what you did was destroying my life and I had too much at stake to lose."

"I don't expect you to understand, but I'm just a man and subject to all the weaknesses a man has and the traps that we create for ourselves through the temptations of the flesh. I was wrong to be with other women. I was wrong to lie. It was not only stupid, it was selfish. I wasn't wise enough to know that I had the greatest woman already with me. It took losing you to realize what a rare and precious treasure I had in my life.

"I tried to convince myself that we didn't mean anything. I had sex with as many women as I could. After it was over, I felt more alone than I did before. When you're not with someone, all you want is to not be lonely, but what I was doing made me lonelier."

Montana nodded. She knew too well the loneliness that nothing could fulfill.

"Out of desperation, I called your mom. I needed to talk to someone who was close to you, and she told me that if I wanted to be a man—a real man—I had to accept the consequences of my actions. I needed to create my own definition of a man, not something based upon what other men said, but upon what my heart said. As she so aptly put it, I chose my bed, now I had to decide how I would sleep in it. Your mother has an uncanny ability to see beyond the obvious."

Montana suddenly missed her mother. It still had not gotten any easier.

"Anyway, when sex didn't work, I tried drugs to fill the void that your absence left, but nothing helped to relieve the pain. Then a friend of mine, Marc—you remember Marc, don't you?"

"Yes." Montana smiled. "He was a really nice guy. I liked him. It's so hard to believe you used drugs."

"It's hard for me to believe too, but sadly, it's true. Anyway, Marc took me to a Man Power Conference and . . ." Garrett became quiet as if speaking would cause him to burst. He cleared his throat and continued, "Montana, I'm telling you, it changed me. I resisted it. I denied it. I tried not to accept it. Then the most amazing thing happened. Bishop Vernon Jacobs said he knew some men were confused about what being a man really meant because they could not grasp the definition of a man as God intended. As a result, they couldn't fulfill the inherent responsibilities of a man and moved about aimlessly, never stopping long enough to notice the destruction they caused along the way."

Listening intently, Montana turned around to face him. She was amazed and skeptical at the same time. God could work miracles, but sometimes Satan created the same illusion. *The snake and the charmer,* she thought.

"He said these men had lost everything of intangible value. The only thing left was their soul, and Satan was ready and waiting with open arms to receive it. Bishop Jacobs said he knew a God who accepts you as you are with all your sins, scars, and blemishes. He erases the pain and forgives you. He will heal your wounds and your heart, if you simply seek Him first. I don't know what happened, but before I knew it, the Holy Spirit moved within me and I cried from the great depths of me.

"Marc asked if I wanted him to walk with me, but I told him if I was going to stand on my own, this was something I had to do alone. As I walked to the altar, I joined nearly every man there. It saved me. God saved me. I still make mistakes, and I'm not the man I should be, but Montana, I am not the empty shell of a man that I was. God told me you were my destiny. I already knew that, but now I really know. You know how you know you know, but you can't explain how you know?"

Garrett stopped the car and pulled over. He took Montana's hand in his, "Montana, there has not been a moment in my life since that dreadful day that I have not kicked myself for hurting you through my stupidity and selfishness. I have always loved you. I never stopped. The light in my heart burns dimly, but it needs your love to rekindle the flame and bring back the glow. My need for you is as essential as breath."

Montana started to say something sarcastic, but the look on Garrett's face was so sincere, she decided against it.

"I don't know how you feel about me, but I want you to know how sorry I am that I betrayed, humiliated, and abused you. I can't answer why I did what I did. I was of the world. I only know that if you live long enough, you are bound to do foolish things. I only ask that you forgive me as God has."

Montana wanted to scream at him. She wanted to take her long-awaited anger out on him, but she could not find it. Montana looked at him with a love that defied understanding.

"Garrett, I don't know what to say. I thought there was so much anger in me towards you that your words would not affect me, but I was wrong. While you were talking, I tried to say something smart, but my spirit confirmed that you were telling the truth. Not that I would know what you look like when you told the truth. Oops, sorry. I guess habits are hard to break sometimes.

This could be something worth having again, don't blow it, she thought. "You seemed to have grown up more than I believed was possible. I really appreciate what you've said because it gives me a sense of relief that I have needed for so long, but it wouldn't be me if I didn't say what I needed to either."

Garrett hesitantly nodded. When Montana spoke, things had a way of taking on a life of their own.

She saw the hesitancy. "I promise to be kind."

He breathed a sigh of relief. "Okay."

"When I was with you, I trusted everything you said, but everything you told me was a lie. I don't know how or why someone would lie about everything, even inconsequential things, but you did. Once that bond of trust was broken, the foundation that was 'us' had shaken loose, and it was only a matter of time until it crumbled. If it hadn't been another woman who separated us, it would have been me."

Garrett's eyes widened in surprise. "You would have left me anyway?"

"Yes, without a thought. When you lied, that meant you didn't trust me. You didn't trust me to love you no matter what the truth was. You didn't think I had the ability to handle the truth or make appropriate decisions based upon it. Lies rob people of honor and dignity. The most powerful weapon we have is the tongue. It can destroy lives or create them, praise God or serve Satan.

"When I walked in on you and that woman, I can't really say I was surprised." She visibly struggled to say what was in her heart and not on her mind.

He could see the pain reflected on her face, but he was surprised by the ache in his heart as he now felt her agony. It seemed as if someone had cut his heart open and left it to bleed freely.

"If I was not exciting enough, you should have told me. If I was no longer what you wanted, you should have said that we needed to go our separate ways. You treated our relationship and me with indifference.

"I guess when you invest in something you expect to see a return on your investment. I never thought that we would experience such a huge loss in value. My world caved in on me and the very thing that used to resuscitate me was now suffocating me and causing me to die.

"It was a lengthy journey to find me again, but I found me when I found God. As horrific and devastating as our breakup was, I am grateful that it happened. It marked the beginning of my life's journey with God."

Garrett knew she looked different somehow and now he understood why. As he looked into her eyes, he could see her light.

"He rescued me. He allowed me to see my value. Jesus saved my life. I have walked with Him ever since, but it is not a journey for the faint of heart. It takes a strength that cannot be measured, only endured.

"I never thought I would see you again in a million years. As much as I wish I could deny it, I am happy to see you again, but I'm a little gun-shy now. Though my mind and soul have forgiven you, my heart is not so trustworthy. To be completely honest, this will take time. Words come easy, but it will be your actions that will be judged."

The pain he had caused her stabbed sharply at his heart, but her words provided the healing he needed. Garrett felt every scar that was etched into his soul being restored.

"Thank you for listening and considering to be with me again. A man rarely gets another chance at true love. Let's just enjoy ourselves and see what the night presents."

He placed Montana's hand in his and lifted it to his lips. He started the car and they drove to Rothchild's in silence until he pulled into valet parking.

"I didn't expect you to jump into my arms, but I do want you to know that I realize the harm I have caused you and I am so sorry," Garrett confessed.

With each word, Montana's heart was made whole. People made mistakes—Lord knows she had made her share—but she was going to be wisely careful about opening her heart again. She felt herself hoping, no thankful, for the joy that started to fill her heart and she could sense that the same was happening to Garrett's.

Garrett walked over to the passenger's side to open the door and help her out of the car. His lips brushed her cheek as he reached for his jacket. The embers caught fire and both of them were burned in the flame.

CHAPTER SEVEN

"If you really love something, your fate is in its hands."
Tupuri Proverb

Rothchild's was an old warehouse that had been renovated into an elegant restaurant with an ambience that was romantic and intimate. Spotlights illuminated the lily pond, candle flames glistened softly off the hardwood floors, and French sconces decorated the walls. Reproductions of Van Gogh, Picasso, and Renoir were scattered throughout while smooth jazz drifted through the speakers. Garrett opened the door allowing Montana to enter first. As he strolled leisurely behind her, he marveled at the way her body moved.

"Um, um, um. That shake should be in the Ice Cream Hall of Fame."

Montana looked at him. "Down, boy, down."

"Good evening, Mr. Rivers," a black Englishman said.

"Hello, Evan. How have you been?" Garrett asked.

"Fine, sir. I see you're doing well yourself." Evan smiled as his eyes found Montana. "Right this way sir, ma'am." He gestured to a candlelit table in the corner.

An antique eighteen-inch hand-cut crystal vase dressed the table filled with a stunning bouquet of white flowers including calla lilies, orchids, roses, camellias, magnolias, and stargazers—all of Montana's favorites.

Montana saw the vase and immediately knew that Garrett had done this. "Oh, my." Emotion stirred inside her as she fought to maintain control. "They are beautiful, Garrett. Thank you so much." She looked at Garrett with such tenderness he felt he had been kissed.

"You're more than welcome, but be kind to them. They pale in comparison to you." Garrett pulled the chair out for Montana, removed the napkin from the table, and placed it in her lap.

Evan placed the menus in front of the guests. "If I'm not being too forward, madam, I must say this evening is surpassed only by your presence."

"Uh, thank you, Evan," Montana said shyly.

Garrett smiled. He knew Montana became obviously uncomfortable when people commented about her looks. Thinking back, he remembered her reaction the first time he complimented her as she stumbled trying to find her voice.

Evan could see that she was uneasy. "If I was too forward . . ."

"I understand. It's just that I don't see what others do."

"And that is what makes you even more enchanting." Evan nodded and excused himself.

"I know looks aren't everything, but you have to understand people are drawn to beautiful things. Don't get me wrong, you've got to have a connection, and most people would prefer someone who is attractive, but it can't be the only reason for your choice. And, Lord, I'm sorry, but it is a little difficult to have chemistry with someone who looks like a cow's behind turned inside out." Garrett laughed.

Montana looked at him and started laughing, too. "You are so silly."

"Personally, I'm glad we found each other because I could be talking to the rear end of a cow right now. You might still be a cow, but at least you're the front end," Garrett said, smiling

"Gee, thanks for the compliment, honey."

"Anytime. Glad to help."

"I just know you are." The intoxicating fragrance of the flowers filled the air and lifted her heart.

"Seriously, thank you so much for the flowers. As usual you have outdone yourself."

"The vase comes with it, you know," Garrett said, pleased.

They had seen a similar vase years ago while browsing through antique shops, but it was much too expensive for either of them then. Now, he could buy her the world, and he was going to give it to her on a silver platter—no, make that a platinum one.

She was thoughtfully quiet for a moment. Her eyes turned dreamy as if she had looked out to sea and discovered an uninhabited island that marked her past and established her future.

Toying with the silver at the table, Garrett turned over his thoughts as easily as the fork that was in his hand. He wore a look of pensive trepidation.

"I'm really sorry about your mom. Anne, my secretary, told me what happened. Your mother was such a splendid treasure. Somehow, I don't think the world will shine as brightly without her."

Incapable of responding, Montana remained silent temporarily leaving the newly discovered island.

Garrett watched her until he thought she was ready. "I was surprised Anne knew. Why didn't you tell me?"

"I really didn't mean to tell Anne, but she caught me on a bad day. She was compassionate and gave me such wonderful words of comfort. I cannot begin to tell you how much I miss her. Some days it takes a lot more out of me than I can handle." Montana was on the edge of tears.

"I know how close you two were. I wish there were something I could have done. I would have given my life for her. She was such an inspiration."

Montana shifted uneasily and changed the subject. "Have you been here all this time?"

"Yes, at least in body."

Montana resisted the urge to speak feeling that Garrett needed to talk.

"A lot of guys envied my life, but I was empty and drowning in my own misery. I tried to talk to my boys, but they were as messed up as I was. It was like taking advice from a drug dealer on how to stop using drugs.

"My soul desperately cried out as it slowly burned in hell. I could almost feel Satan riding my back and trying to whisper to me. I guess if you're on the outside looking in, it may have looked like my grass was greener, but even Bermuda turns brown in the winter.

"When I tried to talk about Satan, I got dissed, and Satan got dismissed. It is amazing how many people deny his existence. He is powerless without our help, but when people don't believe he exists, he can sneak up on you without warning. He manipulates you so much that the line between right and wrong starts to blur and over time disappears. It's scary when you think about it. Satan has so consumed this world that society is politically correct, but spiritually corrupt.

"It's funny in a way," Garrett continued, "We convince ourselves that a little bit won't hurt, and before you know it, it's a part of your everyday routine. I'm not sure if it's our free will or Satan, but a lot of the time it can bring us to the same destination."

Satan's interest was raised when he heard his name.

"I got you as high as you wanted to get. I gave you as much sex as you wanted, any way you wanted it, with anyone you wanted. Wasn't the sex the bomb? Women giving you blow jobs just for the asking. Man, you were living large. You couldn't have asked for anything more. You ungrateful idiot! It was not enough to just sit back and enjoy it. You had to start questioning everything, looking for relief from your affliction. What is so important about knowing Him anyway? I don't know why I waste my time on humans."

Satan overheard one of his workers say that a man had lost his father and was blaming the doctors for his death. The man became belligerent and started to wildly wave a gun around screaming he would make them pay even if it was with their funerals.

Um, Satan thought, *this could prove interesting.* He quickly left to see what new opportunities awaited him as the vile smell of death and decay remained behind.

"Garrett, I am so sorry about what happened to you. We all have our crosses to bear. The important thing is that you have committed yourself to God."

"You aren't going to judge me?"

"I can't afford to throw stones. I, too, live in a glass house. Here we are friends and strangers. You seem the same, yet so different."

"I remember once I was in my bedroom on my knees looking for anything that looked like a rock. Everything I saw that was white and hard, I tried to smoke it. I had gone on a binge and hadn't eaten, slept, or bathed in days. I looked up and glanced at myself in the mirror and I didn't know who I was. The face resembled someone I knew once, but not enough to remember whom. I broke down and cried. All the hurt, fear, and pain were given life through my tears. I screamed out at the top of my lungs, 'Jesus, please, if you're there, I need You, I need You to carry me. Please save me.' "

Seeing the pain on Garrett's face, Montana was moved. When he looked up, his eyes were moist. "I was lost, but God took me back and led me home, no questions asked."

Montana spotted the waiter for the third time out of the corner of her eye. "I guess we better order before they start to charge us rent for taking up space,"

She wanted Garrett to know she accepted him and reached across the table to touch his hand, gently holding it. "I'm proud of you," she whispered.

Garrett caught her eyes, and the sincerity in them reached out to him, only him. At that moment, more than any other, he was glad to just simply be. Tears slid down his face as he gingerly kissed her hand.

CHAPTER EIGHT

"A long voyage begins with just one step."
Philippine Proverb

"Would you like to listen to some jazz at Sambuca? I'm not ready for this evening to end yet," Garrett said.

"I would love to some other time, but I need to get home soon. I had a wonderful time. Thank you so much. I hope I'm not spoiling it for you," Montana said apologetically.

"You aren't spoiling anything. I would give my life for one chance to touch your hand, hear your voice, or see your smile than to spend a lifetime without it."

Montana blushed. It seemed her heart leaped out of her chest to join Garrett's. "Thank you. I haven't been touched by words like that since . . . since you." Her cheeks began to glow, enveloping her face in radiance. "I forgot how romantic you were."

"Well, I'm glad I was able to refresh your memory."

Garrett became still for a moment as if readying himself for battle.

"Montana, I'm not trying to get in your business or anything, and if you'd rather not tell me, I can respect that, but who lives in the house next door to you?"

"The lady who lives there is named Olivia. She's one of the most fascinating people I know."

Montana felt a wave of butterflies change direction in her stomach. "Garrett, I need to tell you something." She cleared her throat.

"Okay, shoot."

"I haven't seen you in years, and in that time a lot can happen. One of the things that happened to me is I have been blessed with a daughter." Montana watched his expression.

"Is she adopted?"

"No. Why would you ask that?"

"It's just that I know how careful you were about not getting pregnant, at least you were with me. I just never pictured you having a child and not married."

Montana became enraged. "Well, perhaps you don't know me as well as you think. Unplanned pregnancies do happen, you know. I am completely capable of raising a child, thank you very much." Frustrated, she immediately reconstructed the brick wall. Yes, she needed to tell Garrett, but this was not the time, not when she was angry. Upset by his response, she wondered why it never occurred to him that Chesne could be his, but knowing Garrett as she did, the thought probably never occurred to him since he knew in the past, she obsessively practiced safe sex. *But how could he not know? I sent a letter and left several messages for him.* She was tossed between anger and guilt, but despite her feelings, Chesne and Garrett had a right to know. She would not deprive them of the truth and hopefully, their happiness.

Garrett was confused. He did not know what he said that would have upset or hurt her as much as she appeared to be. Hundreds of thoughts ran through his head. Did something happen between her and the father? Did the child have some challenges? Did Montana have a difficult time raising her child? Was the father still in her life? One thing he knew for sure, if he did not say something quick to tear down that brick wall, he would never have a life with her.

"I'm sorry if I said something that offended you. I just remember when we were together before, you were so adamant about not having children without the benefit of marriage. I know people change. I guess I retained a certain image of you. To be honest, I thought that if you did have children it would be with me. I know that's selfish, but I just never imagined you having a life without me even with our past. I know I did things that were wrong and I didn't always show it in the right way, but I have always loved you. That has never changed. Will you please forgive me?"

Montana looked at him and then through him. She was working something out in her mind as the flow of thoughts formed themselves into an acceptable outcome. "I didn't mean to come off so harsh. If anyone should apologize, it's me. Do you forgive me?"

"Nothing to forgive." Garrett still didn't understand. *Better not press the issue*, he thought. He released a huge sigh of relief. "I thought you were going to say you were engaged or married. So are you and the father still together?"

"No, we're not together. We broke up many years ago. He left before she was born."

"I'm sorry to hear that. Does he know he has a daughter?"

"I tried to tell him. I sent a letter to him at his parents' address since I didn't know where he was living, but he never acknowledged it. I also called his parents' house and left messages asking him to call me, but he didn't so I gave up trying."

"Do you think he got it?"

"Of course, I don't see why he wouldn't have. I know his parents would have given it to him."

"Maybe, but I wouldn't be too sure. In every family, there is always someone who tries to destroy anyone who may have a sliver of happiness. For me it was my sisters. They hated you. It was nothing you did, but at the same time, it was everything you did. You had your life together. You were beautiful, successful, financially secure, and you were genuinely kind to everyone. You were a constant reminder of what they were not. They're my sisters, but I wouldn't put anything past them. Remember when you *lost* that eighteen-karat gold medallion with the elephants on it that your mother brought back with her from Thailand?"

Montana nodded.

"I never wanted to tell you this, but I have always wondered if Gwen stole it from you or had her daughter to."

"Garrett! She wouldn't have!"

"I've seen her do worse."

"But after everything I did for her and her children. I didn't do it because I wanted to be repaid or wanted thanks, I did it because they were in need," Montana said, confused.

"And that, my dear, is exactly why she stole it. Envious and greedy people always want more, no matter what they have to do to get it. She and Brenda probably felt you could afford to lose something. You would simply replace it. Sentimental value would have never entered their heads. It's sad when you think such things of your own family. Sometimes you have to love those closest to you from a distance. They'll undermine anyone, even me, if they think you have one more crumb than they have. Crabs in a bucket."

"I'm sorry. I didn't know. That's so unfortunate."

"Yes, it is, but sometimes you just can't divert someone's path to hell no matter how hard you try."

"You're right," she said barely able to get it out. *If that's true, he may not have gotten the letter or messages at all. This is like starting all over again. He might not have any idea. How can I bring this up years later and he believe me?*

"Let's get back to something worth talking about. What do you tell her about her father?" Garrett asked.

"It's hard for her to understand why he has never seen her. I explained that I had tried to reach him, but didn't know where he was now. At first, it was hard for her, but I assured her that if he knew he had a daughter, he would do anything in his power to see her. I make sure I don't say anything negative about him. I want her to form her own opinion. I've explained that we just couldn't work things out, but she was not to blame nor was she the reason. You know, it's funny how you can have an opinion of how certain events happened and be wrong yet have no idea how wrong you are." *If I ask him if he got a letter from me, he's going to want to know what did I write and why is it still important after all these years. I'm not ready to start at the beginning. I can't believe this. I may have been bitter this entire time for nothing. Please forgive me Father.*

"Yes, it's something how the mind works, but I think when you have limited information, it's easy to reach the wrong conclusion. Does he see her?"

"No, he's never seen her," Montana sighed.

"That's unfortunate." He reached over and held her hand. "That must be hard for her and for you. Raising a child alone takes a lot of work."

"I'm not alone. He–," she lifted her eyes towards the sky, "–has been the father she needs."

"What I mean is that it must be hard from a physical standpoint when you're all she has. I can imagine that it would be difficult to work all day, come home to care for a child, and find time for you, too."

"It's not that hard. Chesne's worth it. She's a great kid."

"Chesne, that's a beautiful name. Perhaps I can meet her one day." He had always hoped that he and Montana would have their first child together, but it seemed that honor belonged to someone else. He would just have to work harder to be the father figure Chesne needed.

"Garrett?"

"Yes."

"I thought I had lost you for a minute there."

"No, I was just thinking.

They talked the entire evening, catching up on each other's lives. There were sparks, both friendly and unfriendly fire, but it was needed medicine for them to feel comfortable and reach a place of mutual resolution. Garrett had obviously changed. He had grown into a man of honor, and he wore it well. She just hoped that he would be happy to learn that Chesne was his, but first she had to ensure that he was everything he presented himself to be. Otherwise, the effect on Chesne might be more detrimental. A father full of broken promises was worse than the absence of one.

It was a magical evening, but like Cinderella's ball, midnight was approaching, and Montana had to get home.

"Garrett, I'm sorry, but I need to go."

"I hate for it to end, but I understand."

"Thanks. I knew you would."

Garrett paid the check and they rose to leave. Montana lifted the vase, but it was too heavy and hit the table a little too hard. Garrett carried it for her to the car. "I didn't think damsels needed rescuing."

"Okay, my words come back to haunt me. Leave it to you not to forget anything. I guess there are always exceptions," she said, smiling.

The drive back to Montana's house was quiet yet filled with conversation, as they were able to communicate on intricate levels without the benefit of speech. Garrett pulled into her driveway, but before he could walk around to let Montana out, the door of Olivia's house flew open with a thud. Instinctively, Garrett ran to Montana pulling her close behind him to protect her.

Chesne ran outside. "There were three car accidents on the news, but they didn't say who it was. I was worried about you. I'm glad you're okay, Mommy."

"Of course, I'm okay."

Olivia walked onto the porch making her way to the sidewalk. "I'm sorry, Montana. She's been on pins and needles ever since you left. She would not go to sleep."

"That's okay, Olivia."

Montana turned to look at Chesne who bore the appearance of a young woman sooner than Montana wanted. "How's my little lady?" Montana shifted easily into motherhood.

"Fine, but I sure did miss you."

"And I missed you, too. I'll be right back, baby."

Montana tapped Chesne on her nose with her forefinger. Chesne then turned to look at Garrett, quickly sizing him up. He smiled in response.

Snapping his fingers as if he had forgotten something, he opened the passenger's door and picked up the vase of flowers. When Chesne saw them, her eyes became as bright and big as full moons. She looked at her mother who was on Olivia's porch.

Walking over to hug Olivia, Montana said, "Thank you so much for everything you do." She kissed her on the cheek. "I'll come by in the morning to check on you."

"Alright, baby." Olivia tried to steal a glance at the young man near the car. "Good night, Chesne." She turned to walk back toward her house.

"Good night. Thanks for taking care of me."

"You're welcome, love," Olivia said as she closed the door.

Montana walked back to Chesne and Garrett. "Chesne, I'd like for you to meet Mr. Rivers."

"Hello," Chesne said in her best grown-up voice.

"And hello right back to you. Your mother didn't tell me you were such a beautiful young lady. You look so much like your mom."

"I know. That's what everyone says. She's just a little bigger," Chesne said.

"Just a *little*," Garrett said, looking at Montana. Chesne smiled at the expression Montana gave him.

"Well, it wouldn't be nice to keep two ladies out in the middle of the night, so I will bid you farewell," Garrett said as he bowed.

Chesne giggled when Garrett kissed her hand. "Good night, fair princess. Good night, my queen," he said, looking deep into Montana's eyes.

This man really could charm a snake, Montana thought. She was amazed by his gentle, nurturing manner, and realized only he could break the ice with a child in that way.

Garrett walked them to the door. "Aren't you coming in?" Chesne asked.

"Oh, no. It would be improper to enter a lady's house at this hour. I'm walking you to the door because that is what a gentleman is supposed to do. Remember that, okay?"

"Okay."

"Well, good night again."

"Good night," Chesne and Montana replied simultaneously.

Montana floated inside as she closed and locked the door smiling to herself. It had been an eternity since she was this ecstatic and of course, God created exactly what she needed to renew her heart. How thankful she was that God was a God of second chances.

"Mommy?"

"Yes, baby?"

"I like him. He's nice and very handsome."

"I like him, too."

She glanced down at Chesne. "Time to go to bed, young lady."

"But Mommy, I'm not sleepy."

"But I am." Though in actuality Montana was not sleepy, but wanted time to reflect on the evening.

Chesne looked at her with pleading eyes.

"Since it's the weekend, you can stay up and watch TV, but don't expect me to watch it with you."

"Okay. Thanks, Mommy."

Montana knew Chesne would be asleep before the first commercial came on. Then she could relive every moment of the evening all over again. *Thanks,* Montana thought, directing her attention to God.

"You're welcome," Satan said when he overheard her, although he knew she was not speaking to him. Jealousy ran through him like a surge of electricity. "How dare he touch her! She is my betrothed, and I will be the one she unites with. Who does he think he is? He'll get a second chance alright."

He gazed at Montana and ached. She was so beautiful. "He can still create the most magnificent works of art," Satan reluctantly admitted to himself.

CHAPTER NINE

"There is no better mirror than a best friend."
Cape Verde Proverb

ontana woke up early and could not believe how energized she felt. She made a pot of coffee, took Scottie for a walk around the yard, and got the paper. As she and Scottie reentered the house, she heard Chesne upstairs.

"Good morning, sunshine," Montana called out as she closed the door.

"Good morning, Mommy. I'm hungry."

"You're always hungry."

"What do we have?"

"Let's see, we've got eggs, bacon, turkey sausage, pancakes, cereal . . ."

"Pancakes and sausage."

Montana had poured food into Scottie's bowl and was putting his dish down in the laundry room when the doorbell rang. *Who could it be at this hour? It's probably Olivia.* Since the peephole was absolutely useless, she just opened the door. "Good morning, Oliv–," she stopped abruptly as she stood staring at Garrett.

"Well, good morning. Correct me if I'm wrong, but when I got dressed this morning, I was a man. Have I changed?"

"You're amusing. What are you doing here? And without calling I might add."

"What good is it if the people you're trying to surprise know?"

"And what kind of surprise would this be, Garrett?"

"The Happy Saturday Morning Surprise."

"What is all of this?" Montana motioned to the bags and basket in his arms.

"It's a picnic." He frowned as if she had just asked the strangest question.

"At eight-thirty in the morning?"

"Who said you can't have a breakfast picnic? Are you going to let me in, or do I have to serenade you, too."

"Come in, please, crazy man. We only like the dogs to howl at night."

He smirked at her ignoring her comment. "Please tell Chesne, I am here to see *her*."

"Whatever you say, your mindless one."

"Hey, that hurt."

"Sorry, haven't had my coffee yet."

"You were always a grouch before coffee."

"At least you were already warned. Why don't we take these into the kitchen?"

Montana helped him place everything on the table then walked to the maple cabinets to get the plates and silverware. She also grabbed three leaded crystal glasses and poured orange juice.

Garrett looked around the kitchen. "I see you still have excellent taste. You've always had a discriminating eye for interior design. It's got you written all over it,"

"I'll take that as a compliment."

"That's how it was meant."

"Thank you. It was hard work, but it was fun. I love these kinds of design projects."

Montana walked to the steps. "Chesne, there is someone here to see you."

"Who?"

"You have to come and see."

"But I'm watching TV. Is it Kayla?"

"No."

"Amani?"

"No."

"I don't know anybody else."

"It's Mr. Rivers, the man you met last night. Just come downstairs," Montana said, slightly annoyed.

Chesne jumped up and raced down the stairs.

"Hi," she said shyly as she rounded the corner. "Oh, wait." She ran back upstairs and walked into the kitchen a few minutes later fully dressed. "I'm so glad to see you." Chesne extended her hand.

"And I'm glad to see you." Garrett was going to shake her hand when a small frown crept onto her forehead between her eyebrows. He kissed her hand instead. A smile as bright as the morning star appeared on her face.

"I have brought food fit for a princess. Do you know if one lives here?"

"No. No princess, but I do," Chesne said.

"Then *you* are perfect."

"Well, what did you bring?" Montana inquired.

"It smells good," Chesne said. Her stomach growled in agreement.

"Well, I have pancakes, sausage, bagels, and hash browns."

"Pancakes and sausage. That's just what I wanted. How did you know what I wanted to eat?" Chesne asked.

"What else would a princess want?" Garrett asked.

"Do you want some coffee, Garrett?" Montana got up to pour herself a cup.

"Sure." He followed her to the counter. "I see you still like a little coffee with your cream and sugar."

"And you still drink yours black."

"Black like me, pure and simple. Nothing to hide."

"Oh, please! I was thinking more like hot and bitter."

Garrett looked at her with a menacing grin.

"How are you this morning, Chesne?" Garrett asked.

"I'm fine." She watched the two of them. They seemed intensely comfortable with each other. "Mr. Rivers, I'm glad you came to see me, but would you mind if I finish watching TV."

"Well, I'll miss you, but I'll try to wait." He held his heart feigning hurt. Chesne gave her mother's smile.

"I'll see you later." Chesne quickly disappeared and ran upstairs.

They walked back to the table. Montana looked at him with raised eyebrows.

"What?" he asked.

"You know very well what. What are you trying to do? Steal my daughter?"

"No, but she would be worth stealing."

"You would give her back once you took her shopping. So, to what do I owe this pleasure?"

"I couldn't stop thinking about us last night. Every time I drifted off to sleep, I woke up dreaming about you. You were everywhere.

The smell of you was on me and I couldn't separate you from me. It was torture."

"Good, I'm not the only one who had a hard night." Montana smiled. "Thank you so much for last night. I had a wonderful time."

"The pleasure was all mine."

Montana looked at Garrett, and her love for him tugged at her heart. She realized she had forgotten the napkins. She got up and as she stood, Garrett stood, too. They were face-to-face, their lips barely a whisper apart. Garrett wrapped his arms around her and kissed her gently with great passion.

"Chesne is here, Garrett."

"I know. That's why this is all I'm doing," he teased.

Montana broke the embrace. "What was I doing? Is it hot in here?" She walked to the pantry and saw him smiling out of the corner of her eye.

"You think you're something, don't you?"

"What?"

Frustrated with her inability to hide her feelings, she said, "You think you can come back into my life after all these years and just pick up the pieces." Tears formed in the corners of her eyes.

Garrett quickly noticed her mood. He walked over and said, "Baby, I am so sorry for hurting you. I don't know what I can do to make it up to you and show you that I've really changed. All I know how to do is love you and I promise to protect your heart and to honor you always. I make this vow before God and He stands as my witness. I want the love we shared again only better. I want us back. If there is a speck of love in your heart for me, please take a chance on me now. My soul cries out for you."

Montana felt her hold quickly slipping until she lost control, and the rivers that were held back by the dams she had created gave way. "I love you, Garrett. I always have, and it seems I always will."

Montana's cheeks were as moist as blades of grass from the morning dew. Garrett looked at her and realized his own cheeks were moist, too.

"Well, this is a fine mess you have gotten us in," Montana teased as Garrett wiped her cheeks.

"But at least we're in it together," he said, more as a question than a statement.

"Yes, we are."

"We are?" Garrett was so excited, he picked her up and swung her around.

"Put me down."

"You like it when I *handle* you. I remember."

She smiled in response. "I do need to talk to Chesne. I think we should just keep things a little light until then. I just need a little time, okay?"

"Okay." They walked back to the table arm in arm.

Garrett and Montana were talking when Chesne walked in wearing different clothes.

"Sorry I took so long. Did you miss me?" Chesne asked.

"Of course. Are you ready to eat?" Montana asked.

"Yes."

"I'll probably have to heat it up as long as it took you to come back downstairs. I thought you were hungry."

"I am, but sometimes, people are hungry for different things. At Sunday school, the teacher said believers should be hungry for the Word of God. So I guess there're different kinds of hunger. Weren't you hungry, Mommy?"

"Uh-huh," was all Montana could muster. "Go wash your hands, baby," Montana said, turning to Garrett. "She says some of the strangest things."

"But she's only nine. She's right, though. We were both hungry."

Montana looked into his eyes, feeling the hunger he had for her. It sent ripples of warmth through her body. She blushed and clumsily tried to regain her composure. Garrett saw the emotion on her face, but decided not to say anything.

"Chesne knows things I can't begin to explain. All I can say is it must be the wisdom of the Holy Spirit. She has always been profoundly spiritual, very above this world, but also interested in things that are age appropriate. It scares me, and yet, I am in awe that He has so much faith in her to bless her as He has. I'm extremely proud of how she handles her responsibility to Him."

"She is something," Garrett said as Chesne walked back in. "So, Chesne, what grade are you in?"

"I'm in the fifth grade, but I could've been in the seventh."

"In the seventh? How?"

"They had an aptitude test at school that measured your intelligence and your academic ability. My test scores showed that I should be in the seventh grade, but my mom didn't want them to promote me."

"Your mommy was right not to let them. Sometimes when you're with kids a lot older than you, it's hard to fit in because you like different things at different ages."

"That's what Mommy said, but she told me it was my choice. All she wanted was what was best for me."

"Don't tell your mother, but she's pretty smart."

"Okay, I won't," Chesne promised.

They sat down to eat and Garrett blessed the food. Chesne talked incessantly about her dreams. She wanted closets filled with clothes so she would always have something to wear, to travel all over the world, and minister to people about God. She felt starting her own company would allow her to make enough money to bless other people. Chesne took a deep breath for the second round of discussion. She said it was like what her teacher told her at church, 'If you give a man a fish, he can eat for a day, but if you teach him how to fish, he can eat for a lifetime.' Since Jesus was a fisher of men, it was her responsibility to be a fisher also.

"Thank you for a great breakfast, Mr. Rivers."

"Yes, thank you, Garrett. That was thoughtful of you," Montana said.

"Don't thank me yet, I have my own agenda."

"Here we go, Mr. Spontaneous."

"I just happen to have two extra tickets to Disney on Ice this evening. You wouldn't happen to know anyone who might want to go? If you have something planned . . ."

"Planned, oh my goodness, Noelle is going to disown me. I'll be right back," Montana ran upstairs to call.

"Noelle, this is Montana. I've got some good news and some bad news. I know we're supposed to go shopping this morning . . ."

"Yeah, and?"

"Well, Garrett surprised Chesne and me with a breakfast picnic basket and . . ."

"Garrett is there now?"

"Yeah."

"How does Chesne like him?"

"They act like old friends."

"Look, I don't do this often, and don't even think about asking me to do this again, but you and Chesne need to spend some time with Garrett. I can go shopping by myself even though it won't be as much fun."

"Noelle, I can't do that to you. I promised."

"You can't do that to yourself. You missed out once. Don't lose this chance, too. Anyway, Chesne likes him and you know how picky she is. That's half the battle."

"Noelle, you are a real friend. I love you."

"Who wouldn't? Besides, what are friends for? You're more like a sister than my own sisters are, and I love you, too. You've always been there for me. It's time I returned the favor. I am genuinely happy for you."

"Thanks. Me, too."

⟡ ⟡ ⟡ ⟡ ⟡

Satan sat on Noelle's knee. "You know you're jealous. You want her to be alone so she can be lonely like you. What are you going to do without her? You know Garrett is not going away. You'll have to compete with him for her time. She didn't want to be bothered with you anyway. She just felt sorry for you."

⟡ ⟡ ⟡ ⟡ ⟡

Noelle frowned as if she had smelled something rotten. *I'm so happy for Montana. God's favor is with her, and I can't think of anyone who deserves it more*, Noelle thought.

⟡ ⟡ ⟡ ⟡ ⟡

Disgusted, Satan slithered away. "Stupid girl, I'll be back."

Montana was grateful to be alive and loving God. She got on her knees.

"Father, I humbly come before You to just say thanks. Thank You for loving me even when I don't deserve it. Thank You for blessing me with Chesne. I pray that she will always belong to You. Protect her as long as she lives. Thank You for Garrett. It's been a long time. If nothing else, it will give me closure. Most importantly, dear Father, I want to thank You just for being You all by Yourself. You are truly awesome. I love You."

Smiling, she glowed as she descended the stairs. Walking with God was the best journey on Earth.

As she entered the kitchen, she heard Chesne and Garrett talking about Santa Claus. Montana did not want to disturb them so she stood in the doorway and listened.

"When I was little, my mommy told me that there's no such person as Santa Claus. I believe in the magic of Christmas, that comes from the birth of Jesus but Santa Claus is another way Satan distracts the world from God. Did you know that Santa is just Satan spelled another way? I don't like Satan. He's an ugly, bad man. I love God. He created me, you know," Chesne said.

"Yes, I know."

"And another thing," she added, "Satan never did anything for me. He doesn't love anyone except himself, but God shows me He loves me every day. Jesus suffered and died for me as proof of God's love. Satan does things *to you* not for you. See that doormat?" she asked seriously.

"Yes."

"That is what Satan is to me. I wipe my feet on him every chance I get," Chesne said defiantly.

"That's right, baby." Montana walked back in. "Satan is our footstool, and the enemy cannot defeat us."

"She is an extraordinary young lady. She is so precocious," Garrett said.

"Yes she is. That's what was happening at school. When they asked me about accelerating her, I didn't want them to. I skipped grades in school, and I always felt different. I didn't want her to feel that way. I suggested that they enroll her in a gifted and talented program instead. At least that way, she would have the advanced studies to keep her stimulated and still be with children her own age."

"So what about today?" Garrett asked.

"We're all yours," Montana replied.

Chesne's face lit up like a Christmas tree. "Alright! I can't wait!"

Garrett was pleased he had made Chesne happy. "First, I thought we could go to Fernbank or IMAX and the Apex Museum has an African-American invention exhibit."

"I love dinosaurs. They just amaze me. I even thought of becoming a paleontologist. And I'm always happy to learn more about my ancestors. They sacrificed a lot," Chesne said.

"Yes, they did. You want to be a paleontologist?" Garrett asked.

"I used to, but I really don't like getting dirty so I'm going to be a doctor and an attorney. I can do more to help that way," Chesne said.

"Both?"

"Of course. A doctor to help heal people and an attorney to defend patients who are misdiagnosed or didn't get the right medical treatment."

"Isn't that contradictory?"

"Kind of, but I remember learning about the Tuskegee Experiment, and humans should not be guinea pigs. I want to do what I can to make sure people know we, black people, aren't property or disposable."

Garrett shook his head at Chesne's wisdom that was far advanced for her age. He had no words to express his thoughts.

"Well, it seems we have a full day in front of us," Montana said. "Let me clean up and then we can go."

"I can help you with that," Garrett volunteered.

"Thanks."

"Chesne, while we're cleaning up in here, would you take Scottie out?"

"Sure. Come on, boy." Scottie ran to her thinking she had scrapes from the table for him. When he realized her hands were empty, his tail stopped wagging. Then he heard the leash and his tail started wagging all over again.

When they were finished cleaning up, Montana peeped out the window to see what was taking Chesne so long. She saw her talking to Olivia and opened the door.

"Good morning, baby." Olivia walked up to the house with Chesne as Scottie tagged along.

Chesne unleashed him and ran to her room.

"Sorry I haven't gotten over there this morning," Montana apologized.

"That's okay. I see you've got company." Olivia smiled, recognizing the Mercedes CL600 from the previous night. "I guess your house has been cleaned." She winked.

"Well, Mother Olivia, I cannot tell a lie. The house has more cobwebs than ever," Montana said, laughing.

"That's my baby."

"Come on in. We were just finishing breakfast. Are you hungry? There's plenty left."

"Thanks, baby, but I've already eaten. You know I get up before the birds do, and morning just isn't morning until I smell bacon frying. Actually, I came over to see if you wanted to go and browse through antique shops with me, but we can do it some other time."

"Olivia, I'm sorry. Garrett just invited us to go to the Fernbank Museum, Disney on Ice, and the Apex."

"Oh, then don't mind me. That sounds like fun. Who wants to go looking at old dusty furniture anyway? You should have a wonderful time. Go on and enjoy yourselves."

Montana could see the disappointment on Olivia's face. "Where are my manners? Let me introduce you." She tucked her arm into Olivia's as she walked with her to the kitchen.

"Garrett, I'd like you to meet an extraordinary woman. This is Olivia Doucette."

Garrett stood. "Hello, Olivia. It's nice to meet you. I've heard a lot of good things about you."

"Ain't none of it true. You can't believe everything you hear."

"Well, in your case, I believe it."

Garrett noticed she had a smile that could melt butter. "Would you like to have a seat?" He pulled a chair out for her.

She noticed Garrett's gesture and nodded approval. "Thanks, but I just came to check on Montana and Chesne and to see what they were up to today. You know, they're all I've got except for my sister and niece. I love them, and if anything were to ever happen to them or they were hurt, I would take no mercy on who did it, and I would pray that God destroys them," Olivia said sternly.

"I get your point, but I would never intentionally hurt them. I promise."

"And I'm gonna hold you to that, young man."

"I know you will." Garrett smiled. Olivia was a woman who spoke her mind.

"Olivia, we'll be just fine," Montana said.

"Sometimes it's hard for you to see the bad in people, baby. You always give them the benefit of the doubt, and sometimes the only benefit they're looking for is what they can get from you. When you've lived as long as I have, you will learn that there is a little bad in mostly everyone. Don't get me wrong, there are a few special people that God has placed here to help us on our journey, but those people, like you and Chesne, are vulnerable and need to be protected."

"You're right, Olivia, they are certainly special," Garrett said.

"You just make sure you treat them that way. You get my drift?" Olivia lifted her eyebrows when she looked at Garrett.

"Yes, ma'am, loud and clear." Garrett felt as if he had just been reprimanded.

"Well, I'll be on my way. I've said my peace." She turned to look at Garrett. "I hope to see you again, young man."

"I would love to, Ms. Olivia." He bowed slightly. "And thank you."

"Thank me? For what?"

"For loving Montana and Chesne. We all need someone like you in our lives."

"Thanks." She reached out to give his hand a slight squeeze. "You take care."

"You, too."

Montana peeped at Garrett and gave him a look that said *I told you she was sassy.* Garrett smiled and said goodbye to Olivia as the two friends walked to the door.

"Olivia, you are something else."

"You got that right."

Montana hugged her. "I love you, you know."

"I know, baby, and I love you right back. Bye, Chesne," she yelled upstairs.

"Bye, Grand Livi."

"He's okay, baby. He loves you. It's all in his eyes. You two, rather three, will be just fine."

"I know. I'll talk to you later," Montana said.

"Okay, but if you don't call me right away, I understand. You might be cleaning house or something." Olivia had a mischievous smile on her face.

"You are a naughty young lady." Montana shook her head and laughed as she closed the door.

"Now that's one lady I don't ever want to cross," Garrett said as Montana reentered the kitchen.

"You'd better not either. When she said she would ask God to strike down her enemies, she means it. I can't begin to tell you the stories she's told me."

Garrett looked at his watch. "Time is slipping away. We'd better hurry if we're going."

"I'm ready."

"Me, too." Chesne said, bouncing down the stairs.

They left holding hands as if that was the way it had always been, and somehow to each of them it was.

CHAPTER TEN

"A mother's tenderness for her children is as discreet as the dew that kisses the earth."
Nilotic Proverb

Chesne glanced down the aisle of the grocery store. "May I have some cookies for our girls' night out?"

"Yes."

"Let's see, I like Oreos, but I don't always want chocolate. I could get some Teddy Grahams, they're cute. No, I'll get the Pecan Sandies. Simple, yet rich just like me."

Montana looked at her daughter and shook her head. "Yeah, and also nutty just like you. Girl, you are a mess."

"She is so cute," a woman said as she watched Chesne deciding on the cookies.

"Thank you," Chesne said.

When they walked farther down the aisle, Chesne saw the candy. She looked at Montana and was stopped in her tracks.

"Don't even think about it."

"What? I didn't say anything."

"And you didn't have to. Don't give me that look."

They moved over to the next aisle and Chesne saw the juices.

"May I have some juice? It says its one hundred percent juice. That will help me grow big and strong. Look," she said, as she picked up a bottle, "Vitamins C and E."

"I get the point, Miss Chesne. You can have one, but you'd better make sure it has everything you said. That's it for you. Nothing else. *Nada*."

"Alright. Thanks, Mommy."

"She is a beautiful child," a man said as he struggled with his own.

"Thank you," Chesne said.

"Mommy, why do people always say that?"

"Say what, baby?"

"That I'm cute or pretty."

"Well, people admire beautiful things."

Chesne pondered her mother's words. "But being pretty on the outside doesn't mean you're pretty on the inside."

"I know, but some people, most people, aren't interested in how someone is on the inside. They just want to have, or be associated with fine, pretty things."

"But that's not what matters. Satan can transform into a beautiful angel of light, but he's not and it's not real. Would people really trade God for something that's not real?"

"They do everyday, baby."

"But how? Can't they see it?"

"Some can, like you. You were blessed with an ability to see certain things. God gave you special gifts because He knew you would know what to do with them. God loves everyone and wants all of humanity to seek Him. His spirit lives inside all of us even if we don't acknowledge it, but He wants us to choose Him."

"I guess it's like telling a fish how to find the ocean."

"What do you mean?" Montana asked.

"I mean how can you show someone how to find something when they're already surrounded by it? It's in them. It's not really lost, it just hasn't been found. It's like the Holy Spirit. He dwells in us, but you won't know it until something activates it."

Chesne never ceased to amaze Montana. "Yeah, that's right." Montana glanced upward. *This is Your child*, she thought.

The weight of her responsibility in raising her daughter suddenly hit her. Chesne had so much to give the world and Montana wanted to give her the best she had to offer. *Am I really the right parent for her? Do I give her what she really needs?* Silently within the confines of her own spirit, she heard, *"Yes, my child, you are exactly the one she needs in this life. I am well pleased."*

"Mommy?"

"Yes?"

"Are you okay? Your eyes are watery."

"I know, but it's because God loves me."

"God is a lot like you. He protects me even when I can't see it."

"You mean I'm a lot like Him."

"Yeah, He takes care of me, loves me, and guides me just like you."

"And I love every minute of it." Montana kissed Chesne on the forehead.

An elderly woman was listening behind them.

"Excuse me, ma'am," she said to Montana. "That's a dedicated spiritual warrior you have there. She's going to make you enormously proud one day."

"She already has." Montana beamed like the rays of the sun.

The woman looked at Chesne. "God loves you very much. He's got many great things in store for you. You can't even begin to imagine." Then she turned toward Montana. In a hushed tone she said, "Protect her. I don't mean to scare you, but Satan is after you, and when he gets you, he will have her."

Instead of frightening Montana, the woman's words gave her some relief. From the day Chesne was born, she had always been extra protective of her—not smothering, but making sure Chesne believed in God and walked with Him. Unexplainably, she felt it was the only way Chesne could live in this world.

As the woman walked away, she said, "God loves you, too."

"I know," Montana said, "I know."

Chesne and Montana stood there. It seemed that hours passed, though it was only minutes. There was no need to explain what had just happened. They both knew and somehow, it made them cling even closer to God and each other. There was work to do and like it or not, they were an essential part of that work.

They walked down the aisle in silence, each trying to come to grips with the big dose of truth they were just dealt. As always, in their own way, they turned it over to God. Chesne and Montana looked at each other and smiled. They held hands and walked to the register.

Montana reached in her purse as the cashier scanned their items. "That didn't take too long."

"No, but it was long enough," Chesne replied.

"Patience, baby. You need to develop patience and so do I. It will make us stronger. Now, are you ready to watch our movies and eat some junk food?"

"Yeah!"

"Maybe we could talk a little too."

"About Mr. Rivers?"

"Yes, about Mr. Rivers."

Chesne and Montana watched *The Little Mermaid*, which was one of Chesne's favorite movies. Chesne liked the original story by Hans Christian Andersen better. She asked Montana to tell her the story again before they watched the movie.

"In the original story written in 1836, the little mermaid saw a prince who was drowning, and she swam over to save him. She carried him onto the shore and sang to him. He fell in love with her and her beautiful voice. Over time, she began to love him so much that she desired to become human more than anything else. Her first sacrifice of love was her voice. As she made this decision, she knew that if the prince did not choose her as his bride, she would die. He tirelessly searched for the woman who saved him, unaware that the woman and the mermaid were the same. He noticed the resemblance, but because she was mute, he did not believe she could be the woman he longed for. Continuing his search over many years and many lands, he found a woman as beautiful and gentle as the mermaid who saved him.

"The prince decided to marry her. The poor mermaid accepted that she would never realize her dream of marrying the prince. In light of this, she knew her death was imminent. The mermaid looked out into the ocean, distraught over what she feared would happen. In an effort to save her life, the mermaid's sisters threw a knife to her so she could kill the prince. Thus, by killing him, she would save her own life. As the sun started to rise on the last day of her life, she looked upon the prince whom she had grown to love more than anything in her life and knew that she could not kill him. She could not end his life to save her own. This was her second and ultimate sacrifice of love—to give her life for another. She threw the knife away and plunged to her death into the water. By virtue of her great unselfish act of love, the angels came and took her to live with them in heaven where she received an immortal soul."

Chesne's face suddenly became illuminated as she was inspired by a new revelation. "The mermaid gave her life for the prince just like Jesus gave his life for us, simply because He loves us."

"Yes, exactly."

"Okay, it's your turn to choose," Chesne said when the movie ended a couple of hours later.

Montana loved watching old movies. She could not decide between *Imitation of Life* or *A Patch of Blue*. She finally chose the former.

They watched in silence as Chesne listened, intently ingesting the movie. Montana, as usual, was moved to tears.

"Mommy, why did that girl want to be white so bad? What's wrong with being black?"

"There's nothing wrong with being black. We come from a long line of intelligent, strong people who were an advanced civilization. All the riches in the world were found in our country until the Europeans came and stripped the land and us of our worth. We were traded as cattle and treated worse. During the Middle Passage, we were shipped to America in slave ships. We were packed together so tightly there was no room to move for months. People were chained to one another and robbed of all dignity."

"Did people die?"

"Yes, baby. People died, sometimes right next to you."

"But when the body was moved, there was room. Right?"

Montana was quiet. "No. Most of the time if someone died, that person remained chained to the living. When the smell of death became unbearable, the bodies were then thrown overboard."

Chesne started crying. "That's horrible. How can someone treat another human so badly? That's not right!"

"No, it's not, but that's why we are such a strong people. Slavery made us strong because we had to endure, and Jesus made us strong because He endured. A different culture means diversity, not ignorance, but for a majority of immigrant Anglo-Saxons in this country, that is exactly what it means. They never took the time to recognize the richness that all cultures possess and the loss they have incurred by not acknowledging the value of each.

"Sometimes people can't accept who they are, so they try to be someone else. Throughout our history, some blacks that had very, very light skin and wavy or straight hair decided to pass as white. They sacrificed the loss of their family and themselves for a graven image. That is a difficult thing to deal with because you can change your environment, but you cannot change you. No matter where you run, you take yourself with you.

"Most of the time when someone rejects such an integral part of herself, like race, it is because she is made to feel ugly and unworthy. She thought being white would make her better and erase all of her problems, but instead it only increased them, causing her mother to die of a broken heart."

"But color has nothing to do with making life problem-free. It's God."

"I know, but some people make gods out of things that are earthly or mortal. Ethnicity, money, beauty, sex, material possessions, drugs . . . the list goes on."

Montana waited to see if Chesne had anything else to say. "You ready to talk?"

"Yes."

"Well, years ago, even before you were born, I met Mr. Rivers. He and I were in a relationship for six years. We loved each other deeply."

"Then what happened? Why did you break up?"

"Well, he was not ready to be in a long-term committed relationship. He thought he was ready, but he wasn't."

"Did he hurt you because he wasn't ready?"

"Yes, but it's easy to get hurt when you love someone."

"Why does love hurt, Mommy?"

"When you truly love a person, you love them unconditionally. You open your heart and mind in the hope that you will spend your lives together. Sometimes people don't take care of your heart and you get hurt. A lot of the time people just don't love each other enough to work through the pain. But you know what?"

"What?"

"If I didn't experience hurt, I would never have known love. It's kind of like when you look at a rose and admire its beauty; you also have to accept the thorns because one cannot exist without the other. By an act of God, Mr. Rivers and I have met again. We feel that we should take advantage of this opportunity and try to make what we had better. I know you've just met him, but in time, you will know what I know, and that will make all the difference. Do you think you can try?"

Chesne sat in silence for a long time absorbing everything that was said. "If one of us is sad, then no one can be happy. If being with Mr. Rivers is what you want, I'm all for it. I can tell you love each other, and I will grow to love him, too."

Montana could not have been prouder of her daughter than she was at that exact moment. What she had done was one of the most selfless acts of love anyone could make for the happiness of another. Chesne was her little mermaid.

"Chesne, there's something else I want to tell you. Mr. Rivers . . ."

"You're getting married and you want to know what I think about it?" Chesne interrupted.

"No, but when I was pregnant with you, your father and I were not married. It is a sin in God's eyes to have intercourse when you are not married. I knew it was wrong, and I asked God to forgive me. Now, I'm asking for your forgiveness. I love you more than I can ever express in words, and I am grateful to God that you are here to share your life with me." Montana wanted to tell Chesne about her father but could not without Garrett there.

"I want you to wait to have sex until you find someone worthy of you. I was wrong to do what I did. There may come a time when you really want to have intercourse or someone really wants you to, but that is something you and only you should decide, but please remember that it is not behavior that God approves. It won't be the end of the world if you do, and you won't be sent to hell for it as long as you confess it to God and repent. But like me, He wants you to wait for that special someone who is as spectacular as you."

"I will wait. I know it won't always be easy. The devil is patient and he will wait until I am weak to try and tempt me, but I know my faith and trust in God will keep me strong." Chesne paused. "When I do meet that special person, how will I know when it's true love?"

"Well, you would ask God to send the mate He has chosen for you. Never chase a man or go looking for one because you will never find him. He has to find you. A woman is a man's crowning glory. You will feel God's spirit align with yours and you will know. When someone truly loves you, he will never ask you to do anything you don't want to. He will accept you as you are and will only do what uplifts you without concern for himself."

"God forgave you and so do I. I'm glad you're my mommy. If I had been able to choose who my mommy would be, I still would have chosen you."

"You're a pretty special kid, you know that?"

"Yeah, I know."

Montana looked at Chesne and smiled. "And conceited, too."

"No, just confident."

"Oh, is that what it's called now?"

"Yep."

They both laughed.

CHAPTER ELEVEN

"Where a river flows, there is abundance."
Nilotic Proverb

Excitement nervously tapped Chesne on the shoulder waking her up unusually early. Mr. Rivers had said they would go to the beach during her spring break and he might even teach them how to fish. She had been before, but going together would be more fun even though they were not a family, when they were together it seemed as if they were and that felt good.

Chesne heard the doorbell, but Montana was still sound asleep. She ran to her mom's room. "Mommy, I think it's Mr. Rivers at the door."

Groggy, Montana turned over. "What time is it?"

"Seven-thirty."

"Seven-thirty? Tell him I'll be there in a minute."

Chesne rushed down the stairs. "Just a minute."

"Okay," Chesne heard Garrett say from the other side of the door.

"Hi, Mr. Rivers. It's Chesne."

"No, that can't be Chesne. You sound like a lady."

"I am. I'll be right back." She ran upstairs to her mother's room. "It's Mr. Rivers, Mommy."

Montana tied her robe on the way downstairs and opened the door. "And just what in the blazes are you . . ." Montana stopped when she saw Garrett.

In his right hand was a bouquet of white roses edged in pink; in his left was a bouquet of daisies, carnations, lilies, and roses in the softest pinks, yellows, and purples. Montana started laughing. "Did you buy *all* the flowers?"

"No, I left a few." Garrett smiled and kissed Montana.

Chesne came downstairs smiling when she saw the flowers. She thought they were the most beautiful flowers she had ever seen and she was certain one of the bouquets was for her.

"Good morning, Chesne. How are you?"

"I'm fine. Thank you. Please excuse me." Chesne walked into the kitchen.

"Do you think I could come in?"

"I'm sorry, Garrett. You know I'm not exactly with it in the morning."

"So what's your excuse in the evening?" Garrett laughed.

"Go ahead and laugh. I'll get you back."

"I couldn't resist." Garrett saw Chesne return with a glass of juice. She stood beside her mother.

"I just bet you couldn't," Montana responded.

"Chesne, these flowers are for you."

"Thank you, Mr. Rivers," Chesne said, excited to have her first bouquet of flowers. She walked back into the kitchen to put them in a vase. When she returned she smiled brightly as she went upstairs to get dressed.

"These are for you." Garrett handed the other bouquet to Montana.

"Thank you, sweetie." Montana kissed him on the cheek. "We're all packed. I just need some coffee. Would you like some?"

"Sure."

"Come on in the kitchen. I'll make coffee and a quick breakfast." While the coffee brewed, Montana clipped the stems and arranged her flowers in the vase. She poured two cups of coffee and handed Garrett his cup.

"I can make breakfast while you and Chesne get dressed," Garrett offered.

"You've got a deal. Thanks, I really appreciate it."

"What do you have?"

"Waffles, eggs, bacon, cereal . . ."

"Okay. I'll whip something up."

⊕ ⊕ ⊕ ⊕ ⊕

Montana jumped in the shower and lathered quickly. She was bursting with life as if every nerve ending in her body had been recharged. Looking outside, she felt as bright as the sun and decided to let her clothing reflect her spirit by wearing sky blue low rise jeans and a floral baby blue wifebeater.

"Chesne, you ready?"

"Yes. Something sure smells good."

"Mr. Rivers is cooking."

"He is? If it tastes as good as it smells, he can cook."

"Yes, he can. He cooks extremely well."

They came downstairs and walked into the kitchen.

"Ready to eat?" Garrett asked.

"I am," Chesne said as she took in the feast that he had prepared.

They sat down at the table, and Montana blessed the food.

"Which beach are we going to?" Chesne asked.

"Destin, Florida. It's beautiful there. I think you'll really like it. The sand is so white, you would think it was snow, and the water is crystal clear and looks like glass. You can just reach in and grab a fish," Garrett said.

They finished breakfast and got into his SUV dropping Scottie off at the canine hotel on their way. As they drove on the expressway, they talked, sang songs, and played games. They were having so much fun that it did not seem they had driven six hours.

Garrett pulled into an exclusive gated community called Neighborhood of Caribe. When he turned onto Rue Martin, both Montana and Chesne's mouths fell open as they looked at the house that would be home to them for the next few days. It was a Spanish-style stucco with Mediterranean influences and was a short walk from the beach.

Once they got out, Garrett grabbed the luggage from the trunk while Montana and Chesne headed for the house.

Montana turned around. "You need any help?"

"No, I've got it, but you can take the key and open the door."

"Okay, no problem." Montana met up with Chesne who eagerly waited at the door. As she opened it, their fascination with the house continued. It was fully furnished with amenities for the most demanding traveler.

The Neighborhood had two swimming pools, four tennis courts, and its own private beach access. The upscale Silver Sands Factory stores were just across the street with shopping, dining, and entertainment according to the brochure that was on the living room table along with other information about tourist attractions. There were two master suites with large baths and ample closet space.

Three additional bedrooms were upstairs. The kitchen had a large eat-in area as well as a counter with barstools. The family room was open and comfortable. On the far wall were a widescreen television, DVD player, and every video game system imaginable.

It was about seventy-three degrees in Destin, and the weather seemed to promise much of the same for the next few days. Destin was located six miles east of Fort Walton Beach. The city has a rich historical heritage dating back to Native American inhabitants as early as seventh century A.D. About nine hundred years later, Spanish explorers also visited, adding to the influence of the mixed heritage in the area.

"This is beautiful," Chesne said.

"Yes, it is," Montana agreed as she opened the patio door and walked out with Chesne. Looking back Montana asked, Garrett, are you coming?"

"In a minute." Garrett put the suitcases in the appointed rooms and came out shortly after to join them. They each took a deep breath, inhaling the intoxicating smell of the ocean and the tranquility the beach provided. The breeze off the water was a welcome reprieve from the heat. Chesne, Montana, and Garrett absorbed the breathtaking views of the water and the sugar-white sand.

"I could stay here forever," Chesne said.

"So could I," Garrett agreed.

"You two would be on the beach so much, you would probably turn into sand crabs," Montana said.

"No, I wouldn't." Chesne laughed.

The sand and the water were striking contrasts and one of nature's most dramatic landscapes. The azure sky looked freshly painted and the clouds were scattered throughout and looked like air-spun wisps of cotton candy.

As Montana peered out at the ocean, she saw many fishing boats eagerly trying to catch the daily delicacies required by the local restaurants for their dining guests.

The simplest and purest of pleasures seemed to exist here. There were dolphins performing an aquatic dance and water that glistened like emeralds stretching out for miles. It was exactly what they needed, a little piece of heaven to call their own. The beach possessed its own unique personality—unpretentious, uncomplicated, and remarkably beautiful.

"So what do you want to do first?" Garrett asked.

"I hate to be the thorn in anyone's side, but I want to stroll along the beach, get something to eat, and have a relaxing evening," Montana said.

"And I can look for shells while we're walking. I might even find a special one for you, Mommy."

"That is so sweet of you."

"Well, it's kind of a shell."

"What do you mean kind of?"

"The shell of a sand crab so you can think of Mr. Rivers and me whenever you see it."

"Oh, so now you're a comedian," Montana said, laughing.

Garrett laughed so hard his stomach started to hurt. "I see where she gets her quick wit."

Montana rolled her eyes. "Anyway, if any sensible people want to walk with me on the beach, I'm going now."

They changed clothes and began their stroll along the sandy shore. They were barefoot as they walked, the feel of the warm sand between their toes felt good. The wind gusted for a moment and blew

Montana's hat off, she ran over to get it. When she looked down, she saw a perfect sand dollar and eagerly picked it up.

"Chesne, look what I have for you."

"What?"

Montana opened her hand to reveal the treasure.

"It's beautiful, Mommy. Thanks." Chesne hugged her and put it safely in her pocket.

Garrett picked Chesne up and ran into the water acting as though he were going to throw her in. She screamed, yelled, and laughed. He put her down and tapped her on the shoulder.

"You're it," he said as he ran.

"Oh, that's not fair!" Chesne started after him. By the time she caught up, he was bent over trying to catch his breath.

Montana shook her head. "See, that's what old age does to you." She looked at how natural Chesne and Garrett were with each other and smiled. *How am I going to tell them now? They will wonder why I waited so long, and I don't have a good answer.*

"You're right. I thought I was in shape."

"You are, dear. You just can't keep up with a nine-year-old."

"I'm nine and three-quarters."

"Oh, I'm sorry. How could I forget?" Montana said, smiling.

Chesne looked out toward the horizon. "Look, more dolphins! They are so smart and graceful."

The sunset was starting to display its magnificence. The sky expanded itself and displayed muted colors of crimson, saffron, tangerine, and varying shades of indigo. Garrett looked at his watch. Three hours had passed since they started walking. "It's 7:45."

"It's that late? Boy that went by quick," Montana said.

"Is anybody hungry?" Garrett asked.

"I am. I am," Chesne and Montana chorused.

"Then what are we waiting for? Let's go."

"The sunset is gorgeous," Montana said, slipping her hand in Garrett's. She looked at him and stood on her tiptoes to kiss him.

Chesne ran up in front of them chasing the tide as it kissed the shore and then shied away.

When they were almost at the house, Montana said, "Chesne, wait a minute, baby. We need to rinse the sand off."

Garrett pulled the showerhead off the rack and aimed it in Chesne's direction.

"Oh, it's warm. It feels good on my feet," Chesne said.

"Now for you," Garrett said to Montana as he discreetly adjusted the temperature of the water. She lifted her foot and held it out.

"Ooh, that's freezing. Get that thing off me! Chesne, I thought you said it was warm."

"It was."

They heard Garrett laughing as he quickly ran inside. Montana ran after him. "I'm going to get you."

Chesne laughed as she watched her mother in love with the man she had also grown to love.

Montana quickly took a shower and changed clothes. She walked into the family room to browse through the brochures and find a restaurant.

"Mommy, why are your clothes in the same room as mine?" Chesne asked as she walked into the family room fully dressed.

"Because Garrett and I aren't married."

"But we act like a family."

Garrett walked into the kitchen as he heard Chesne's comment. He was touched that she felt close to him. Montana smiled as she interpreted Garrett's thoughts from his expression.

"Well, sweetie, acting and being are two different things. You have to be married by a minister or appointed official. Once you start justifying your actions and straddling the line, it becomes harder to tell right from wrong."

"I know, but God knows our hearts."

"Yes, but He also wants to know that no matter what, we will obey His word without wavering. He wants us to choose Him as our guide, not society or our own desires," Montana said.

"I can't believe how easy it is to be misled. Satan really is busy," Chesne said remorsefully.

"Yes, he is, but God knows you're a good steward. He forgives you, but that's why it's so important to talk to Him every day. Do you understand?"

"Yes." Chesne walked back into the bedroom realizing that she forgot her shoes.

"What do you want to eat?" Montana asked Garrett.

"Seafood is fine."

Montana chose The Back Porch mainly because the brochure stated it was a beachfront restaurant and served only the freshest seafood. Montana carried a map as they got into the SUV while Garrett was armed with an extra dose of testosterone, which announced, "I am man, I don't need to ask for directions."

Montana looked at him after they drove down Highway 98 East for the second time. "I think you made a wrong turn. Are you sure we're on Old Highway 98?"

"You didn't say Old Highway 98."

"Yes, I did." Montana looked around for signs. "Old Highway 98 is right over there," she said, pointing.

"If you had told me it was Old Highway 98, we could have been there by now."

"Oh, really?"

"Yeah."

Montana looked at him and they both started laughing.

"You just don't like to admit you're wrong," Garrett said.

"And you do?"

"I've only been wrong once in my life. That's when I thought I was wrong and I wasn't."

"Yeah, right."

Garrett finally pulled into the parking lot of the restaurant and walked around to open the door for Chesne and Montana.

"Good evening," the hostess said as they entered.

"Hello," Garrett said.

"Three for dinner?"

"Yes."

"This way please." The hostess led them to their seats and placed the menus on the table. Chesne pulled out her chair and sat down.

"A gentleman should always open the door and pull out your chair. Now if you would allow me," Garrett said.

Chesne stood while Garrett pulled out the chair, then she sat down and he placed the napkin in her lap.

"Are you okay?"

"Yes." Chesne smiled and watched Garrett do the same for her mother.

"Everything sounds good," Montana said, reading over the menu.

"Yes, it does. I'm having a hard time making up my mind," Garrett said.

"I'm not," Chesne said.

"What do you want, Chesne?"

"Shrimp, fries, and a vanilla shake."

"A woman who knows what she wants," Garrett said.

"I want the grilled shrimp, drawn butter, rice pilaf, and asparagus. And you, love?" Montana asked.

"Uh, I'll take the Seafarer's platter. No, the salmon. Wait a minute." He heard Montana laughing.

The server walked to the table. "What can I get you to drink, honey?" she asked, smiling a little too friendly at Garrett.

"I'll take a Sprite."

"And you?" she said to Montana but kept her eyes on Garrett.

"I'll take a Pepsi, please."

"I want a Sprite, too," Chesne said.

The server bent over and spoke seductively to Garrett, "I'll get *that* right up for you." She turned to walk away.

Montana couldn't believe what she was hearing. "Uh, excuse me, ma'am, if I can call you that."

The waitress turned obviously annoyed.

"If you want to live beyond today, I would suggest..." she stopped and turned her attention to Chesne. "Chesne, don't you need to use the restroom?"

"No," Chesne said, smiling, anxious to hear. Montana looked at her and Chesne quickly left.

Montana sighed. "As I was saying, I would suggest that you put some ice on that hot tail of yours and regain some semblance of self-respect and decency."

"Oh, I'm sorry. I didn't realize . . ."

"Save it." Montana held her hand up signifying that she didn't want to hear any more. The server dismissed herself quietly.

Garrett started laughing. "Well, she certainly knew what she wanted," he teased.

"And if she's not careful, she'll get more than she ever imagined."

When the server brought the drinks, it was a different woman. "Susie wanted me to take care of you for her."

Montana looked at Garrett who smiled.

✧ ✧ ✧ ✧ ✧

After they ate breakfast the next day, they got ready to leave. "Is everybody ready to learn how to fish?" Garrett asked.

"I am," Chesne said.

"Yeah, me, too." Montana was not excited about fishing, but knew Chesne and Garrett were. All Montana could think of were the slimy worms she would have to put on the hooks and the stuff that oozed out of them. She didn't even want to think about looking into the poor fish's eyes as she tried to get the cold, flipping thing off the hook and into the cooler.

"I chartered a boat for us to go out onto the water. We'll be sharing it with some other families. Is that okay?"

"That's fine," Montana said.

When they got to the dock, there were about five other people standing around the harbor. Garrett drove up to the crowd. "Do you know if this is where we catch the charter boat *Sure Catch*?" Garrett asked, not directing his question to anyone in particular.

"Yeah," a man said, "y'all getting on?"

"Yes. I'm going to teach my family how to fish," Garrett said.

The man started laughing. "This may not be where they want to learn." He extended his hand. "How ya doing? My name is William." Garrett introduced himself then went to park. He walked up to William while Chesne and Montana walked to the other side of the parking lot.

"Man, the fish I caught here last year were so big, it took me hours to reel them in. All I could do after it was over was drink beer," William said. "Nothing like it."

"No, you're right, it's nothing like the feel on your line when you know you've got a big one. It's a test of wills between you and him," Garrett said as his excitement grew.

"This is my wife, Vickie, and my daughter, Courtney," William said.

Garrett turned around to check on Chesne and Montana, but they were still on the other side looking into the water. He saw Chesne pointing to something.

"That's my family over there, Montana and Chesne. Chesne is nine."

"My daughter just turned ten. Maybe they'll have something in common. I wasn't sure about her coming. You know how kids are."

"Yeah. I'm sure they'll get along. Excuse me. I'll be back." Garrett walked over to them. "What did you see?"

"I saw a school of fish. They were cute."

Garrett looked toward the crowd and saw the boat pulling in. "Looks like we're ready. I'll introduce you to William and his family once we board." They headed toward the boat, which was being tied to the dock.

"This is nice," Montana said after they climbed aboard.

"Hi," a woman said.

"Hi," Montana responded.

"I'm Vickie, William's wife," she said, pointing to her husband who stood next to Garrett.

"Oh, you were dragged along, too, huh? I'm Montana. Nice to meet you."

"No, I actually like fishing sometimes. The first time we came out, I caught a three-pounder and I was hooked. It took me forever to bring him in, but it was fun. You wouldn't think something that small could make you work, but when your life is on the line, no pun intended, I guess you fight like crazy."

"Well, I like the ocean, but I don't want to put a slimy worm on a hook just to get a slippery fish off of it."

Vickie laughed. "Out here, you can use shrimp or artificial bait. You don't really use worms unless you go pier or jetty fishing."

"In that case, I might try it."

"You should, it's fun. It's also calm and peaceful. It gives me time to reflect, which is what I like most of all."

"Well, I could definitely use that."

Montana suddenly realized she had lost sight of Chesne. "Where did my daughter go?" She asked, looking around.

"I think I saw her go downstairs trailing behind my daughter, Courtney."

Montana heard Chesne's voice coming from below deck. Rising, she walked to the stairwell and caught a glimpse of her daughter as she looked into the deck below. "Chesne?"

"Yes, Mommy."

"Just checking. You okay?"

"Yes, I'm fine. Another girl is down here with me. Her name is Courtney. We're playing."

"Okay. Have fun. If you need anything, let me know."

"Alright."

"Kids just don't understand all it takes is a minute for something to happen," Vickie said when Montana returned.

Montana nodded. "People are so crazy these days; I don't put anything past them. I worry about Chesne every time she's out of my sight."

"You can only be with them so much. Then you just have to ask God to protect them," Vickie said.

"You're right about that. That's the only way you can protect them."

Montana saw Garrett and William engrossed in conversation sitting on the other side of the boat as its engine started and headed out.

"I see the guys have settled down," Vickie said as she saw them seated with fishing rod in one hand and a beer in the other.

"And did they think of us?" Montana asked.

"No."

Vickie and Montana walked over to where the men were seated.

"So are you planning to catch all the fish?" Vickie asked.

"No, baby. We thought we'd leave a few small ones for you to catch," William said, smiling.

"Thanks, baby. That is *so* thoughtful of you."

Vickie showed Montana how to bait her hook when they reached their seats. "I guess it's just us girls," Montana said. She sat back, closed her eyes, and inhaled deeply, allowing herself to relax and take in the magnificent view.

"This *is* wonderful," Montana said, holding her rod in anticipation.

"Yes, it is. Being out here makes all your troubles melt away," Vickie said.

Montana looked out as far as she could and saw the vast beauty of the ocean. She reached down to grab her water bottle and felt a tug on her rod.

"You've got a fish!" Vickie said excited.

"A fish! How do you know?"

"It pulled your line. Wait to see if it tugs it again." Just then, Montana's rod bowed.

"Don't jerk it. Just pull it in as quickly as you can," Vickie advised.

"I got a fish!" Montana screamed, reeling in her line. Garrett overheard her and turned to look.

"It's a big one!" Vickie said just as excited.

"Alright, baby!" Garrett said proudly.

"Must be one of those small ones you left us," Montana teased as she struggled with the line. "Man, this is work." She caught a glimpse of the fish. "Oh goodness, he is huge."

When she pulled him up, she heard William say, "That's got to be at least an eight-pound grouper."

Montana tried her best to control the wriggling fish. "Garrett, could you please help me?" she asked breathless. "I'm not taking this thing off the hook. Now *you* get a chance to work, baby," she said sweetly.

Garrett laughed. "Some people should not be taught," he teased. He took the fish off and tossed it into the cooler.

"Those who can do and those who can't teach," Montana teased back.

"Hold the presses," Vickie said as she started reeling in her line. She caught a twelve-pound Amberjack.

"Wouldn't you know? The women have to catch *and* cook the fish," Montana said.

"Not this time. We catch them, they cook them."

"Now that's an idea I can live with," Montana said, laughing.

Montana heard William say, "Got it." She looked up and watched William struggle to pull in a twenty-two-pound Amberjack. She was about to say something when she saw Garrett out of the corner of her eye pulling in his rod. At the end of his hook was a thirty-pound Cobia.

Sunset was quickly arriving as the boat slowly returned to the harbor.

"I can't tell you when I've enjoyed talking with someone so much. It was really nice to meet you. I'll give you my number. Maybe we can keep in touch, but I understand how it is sometimes," Vickie said.

"I enjoyed talking to you, too. It's nice to meet another phenomenal woman. I'll call you later," Montana said.

"You've got a deal."

Montana glanced at her number. "You live in Georgia?"

"Yes, in Athens. Why?"

"We live in Atlanta."

"We'll definitely keep in touch."

As they walked to the car, Chesne said, "I had the best day playing with my new friend."

"Me, too," Garrett and Montana replied.

CHAPTER TWELVE

"A son will be what he is taught."
Swahili Proverb

ontana drove to Woodlawn Preparatory to pick Chesne up from school. When she arrived, she saw Chesne sitting on the bench with her teacher, Ms. Flynn.

Megan Flynn was well respected among peers, students, and parents. Loving all of her students equally, she fought for, motivated, and inspired them. In Montana's conversations with her, she never believed Ms. Flynn gave preferential treatment to any student. On numerous occasions, she had told Montana that all of her students were winners.

When Montana saw Chesne with Megan, she knew something important had happened. Chesne was an honor student and never had a behavior or disciplinary problem, which left Montana to assume the worse.

On the surface, there was nothing apparently wrong, but Montana could feel the hairs on the back of her neck rise. Montana instinctively got out of the car.

"Hi, baby."

"Hey."

"Hello, Ms. St. Claire."

"Hello, Ms. Flynn. What's going on?"

"We tried to call you at work, but they said you had already left. We didn't have your cell number, so we couldn't call you."

"But they have it at work. The receptionist would have given it to you. Did you tell her who you were?"

"Yes, Ms. St. Claire, and I also told her it was an urgent matter, but she did not give me your number."

"That's strange, but that's not important right now. I'll take care of that later. What happened?"

"There was an incident at school today. Would you mind coming with me so we can discuss it," Ms. Flynn said.

An incident, Montana thought. It sounded so benign yet earth-shattering at the same time. They walked into Ms. Abernathy's office, the principal at Woodlawn.

"Hi, Montana. I'm sorry to have you come in like this, but we've had a situation at school. Have a seat," Joan said.

"No, thank you. I think I need to stand." Montana felt her stomach building speed as the butterflies in it went on a hair-raising roller-coaster ride. "Continue."

"While Chesne's class was outside playing, Collier Yadrow, a young boy from the sixth-grade attempted to sexually assault Chesne. She . . ." Joan was stopped in mid-sentence.

"He did what? Where was everyone? Why didn't you try calling me again? Where is he?" She rushed over to Chesne. "Are you okay, baby?"

Chesne nodded.

Ms. Flynn saw the despair and terror on Montana's face. "Chesne, why don't we go and get something to drink? Would you like that?"

"Yes," Chesne said softly.

Montana waited until they closed the door. "This feels like a nightmare. How did this happen? When?"

"Well apparently, some children were playing hide and seek, and he assaulted her behind the trailer. We immediately contacted the hospital and took Chesne in to be examined by the doctor. The hospital contacted the authorities."

"Has she . . .did she?"

"He didn't penetrate her," Joan said, aware of what Montana was trying to ask.

"I have contacted the school board and set up a meeting with his parents and you. We have also reported it to the police, Department of Children Services (DCS), and the Office for Civil Rights. We will not go behind closed doors to discuss this. It will be open to you and his parents initially and then we would like to have an open meeting with all the parents, if you and his parents agree."

Montana didn't respond.

"As much as I respect you and can empathize with Chesne's situation, I must remain objective. By law, we also have to protect Collier's privacy."

"What is it you have to protect him from? Anally assaulting himself? His victims are the ones who need protection. I understand you're caught in the middle, but it's not your child."

"I totally understand. This molestation has cast a pall over the school. As you know, the staff here loves these kids, especially Chesne." Joan hesitated, then continued, "The media knows about this now. I can guarantee that Chesne won't be violated while she's here."

"How can you guarantee that when she was *already* violated here?"

"I know you're angry, but please understand my situation. I am caught between my affection for Chesne, my duty to the school board and my obligation to the other children, even Collier. You can press charges against Collier, if you wish. The school superintendent will send a letter out to all parents saying that we are carefully investigating this matter and affirmative measures have been taken. We are also adding security to ease parents' concern. The DCS will be on hand to speak with you and the Yadrows after the meeting. They will soon start to interview all the children involved in the matter. The media may pounce on Chesne once they hear of this so you may want to prepare yourselves. They can be a little insensitive to victims sometime. I will give you copies of all the reports we received. Collier is a minor, but this is still a serious offense that will be placed on his permanent record."

"You knew about the letters that he wrote to Chesne last year and you promised me that it would be resolved and I wouldn't have to be concerned. You assured me it was only infatuation, but it wasn't, was it? If I didn't think you were acting on Chesne's behalf, I would sue the school, but if anything happens, I am holding you personally responsible, Joan."

"So am I," Joan said, feeling the sting of emotion stirring. "One last thing, you might want to consider counseling, just to make sure Chesne's okay. Oftentimes, the full impact doesn't hit until much later. Just watch her." Joan walked over to sit beside Montana. She reached out and held her hands. "You know I would never endanger Chesne," she said with moistened eyes.

"I know."

"If you need anything, anything at all, just call me. Just so you know, I did speak with Collier's parents about the letters, and they

promised me that it would be handled. Evidently, It wasn't, and for
that I am truly sorry."

"Thank you," Montana said barely above a whisper.

Montana and Joan walked into the hall. "Ms. Flynn, would you
walk them out?" Joan said.

"Sure."

They walked in silence until they reached the car. Ms. Flynn said,
"I'm here for support and any assistance I can offer. I love Chesne,
and I hate this happened. Here is my home number, please call me if
you need me. It doesn't matter what time."

"Thank you so much, Megan. I may take you up on that once I
speak with Chesne. Good-bye."

"Good-bye." Ms. Flynn gently squeezed Chesne's hand, giving
her a look of encouragement.

Montana could not breathe. She did not know what to say. All
sorts of things ran through her mind. Her stomach was turning
Olympic-size somersaults, and she felt as if she were going to be sick.

"Sweetie, do you want to talk?" Montana held Chesne's chin in
her hand.

"Not yet. I want to wait until we get home." Chesne tried to be
brave, but she was scared, and no matter what she did, she could not
stop the tears that rushed down her cheeks. Montana slid over and
embraced her gently.

Montana looked at Chesne. Her heart longed to make all of this
disappear, but she knew she was powerless. It was yet another
episode in her life that forced her to exercise every ounce of faith and
strength that she possessed. She knew Chesne needed to cry so she
let her continue. "Okay, baby, whatever you want. I need to call Mr.
Rivers and tell him not to come over because we need some time
together."

"No, Mommy, I do want Mr. Rivers to come over. I want to feel like a family with a mommy and daddy, even if it is just pretend for one night."

Montana's heart screamed out in pain. She knew Chesne did not mean to hurt her, but it hurt just the same.

"Alright, Chesne."

Montana could not get home fast enough. It seemed that every red light caught her, and she was stuck behind every Sunday driver in Atlanta. She silently prayed to God for strength and encouragement, but it seemed slow in coming.

They finally pulled into the driveway and for once, she was grateful Olivia was not in the yard tending to her garden. At the moment, the only thing that mattered was Chesne. They walked into the house, and Scottie jumped on Chesne begging to be picked up. They knew Scottie had to go out, but they needed to talk. Seeming to sense the darkness that surrounded them, he was patient and waited.

Out of habit, they walked into the keeping room adjacent to the kitchen. It was their tranquil place.

"Do you want something to drink?"

Chesne shook her head.

"So tell me what happened, baby." Montana tried to sound as calm and casual as she could. Scottie walked in as if he needed to hear what happened as well.

Chesne sighed deeply as if talking about it would cause it to start all over again. She brushed the hair back from her face with trembling hands.

"Well, it all started when we were outside during recess. All of us were playing hide-and-seek. We took turns counting and hiding. Kayla and I were hiding behind the trailer. You know the one that's sometimes used for the book mobile?"

Montana nodded.

"We hide there all the time because it's a good hiding place. The other kids have started hiding there, too. Anyway, Collier..." Chesne paused to regain her strength.

Montana's mind reached back trying to remember his face. Suddenly she remembered the boy who wrote notes much too mature for someone his age and much too intimate. Initially, when she met him, she noticed how handsome he was, but there was also a sadness that seemed to be deeply buried.

When Chesne showed Montana the letters, she was appalled. Montana called Woodlawn the next day to set up a meeting with Chesne's teacher and the principal. They were shocked that someone so young could describe sexual activities with such graphic detail. Collier's parents were asked to meet with the counselor, teacher, and principal. The counselor, Vivian Baker, strongly suggested that they speak to Collier about his behavior and the need for counseling. Vivian told them that behavior of this magnitude generally got worse before it got better. *Well, here is worse,* Montana thought.

"Collier was it, and he was trying to find us. Kayla told me later that he touched her on the shoulder and motioned for her to be quiet. She said he acted like he was going to play a trick on me and told her that we would catch up with her later."

Here it comes, Montana thought as her throat caught up with her stomach and they both hit bottom as the taste of bile reached her tongue.

"He came up behind me and placed his arms around mine locking me in a bear hug." Chesne stopped. She put her face in her hands and cried wretchedly. Giving her the freedom to weep, Montana waited to embrace her.

She held Chesne tightly as love turned her arms into warm, comforting blankets, chasing away the evil that had attacked Chesne's heart and spirit. "We can finish this later if you want."

Chesne shook her head fiercely. "I need to get this out. It feels like if I don't, I'll just burst. I'm so ashamed, Mommy."

"Baby, you don't have anything to be ashamed of. You didn't do anything wrong. He was the one."

"But I must have done something to make him . . . to make him think he could do that to me." Chesne sobbed.

"It is so hard to make sense out of what people do. Sometimes people are mean because it's what they learned and other times, I hate to say this, but I believe some people are naturally evil. This is a harsh and cruel world sometimes, baby, but no matter what happens, God will always protect you. He will not fail."

Chesne seemed to gain some strength and continued, "I knew he was trying to do something ugly, and I was scared. I was about to tell him to let me go, when he held me and forced me to the ground. He told me he had never seen a black girl more beautiful than a white one. He said that I was sweet and he wanted me.

"I was so afraid. I didn't know what he was really going to do. All I could think of was I would never see you again. I thought I was going to die. I tried to scream, but nothing came out and then when it did, no one heard me because all the kids were playing and screaming.

"He was breathing hard like he was out of breath. He unzipped his pants and pulled out his penis. He tried to pull down my panties, but I kept my legs closed as tightly as I could and kept moving. There was something wet on the tip of his penis and he pulled my panties to the side. He was trying to put it in me." Chesne hesitated as tears were barely contained. Scottie whined as he lay on Chesne's feet to comfort her.

"I wrestled with him, but he's so much bigger than me. All I could do was pray. I asked God to forgive him. Then we both saw a huge image of light appear. At first I didn't know what it was, but I think he was an angel. He was nine or ten feet tall and more real than anything I've ever seen. He had hands and arms, kinda, but they were more. They were like mine, but they weren't. I don't know how to describe it. He was talking to Collier in a language that I couldn't understand. Then he said to me, 'Fear not, precious child, God is with you.' "

Chills ran down Montana's spine and then resonated through her entire being. She was horrified that Chesne had come that close to evil, but she was grateful Chesne was protected by the loving arms of God. Now she knew, really knew, there were angels, but to actually see one had to be a phenomenal experience.

"Collier turned white like a ghost and he looked really scared. He tried to move, but couldn't. After a while, when Kayla didn't see me, she, Gabriel, Michael, and the other kids ran behind the trailer to where I was and they saw what Collier was trying to do. I was so embarrassed.

"Then the angel released him. Collier jumped up and looked at everyone. He tried to run past the other kids, but they jumped on him. Michael and Gabriel started to hit him. I wanted to say no. I know I should have, but I didn't. I wanted him to hurt like he tried to hurt me. Kayla helped me to stand up, and I pulled my panties back on then Amani ran to tell Ms. Flynn what happened.

"Ms. Flynn asked the nurse to stay with me until we left for the hospital while she talked to Ms. Abernathy. I have never been so frightened. I don't want to go through that again. It was horrible. I felt like some ugly, used thing. I know he didn't penetrate me, but if he had, I don't think I could go through anything like that. I don't know how anybody could. I don't know what I would do without you and God.

"Ms. Abernathy talked to me and told me she asked Collier's parents to come to school. When they got there, she told them she had reported the incident. The counselor, Ms. Baker, came to talk to me. I told her I was okay, but she still insisted on talking to me. She talked to Collier, too and told him that he would be enrolled into mandatory counseling. Ms. Abernathy told Collier's parents that he was suspended indefinitely and could not return to school until he completed the six-month boot camp program. She told them they would have to attend counseling with him.

"His parents were angry, but Ms. Abernathy said she didn't care. She told them that they ought to be more concerned with their son's behavior. She said that they needed to be worried that we wouldn't press charges against him and them." Chesne was quiet for a minute. "Mommy, I know you told me if anything bad ever happened, I should be brave and stand up for myself, but I don't feel so brave."

Montana sat there as if she were in a catatonic state. She imagined herself looking straight into Collier's eyes, emotionless while she violently choked the last breath of life from him. She reluctantly snapped herself back to reality for Chesne's sake. Thank God, she was not physically hurt, but the mental and emotional damage was often always worse.

"There's nothing wrong with being scared. It's normal after an ordeal like this. We will work through this together. We will do whatever it takes to make sure you are all right. Baby, I can't make this go away, but I will be right here by your side whenever you need me, and I promise to hold you close."

Chesne smiled ever so slightly and hugged Montana. "I'm okay," she said, more for her mother than herself. "I just don't understand how people can do such horrible things to each other."

"I'm grateful to God that you're alright, but people have been inhumane to one another since the beginning of time. It's not about to change overnight. It will take someone like you to change the world, one person at a time."

"I know I need to forgive him, Mommy, and I will, but I'm not ready to do that just yet. You always said if I want God to forgive me, even when I don't deserve it, then I have to forgive someone even when I feel they don't deserve it."

"You've listened well. You're a terrific young lady. God always understands." Montana hugged her. She was proud of her daughter. Montana didn't think she could ever be that forgiving, but she was glad that she helped to raise a child who was.

In her mind, all Montana could think about was going over to Collier's house to confront him and his parents. She understood Chesne's apprehension and prayed that they both would have some peace, but for now, all Montana could taste was vengeance.

"I have to be honest with you, I am terribly angry that someone tried to hurt you. But right now, all that concerns me is making sure you're okay. I want to do everything I can to ensure that. I think it's important that we talk to someone about this. You can change your mind later, but we do need to see someone. If you want, we can talk to Pastor Brooks."

"Okay," Chesne said.

Montana patiently waited for Chesne to get it all out.

"Mommy, I'm tired of talking about this. It's all I've talked about all day."

"You sure?"

"Yeah.

"Well if you want to talk any more, as always, I'm here for you."

Chesne nodded.

"Do you want anything? Are you hungry?"

"I'm a little hungry."

"I'll heat something up for you." Montana kissed her on the forehead and gently touched her cheek. Shakily, she walked into the kitchen to prepare Chesne's meal.

"Will Mr. Rivers be here soon?"

"He should be here any minute now. Why?"

"I just want to know if all boys are like that. I know you've told me about my daddy, but is he the only one?"

"No, baby, Mr. Rivers is an exception, too. There are not many though. I want you to wait a minute before you talk to him, okay?"

"Okay."

As if on cue, the doorbell rang and Scottie whined to go out. "Okay, you've been patient long enough. Go on." Scottie ran outside.

"Stay in the yard, Scottie," Montana said.

"Hi, baby." Montana flung her arms around Garrett before he could say anything.

"Now that's what I call a greeting," he joked. He saw the distraught look on Montana's face and knew this was nothing to joke about.

Chesne heard him at the door. She ran up to Garrett and jumped into his arms, hugging him tightly. He hugged her and whispered, "Whatever it is, everything is going to be just fine, sweetheart. I will always be here to protect you, no matter what." As if those were the words she needed to hear, Chesne cried softly into Garrett's shoulder.

He held Chesne in one arm and placed the other around Montana. They walked into the tranquil place. Garrett put Chesne on his lap.

"I'm here for you and your mom. I'll always make sure both of you are happy and safe. Is there something you want to tell me or anything you want me to do?"

"No," Chesne said. "I'm just glad you're here." She hugged him tightly.

"I'm here whenever you need me, okay?"

"Okay."

Montana looked at Garrett grateful he was there. "We need to talk," she mouthed.

Chesne stood when she heard the microwave go off. "I'm going to eat. I'll be back."

"Okay." Garrett kissed her on the forehead trying to conceal his worry.

Montana inwardly battled as she repeated the sordid incident. But, before she could finish, Garrett jumped up and started pacing. Veins in his neck contracted rapidly as he gritted his teeth, sharpening them for the prey he would soon devour. "Where does this piece of trash live?"

"Baby, that won't help the situation." Montana knew he wanted to hit something.

"Oh, it will help. I'll make sure it helps," he said. He heard Chesne in the kitchen and remembered she was within earshot. He calmed himself down and walked into the kitchen.

"I'll take care of everything," he assured Chesne. "As long as I live, *no one* will ever hurt you again if I can prevent it. I'm not trying to be your father or take his place, but I care about you more than I can say, and I will do the things a father should do in order to protect those he loves."

"I love you," Chesne told him.

"And I love you, too, princess."

When Chesne finally went to sleep, Garrett and Montana were on edge. "Montana, have you called Collier's parents?"

"Not yet. I was waiting for Chesne to fall asleep."

"If it's okay, I would like to go with you to talk to them."

"I would love for you to." She looked at Garrett lovingly. "I think it's important for you to be there."

"I want to know how they are raising their son. What would make him think this is normal and appropriate behavior?" Garrett asked.

"I want to ask them that and a few other things. I'm glad you're here with me."

"So am I." He gave her a long hug, trying to offer some reassurance, but feeling sorely inadequate.

"When I think of that monster attempting to violate her, it hurts so deeply I can't explain. I know she is not my child, and if I'm overstepping my boundaries let me know, but I think she needs to see there are good men out here. I pray that my being here will help her to understand that."

"It will. She needs you. There is a void in her life that I can't fill. I can only provide the mother side, though I have been both father and mother to her. You can help her with your love and concern from a father's . . . I mean a man's view. That's been missing for so long, and she needs it so desperately right now. I thank God we met when we did. I would probably have killed that boy."

"Don't give me too much credit. I'm not far behind you."

Montana picked up the phone to call Collier's parents.

"Hello, this is Montana St. Claire. I am Chesne's mother."

"Oh hi, Ms. St. Claire," Phyllis Yadrow said merrily.

"I'm sure you know the reason I'm calling. We would like to meet with you and your husband."

"Uh, uh . . . oh my. Honey?" she called. Montana could hear her trying to cover the receiver. "Chesne's parents want to meet with us. Do you think we should?" Montana could not hear her husband's response.

"I know you should," Montana said under her breath.

"Mrs. St. Claire, when and where did you want to meet?"

"At your house, tomorrow morning around 10:00."

"Alright, we'll see you then."

"You know," Montana said in an elevated voice as she replaced the receiver in its cradle, "those people act like nothing has happened. I can't wait to see them."

"Me, either. Guess I'd better go. We've got a long day ahead of us."

"I wish things were different."

"So do I. I hate that someone hurt Chesne," Garrett replied.

"That, too, but I wasn't talking about that. I wish we could find comfort in each other's arms in our own bed."

"I do, too. You don't know how much I want that."

Montana and Garrett looked at each other and sighed deeply. They shook their heads and started laughing.

"Guess I really need to go."

"Yeah, that would be a good idea."

They kissed each other with a luxurious love that had matured and deepened over the years.

✦ ✦ ✦ ✦ ✦

Satan watched. "I just knew I had them then. Lust makes the flesh weak. It's normally so predictable. They're stronger than I gave them credit for, but no man could resist Montana, not a real man. I wouldn't have allowed it anyway. I will be her first before she falls and you will be weak in her eyes. You'll bow down. I'll make sure. She will struggle at first, but she'll come around. I've been known to change the ending a time or two myself," he said, smiling.

CHAPTER THIRTEEN

"Those who sacrifice their conscience to ambition burn a painting to obtain ashes."
Chinese Proverb

A restless night caused Montana to toss continuously, unable to achieve restful sleep. The small amount of rest she did get was repeatedly interrupted with thoughts of Chesne and the trauma that had caused ripples to usurp their peaceful existence. She prayed for understanding, an open heart, and a calmer spirit, but all she could feel was anger.

She glanced over at the clock. It was 4:30. When had she ever been awake at 4:30? It was difficult to resume sleep and she quietly rose to check on Chesne who slept peacefully. The look of innocence on her face made Montana's heart ache at the thought of that look being gone forever—the knowledge of good and evil. Chesne almost ate the fruit of that tree. Chills penetrated Montana's body, then went in search of her soul until her spiritual essence was shaken. Kissing Chesne on the cheek, she was thankful that God had protected her.

She knew it was too early to call Garrett, but he would understand.

"Hello."

"Well, hi," Montana said, surprised. "I didn't expect you to be up at this hour."

"I couldn't sleep. I kept thinking about Chesne and how frightened she must have been. She's such a sweet girl. The thought of that boy assaulting her makes me mad."

"As her mother, it scares and angers me, too. You just don't realize how close evil really is sometimes and if you're unprepared, it's even more frightening."

"I know, baby. We'll get through this and Chesne will be just fine."

"I know. It's just having to watch your child in pain and knowing that nothing you can do will help except God and time."

"Have you called Olivia yet?"

"No. Actually, I was thinking of calling Noelle. She'll do a lot of fun things with Chesne, which will keep her busy and her mind occupied. Noelle won't ask any questions and will wait until I'm ready to talk."

Garrett nodded in agreement. He made an effort to lighten the mood. "But wait, you mean a woman actually exists who is *not* trying to get the latest scoop on you, just to have it broadcasted on the newest edition of *Gossip Network*?"

"There are a few of us, though I must admit not many. People are so busy trying to sweep off your front porch that they forget that dirt accumulates on their own. You have to work on your own dirt before you can criticize someone on theirs."

"Amen. Preach, sister, preach."

"Leave me alone. I'm just tired of misplaced priorities."

Switching gears, Garrett asked, "What time do you want me to pick you up?"

"Well, actually I thought I would pick you up."

"What? I'm flattered."

"Well, before it goes to your head, I need to drop Chesne off at Noelle's anyway. I may as well pick you up. No one else will."

"Gee, thanks."

"I should be there about eight, and please be ready."

"Me, be ready? I don't believe you! Isn't that the pot calling the kettle black?"

"I don't know. My pots and kettles are stainless steel."

"Oh, we are sharp today."

"And it will be nothing compared to what Mr. and Mrs. Yadrow will see."

"Ouch. I smell trouble brewing."

"Yeah, and its name is Collier."

"Montana?"

"Yes."

"Remember, we are Christians."

"Yeah, but that doesn't mean we're doormats. I'll talk to you later. I love you."

"I love you, too."

Montana lazily dropped the phone back in its cradle. Sleep was tapping on her shoulder. *This is going to be a long day and I will need all the coffee I can get.* Walking down the stairs, she heard the soft rushing of the waterfall in her garden. She loved the peace it inspired and wished she had bought one to place inside the house. As she made coffee, she decided to make it espresso-strength and poured another full scoop in.

After dressing, Montana sat on the deck taking in the beauty of the dawn. The birds serenaded her with a bittersweet song as if sharing her appreciation of God's creation and her sorrow.

Montana felt something wet fall on her hand. She thought it was beginning to rain until she realized the drops were her own tears. Her body overflowed with pain and grief. Her mind fluctuated with thoughts of anger, fear, guilt, and doubt. She cried until she was void of thoughts and tears.

"Jesus, why? I know there is evil in this world, but why did it have to touch Chesne? I know you can see the bigger picture, but I need to understand. Please give me wisdom so that I can appropriately convey my hurt and anger to these people. I need strength and conviction so that I can continue to tell Chesne to always seek You. I do not doubt You. I do not question Your reason. I simply need to understand. Talk to me, please."

Yes, I know you want to understand, and I want to understand you, a voice said.

"Lord, but you made me. You understand me even when I don't." Montana was puzzled. The birds stopped singing their praises.

"What I mean child is . . ." Satan stopped. He knew he had made a mistake. Since God was all knowing, He would automatically understand everything about her.

Montana got a strange feeling. "Are you the son of the Living God? Did you rise on the third day possessing all power? Did you go to hell and bring back the keys to death? Were you crucified for my iniquities and transgressions? Can I plead your blood over the enemy rendering him powerless?"

Silence.

"Jesus?"

Silence.

Montana became enraged as her body shook violently. "How dare you try to attack me now, you diseased, fiendish, miserable creature. I know your tricks. You are a slimy, low-life, minuscule being. You are beneath me. The Blood of Jesus rebukes you. You are a good-for-nothing, self-righteous, pestilent gnat. Your end has already been foretold. Get thee behind me, Satan. Through Jesus Christ, I have power you can only dream about. Now, be gone."

"Peace be still, my child. I am the Beginning and the End. The Alpha and Omega. I am that I am," He said. The birds resumed their singing. The voice of God continued, "My most precious Son was tempted for forty days in the wilderness by Satan and through the evil of men, He was crucified and died because they were ignorant and full of sin. Through it all, He still sought to do My will. You, too, must communicate with love to these people who are ignorant of me."

Montana sat for a long time. The tears that were blurring her vision released themselves until she was free and could see with the eyes that God had provided.

Satan watched intently, having experienced failure again. He knew God was watching him closely.

"Yeah, yeah, we've heard the story a million times. So He died. Everyone in your creation dies. People don't believe in You. They only call on You in times of trouble. And if He truly was your son, you would have never allowed him to endure that kind of pain."

"I will deal with you when the time comes. It is almost over, and you will be cast into the lake of fire and bound for a thousand years. You will use anybody or anything to gain what? A bigger piece of hell? You were as ridiculous then as you are now. As it is written, so shall it be. My Word lives forever in the hearts of those who love me. You are the cause of your own destruction," God said.

A bolt of lightning as wide as Texas shot through the sky into the depths of the Earth for Satan's eyes only. "This is a warning."

Chesne awoke a few hours later, dressing quickly and needing to get this ordeal over immediately. "I'm ready."

"I'm going to drop you off at Noelle's, but she'll bring you home. Okay?"

"Okay?"

Thirty minutes later, Montana was waving good-bye to Chesne and Noelle.

Driving to Garrett's house, Montana realized this was the first time, she had ever seen it. It was in the heart of Buckhead, a lavish community of coveted homes. As she pulled up to the wrought iron gate, she pressed the intercom and Garrett allowed her access. *Magnificent house*, Montana thought as she pulled into the circular drive. Garrett was unpretentious, but to look at his home with its gated entry, you would not know it. It was a European stucco and stone with abundant arches and breathtaking gardens. Four chimneys, a portico, and Palladian windows could be seen from the front of the house. *This is stunning! It seems I don't own the corner of the market when it comes to good taste*, Montana thought admiringly.

Garrett owned his own financial planning company, but the thought of how much money he made never entered Montana's mind until now. She was happy all of his hard work had paid off and it made her feel more secure knowing that if they were to get married, they would be able to take care of the things they needed as well as much of what they wanted.

Walking into the house, Montana's mouth fell open.

"If I had known it would have made you speechless, I would have invited you over long before now," Garrett said.

"You know, some things are better off ignored. You have a beautiful place, Garrett."

She looked around, admiring the discriminating architecture and furnishings. A massive, yet magnificent Baltic neoclassical gilt bronze and cut crystal chandelier hung from the ceiling. Italian black and ivory granite created the floor in the foyer and was adorned by spiral wrought iron staircases on each side. The walls were ivory with hand-painted Egyptian inspired motifs in gold leaf. An exquisite round Empire table was in the center of the foyer with an enormous bouquet of flowers. A grand piano, Biedermeier chairs, plump loveseats and enormous palms filled the sunken room behind the foyer. Stately columns stood proudly announcing the entrance to the dining room with a mahogany and rosewood table and twelve chairs. A sideboard and fireplace were opposite each other in the banquet-sized room.

"Thanks."

"Why didn't you tell me?"

"Tell you what?"

"That you lived in such an exquisite house."

"What was I supposed to say? And why? I live in an awesome house in an exclusive area of town. Is that conversation or boasting? You know I'm not materialistic. I look at this as an investment."

"Nice place to hang your hat while you watch the return on your investment. I'm not materialistic either, but this sure does make a statement. Talk about status symbol. It could almost be mistaken for overcompensation if I didn't know better."

Garrett was happy she was able to smile. He knew from their history that she used humor as a way to get through tough times, and this was probably one of the toughest for her.

"I knew you would live in a nice house, I just never thought you were clocking dollars to this extent. I'm so proud of you. How do your neighbors act?"

"They're actually not bad. A few acted as though I was a drug dealer or athlete. I guess they didn't think that a black man could legally benefit from his own intelligence. Mostly, though, they don't seem to have the mentality of some of their suburban counterparts. As long as you can afford to live here, they really don't care what color your skin is only that your money is green. Are you hungry? I don't have much ready except some bagels and coffee, but you're welcome to it."

"No, I'm not hungry. Even if I was, I don't think I could eat anything. My stomach is all tied up in knots."

"Mine, too. Where are we going?"

"To Dunwoody."

"Well, let's get the show on the road," he said.

On the drive to the Yadrows' residence, they were each engrossed in their thoughts. "I think we need to stick to the issue at hand. We don't need to attack them personally, just the actions of their son," Montana said.

"I agree. I could really care less how they choose to raise their child as long as it does not infringe upon the rights and safety of our child."

It took a minute for it to register, then Montana looked at him with surprise. "Our child?"

"You know what I mean. She needs me and you do, too, I hope. I know it sure feels good being together like a family."

"Yes, it does," she said. Montana felt a twinge of guilt for not saying anything about Chesne, but it seemed she could never find the right time or the perfect way. Truth hit her hard as the thought crossed her mind. *I'm just scared and I don't know what it will cause me to lose.* But at this juncture, she did not have strength for anything else and getting through this intact would be a miraculous feat. Garrett reached for her hand and that seemed to have been all the conversation needed.

Montana pulled into the driveway admiring the executive estate.

"Well, they may lack the ability to raise a child correctly, but they sure don't lack the finer things of life."

Garrett agreed, "No, they don't, but most people who are rich in wealth are generally poor in Christ."

They got out of the car and walked up to the mahogany-framed double doors with leaded glass inserts and transoms. When they rang the doorbell, it chimed Beethoven's "Fifth Symphony". A few minutes later, a woman came to the door. She was casually, yet impeccably dressed.

"Well, hello Mr. and Mrs. St. Claire. Won't you come in?" she asked in her prim and proper Southern accent. "Why don't we go into the library? Would you like a drink?" she asked.

"No, thank you," Garrett said.

"Isn't it a little early?" Montana asked.

"It's never too early to drink," Mrs. Yadrow slurred slightly, holding a scotch and water.

"Thank you, but no, this isn't a social occasion," Montana said disgusted.

"Well, no, you're right. Of course it isn't, but I've never needed one to drink. Come on in." She opened the French doors to the library. "Why don't you make yourselves comfortable. I'll get Mr. Yadrow," she said and walked off.

"Thanks for not correcting her when she called us Mr. and Mrs. St. Claire. It's important that we show a united front," Montana said.

"I'm not hung up on titles. She doesn't know our situation, nor would she care. As far as I'm concerned, we are united. Maybe not by name but by hearts."

Montana looked at him lovingly. "I know, but still thanks."

"Mr. St. Claire, Mrs. St. Claire," Mr. Yadrow said as he walked into the room and extended his hand. Garrett stood to shake his hand while Montana remained seated. Montana did not take the time to participate in small talk and jumped right in. "I understand from the school and police reports, and talking with Chesne that Collier tried to rape her. Is that also your understanding?"

"Well, that's what the reports say, but we know Collier," Mrs. Yadrow said. "He would never do anything like that unless . . ." and her voice trailed off.

"Unless what?" Garrett asked.

She hesitated for a moment. "Unless, he was p-p-provoked," she stammered.

Garrett jumped out of his seat.

"And just how would he be provoked?"

Montana grabbed Garrett's arm, trying to bring him back down to the sofa, but he escaped her grasp.

"If she was teasing him or coming on to him. Our boy just isn't like you . . ." Mrs. Yadrow stopped.

"So let me get this right. If you came up to me and called me a nigger, that's provoking me and if I turned around and shot you dead, I'm within my rights because you provoked me?" Garrett asked.

"N-No, that's not what I mean at all," she said.

"Then please tell us what you mean, Mrs. Yadrow."

"What—."

"Please excuse my wife. She has a hard time voicing her opinion sometimes," Mr. Yadrow said in her defense.

"Yeah." Montana said. *When she's trying to down Scotch at the same time.* "That's apparent."

"As a mother, she finds it hard to believe her, I mean, our son could do anything wrong. They have a close relationship and she has always been very supportive of him."

"Even when he's wrong?" Garrett asked.

Mr. Yadrow looked down and then away.

"Aren't you the head of this family?" Garrett asked.

"Yes, but . . ."

"I run things around here. Douglas is a spineless husband," Mrs. Yadrow lisped.

Montana tapped her foot, trying to control her emotion. "Well back to the important issue. Okay so when you said you, you meant you as in Christians, correct? Because that is what we are. As Christians, we have an instruction book called the Bible, which is what we live by. One of the things it teaches is that we are to love you as we love ourselves. That is hard to do right now, but trust me when I say that if a small part of that was not working at this present moment, you would not have breath left."

A wave of courage made Mr. Yadrow's spine less flaccid. "It's hard to believe, but by the evidence, it seems Collier did do these things."

"Well it's good to hear that someone is willing to be held accountable. Your son did attempt to rape my child. There are numerous witness accounts from the other children, the teacher, the doctor, and most importantly, from my daughter. Your boy thinks he has the right to take anything he wants simply because he wants it. Wonder where he got that idea? I do not know how you raised your son, and I really don't give a rat's behind as long as it doesn't harm my child. Judging from how he turned out, I am using the word *raised* loosely."

"He's a boy, he's bound to test his manhood at times. If your daughter provided him the opportunity . . ."

"Phyllis, that is not necessary," Douglas said.

"You don't have the brains to know what's necessary?" Phyllis said.

"Well, I know what's necessary and it doesn't appear to exist here. I spoke with Chesne about this and the whole incident is hard for her to believe. She can't talk about it without crying, but you know the most amazing thing about my child is she wants to forgive him. That is the life of a Christian child, Mr. and Mrs. Yadrow. A Christian child like Chesne looks beyond the evil that resides inside your son and sees him as God sees him. To see God in him or you, one would have to look painfully deep and very far away. At this moment, I am not that Christian, so I'm going to lay this out so you understand."

Montana stood eyeing her prey. Garrett, sensing Montana's building rage and soon to follow attack, intervened. "What Montana means is we will use every recourse available to keep Collier away from Chesne to ensure her safety, and his—by any means."

Mr. and Mrs. Yadrow straightened up in their seats as the seriousness of the situation finally sank in. If Phyllis' father were still alive, she would not have to deal with this. Her father would never concede in battle, he simply paid his way. The Wilmingtons were a respectable family who came from a long line of successful business owners. They had made millions on the backs of others, and status allowed you a long leash in the South.

Her husband, on the other hand, was a diluted version of her father and had grown stale over the years. He grew up poor and as with all poor people, he was brought up in the church. People like her husband, were foolish enough to think there was actually something after death. He wasted his life on earth praying to a god that he could not be sure existed. It took an extensive amount of time for her to convince him that it was your position in life not your position with God that made one successful. After all, once dead, you're simply a matter of dust and ashes that no one will even remember.

"You can't possibly believe that you can do this. I am an important person in this city. My family built most of it and we still own a great deal. Surely, you don't believe that you can get away with this," Mrs. Yadrow protested.

"We have letters that Collier has written to Chesne. Your son is in love with a young black lady, and he has such a low self-esteem that he feels the only way he can get affection is to take it because it is not freely given at home. That's a sad statement for life, and you should be ashamed to call yourselves his parents."

The Yadrows turned so red that Montana thought they would burst. Mrs. Yadrow stood to make another drink. She held onto the sofa to steady herself. She looked at her husband expecting him to finally be a man and make a stand, but when she glanced at him, he sat nervously in his chair like a small boy about to release himself. "It's a shame to be a dickless man," she slurred.

"Now, get the hell out of my house, before I have you locked up. My son will not see one day in jail. For what? Raping a black girl, an insignificant piece of flesh, you must be joking."

Before Garrett could react, Montana lunged at her and clasped both hands tightly around her neck. Phyllis dropped her glass as she was pushed into the antique breakfront. "If I believed in revenge, I would kill you without a thought. This is just my way of letting you know that you have offended me. I wouldn't do it again, okay?" Montana released her grip and straightened Phyllis' clothing.

Mrs. Yadrow cowered close to her husband. "You know, to be a so-called Christian, you sure are acting ugly. God doesn't like ugly."

"Then He really doesn't like you. You know, it's a funny thing about blue blood. The reason it's blue is because it's already dead. Oxygen makes the blood red and gives it life," Montana said.

"We'll walk ourselves to the door. I don't think you can find your legs since your tail is stuck so far up your . . . well, you get my drift don't you?" Montana moved toward Mr. and Mrs. Yadrow who visibly shook as she glared at them intently.

Whiffs of expensive scotch assaulted her nostrils as the vapors seeped from Mrs. Yadrow's pores. Phyllis grabbed the collar of her blouse in a futile attempt to close it as if Montana could see right through her and into an empty, decayed soul.

CHAPTER FOURTEEN

"The sore is cured, but the scar remains."
Ekonda Proverb

S tanding at the sink washing dishes, lamenting over another
lonely weekend in a string of never-ending lonelier ones,
Heather was weary. Her life had never been a satisfying one
or even one she cared to relive, if given the chance, which is why she
accepted the invisible yet ever-present evil force in her life. The
loneliness loomed like darkness in the forest where vision is
incapable of separating the beginning of one mass from the end of
another yet it was distinguishable. It all blended into an impossible
mixture that continued to separate like milk from cream. The only
redeeming factor in her life now was his promise to fulfill her desire
for wealth. And once she had wealth, friends would naturally follow.

But she was tired of being tired, and sat heavily on the sofa in the
living room to watch television mechanically flipping through
channels. The light from her window helped to brighten her
surroundings, but the effect was barely noticeable. Reruns of *The
Cosby Show* flashed across the screen.

"This is definitely fantasy. No black family lives like that, and if they do, somebody is selling drugs. Most white people I know don't live like that."

Disgusted, she continued to change channels and saw *Any Day Now*.

"Someone was really nuts when he wrote this. I would never pollute my world by becoming friends with some darkie unless I could get something from it." She was unwilling to allow her mind to remember that as a child, all of her friends were black, but that was ancient history. Today, she didn't know what she would call them, though friends was not a viable choice. "Real friends don't betray you," she snapped.

The darkness had now transferred from the forest to her living room and the sun that shone brightly from her window, now seemed to have eclipsed.

Heather's mind drifted to Montana and instantly, she was filled with vicious hate and violent envy. *You just can't be nice to some black people. Montana thinks because she went to some private college and graduated at the top of her class that she's better than I am. Because of King, Malcolm X, and Civil Rights, blacks have the audacity to think they are equal to me. They will never be equal to any white person. All they can do is play sports, and that takes no brains. After all, hadn't science proven their brains were actually smaller?* Heather smiled, satisfied that she had inflated her sense of self enough, even if it was at someone else's expense. She paused as if listening to a silent partner, then added one more comment. *I don't care how pretty, or rich, or smart they are, they will always be just a bunch of nigga' savages.*

Satan was perched on the edge of his stool. He slapped his hands on his knees, laughing as he leaned back and crossed his legs. He was arrogantly pleased with his handpicked maiden. "Pride, jealousy, hate, and greed are my greatest weapons."

An escape was needed from the desolate reality that stared her in the face. The brown liquid courage on the table sparkled like bright copper until it lured her to partake of its mellow fluid. Pouring herself a drink, she swallowed quickly to scorch the organs that maintained her life. The familiar warmth rose in her body and she poured another, feeling herself soften around the edges. To make sure the edges stayed soft and pliable, she downed a third. As the spirits numbed her mind, another spirit joined by others whispered to it. Sexual urgency coursed through her and she needed a release, but since a partner was not available she would have to massage the impatient throbbing between her legs that would not wait until later to be satisfied.

Passing a mirror upon entering her bedroom, she admired her body in the mirror—beautiful curves, white skin, blond hair, blue eyes (thanks to contacts) and large breasts. Men's fantasies consisted of her and she was what brought them satisfaction, at least that is what she believed.

As she laid across the cool sheets taking her present situation in hand, she drifted to another place and felt an inescapable desire to be intimate with a woman. It was not the first time she had this fantasy and she was urgently aware that her pleasure would not be quenched until it actually happened. Her moist hand was limp and depleted from its work, but left little in the form of contentment. Fantasy had its place, but the time had come to bring some reality to the situation.

She left the moistness between her legs wanting to attract the right woman who would be aroused from her scent. The time had come for the hunt to begin.

Satan sat back and smiled. He was so pleased with Heather. He had started whispering to her years ago, but she did not hear him then. As time passed, he noticed when he spoke she stopped what she was doing as if she had heard something. The more he talked the more response he saw from her. Then one day he watched her waiting for his voice even though he had not spoken. He knew then that she was ready.

As a child, Heather always felt different not only in the way she looked, but also from her childhood that was absent of love, especially from her mother. As her stepfather's tongue berated and condemned her, the groundwork for an idle mind and an empty soul was cemented. Regardless of the compliments she received, there was never a moment when she felt worthy or loved herself. Growing up, she felt ugly and disfigured, and it was puzzling how no one else could see it except her. Once she accepted this image, she portrayed the attributes that mirrored what she saw in herself and over time, it became normal behavior.

Heather was a rare specimen who did not need much prodding to do or be wicked beyond imagination. Her self-reflecting mirror was her catalyst and she began to enjoy doing the things he said. It was simple really, a thought here, a push there and she jumped on for the thrill of the ride. Heather's animalistic lust was an added plus in Satan's eyes and with her desire for a woman, he could witness firsthand, how his annihilation plan would work.

The initial step was to increase the number of homosexual couples, which would result in a dramatic decline in the birth rate. Then he would put enough temptation in their minds to make many of these partners become secretly bisexual. They would have multiple partners and frequent, frantic, and nefarious sex that was as addicting as heroin. The finale would be the strains of special diseases that would be transmitted sexually to everyone regardless of sexual orientation. The beautiful part was the doctors would concentrate on the widespread exposure of one while the others hibernated on the surface, suddenly exploding into full-scale epidemic diseases incapable of cure and killing millions. AIDS was laughable compared to what he was planning for mankind.

His brilliant plans would prohibit new souls from coming into the world and being converted to God. Satan knew he could then unleash every perversion or twisted thought known to man, and Heather, his most prized possession, was going to help him reach that goal. He would destroy humanity by its own devices.

Heather looked through *Creative Loafing* and stopped when she spotted the advertisement section that tailored to the gay community. Reading about a club called The Corner that caters to lesbians and curiosity seekers, Heather was intrigued and decided to go.

The anticipation of what was to come had her on the edge of climax. She walked in and was able to smell the scent of every woman there. Her perceptions were heightened as if she were an animal searching for prey. The lonely and unending search for fulfillment was everywhere. Smiling, she realized that this was her heaven and she wanted them all. Walking farther into the club, she decided to sit at the far corner of the bar.

Heather must have smelled like fresh road kill to those women. They swarmed around her like savage dogs ready to battle for the last piece of rotten flesh. A woman walked over to her and whispered that there was a special place in the back. The thought of actively living out her fantasy excited Heather. She jumped at the opportunity, but not before asking another woman to join them.

Satan watched as the three women performed. This was going to be good. "Well, that's phase one. It's time for the next phase." He laughed at this stupid woman who was his consolation prize. He could not believe she was so easy. All she needed was someone to show her a little appreciation and he was skilled at that. His timing for giving people what they wanted was impeccable.

Heather woke up the next morning unsure of what happened the night before, and then she remembered. A smile crept on her face as she relived the night. She had exchanged numbers with the dark-haired woman named Jezebel Laird, Jez for short.

"You know Jezebel in the Bible, the one who I think was a whore," Heather remembered her saying. They both laughed at the irony. Seeing Jez again made her anxious as she thought of them creating their own modern Sodom and Gomorrah only better. Heather was confident of it and the anticipation excited her.

She slowly got out of bed and made coffee, smiling to herself. *I am finally happy,* she thought. But then her mind drifted to work, and rested on Montana.

Satan saw his opportunity and planted a seed in her mind, watching her absorb it as her own thought. "Now, we're cooking. I just had to create an itch, and she would do the scratching. Once she dives into this head first . . ." Satan laughed hysterically at the play on words. "She will be so ugly in the sight of God that she will never be able to get close to Him.

"Eve was my first love and deception, Montana will be my greatest, and Heather will solidify my victory. I loved them, but they treated me as if I was some diseased thing that needed to be buried. But you, sweet, idiotic Heather will be the pawn in which I make my most lethal moves. With Montana's fall, I will solidify my rightful place as god. Then Montana will come crawling to me," Satan said boastfully.

✧ ✧ ✧ ✧ ✧

What can I do? I hate her so much. She's got everything—money, intelligence, a nice house, and unbelievable beauty. I think she's got someone in her life. I heard her talking to Stephanie. I have to make her lose everything. I don't want what she's got, I just don't want her to have it. Then another thought crossed Heather's mind. She smiled. This plan was perfect.

Heather looked at her watch noticing it was past noon. Feeling the lustful need grow, she called Jez who would be there within an hour. Quickly showering, she closed the curtains in her room and lit candles to set the mood. *A romantic environment always helped to loosen people up.*

Grabbing two glasses of wine, she waited anxiously, but thinking about the previous night got the best of her. Thoughts of the woman drew her into a dark, forbidden web. She could have sworn she heard other voices crying out, but she couldn't tell if they were cries of pain or pleasure.

Someone forgot to close the door to hell as Satan looked in on Heather.

"Damn those excuses for human life. I would have to be in charge of these imbeciles. They are always screwing up something. Once I get Montana, everything will change," he said as he quickly closed the door.

Sounds erupted from Heather's mouth. She did not hear the knock on the door nor did she hear the door open as someone called out.

"I see you started without me, you naughty girl," Jez said. Heather looked at her, glad to see the woman she had been fantasizing about. Jez walked over to the bed and Heather ripped off her clothes while Jez worked ravenously to please her.

CHAPTER FIFTEEN

"The predator lands on an unknown tree."
Duala Proverb

Seeing Montana walk into the break room, Heather decided to make a small detour before going to her cubicle.

"Good morning," Heather said.

Patiently waiting for the snide remarks to come, Montana hesitated briefly, but when they failed to display their splendid ugliness, she said, "Good morning. This is such a beautiful day. I love this weather."

"Yeah, me, too." Heather looked at Montana and recited what he had whispered to her. "I know you may not believe this, but I believe in God and I know every scripture in the Bible. I walked with God once and served Him, but when I became equal to Him, He sent me away.

"I have been lost for quite some time searching for someone to help make some sense of my life and I have found that person who makes me happier than I ever thought possible."

Unable to speak or feel any real happiness for her, Montana decided it was best to remain quiet. Hypocrisy was not a sin she wanted to add to her growing list.

The moment of opportunity was slowly slipping away and Heather knew if she did not speak soon, she would not receive another chance. "Look, Montana, I'm sorry I've been so hard on you for the last few years. I've just been so unhappy, but I'm much better now. I know it will take time for you to believe, but I really like you and perhaps in time, if given a chance, we can become friends."

Montana was taking a sip of her coffee when she heard what Heather said and almost choked. "Uh, Heather, that's nice of you. I appreciate your apology."

"Okay, well, I'll see you around." Heather had expected Montana to be more gullible since she was a Christian and was commanded to love her neighbor. *If my kindness won't kill her, I'll think of something that will.*"

There is definitely something rotten at Lafayette Drake, but it's not the trash. Better keep my spiritual eyes open. I feel a dark presence. Satan is walking around boldly now. Everything is fair game, Montana thought and shuddered.

Stephanie bumped into Montana as she entered the break room. "What's wrong? You look as if you've just seen a ghost."

"Actually, it's more like coming face to face with evil."

Stephanie looked at her puzzled. She started to ask Montana what she meant, but she was gone before Stephanie could open her mouth.

Montana prayed, *Oh faithful Master, please protect me. I always knew Heather had an unclean spirit, but I've never looked at someone and seen such evil. It was like talking to Satan. I know the time is near for me to drink of this cup You have given me. Please tell my angels to be ready, I think I'm going to need them.*

Shortly before noon, Heather walked up to Stephanie's desk pretending to look for messages.

"Doesn't Montana look nice today? She must be doing something on the side to be able to wear the clothes she does, don't you think?" Heather twirled the message center display.

"Yes, she does, but she looks nice every day. How can you insinuate that she might be doing something illegal? You don't know how much she makes or what her situation is. Montana is not the type of person to do anything that is not above board. She is the most honest person I have ever met and as her friend I resent that remark."

"I don't mean to insult her or you. I've just never known anyone who could do the things she does without doing something illegal. She does have wonderful taste though, and she is painfully pretty. I don't think I've seen her in this light before. I know I have acted really ugly toward her, but I do want us to become friends. I want us to be close, really close."

"Montana's a good friend. I don't know what I would do without her," Stephanie said.

"Look, maybe we can have lunch and you can help me think of ways to become Montana's friend. She is such a good influence on you. Maybe through her friendship she can do the same for me."

"Montana isn't close to a lot of people."

"Not even you?" Heather feigned surprise as she planted a seed of doubt. "But you're so nice. Everyone else thinks so highly of you."

"Montana and I work together, and she has helped me a lot, but she's a private person and I respect her privacy."

"Well, do you think we could go to lunch anyway? I'll treat."

"Okay. I guess it can't hurt." Stephanie surprised herself in accepting the invitation especially when her intention had been just the opposite. Then her stomach growled and confirmed her decision.

"I wouldn't hurt a fly," Heather said sweetly.

Things were starting to look up for Heather and down for everyone she knew. She was glad everything was beginning to fall into place. After returning to her cubicle, she called Jez to make plans for the evening, however, talking to Jez aroused her and she could feel the urge between her loins. She didn't want to ignore it, but she had to meet the deadline on the proposal Paul had assigned to her, but if she arranged it right, she could get out of doing it altogether.

Heather did not feel like working and played solitaire on the computer. Glancing at her watch, she noticed the time. "Boy, time flies quickly and the fun hasn't even started." She picked up the phone. "Hey, Stephanie, are you ready?"

"Uh, yeah, sure."

"I'll be right there."

Montana was walking to Paul's office when she glanced into the lobby and saw Stephanie and Heather talking as they got on the elevator. "Things are getting stranger and stranger around here," Montana muttered.

Heather took Stephanie to lunch at Devlin's. Upon entering the restaurant, they walked toward the empty podium. While they were waiting, Stephanie excused herself to go to the restroom. Heather requested an intimate table in her absence and slipped the man a fifty-dollar bill. She could not afford it, but she knew soon there would be more money than she would know what to do with.

"If you would follow me," the host said when Stephanie returned. He led them to the requested table.

As they perused the menu, Heather said, "Order whatever you like."

"There's so much on here, I don't know how I will ever choose."

Looking at Stephanie seriously, Heather said, "You know, I've been trying to decide if I should tell you this, but if it were me, I would want to know."

"What are you talking about?"

Hesitating for effect, she continued, "Well, you know it's review time and Paul wanted us, Montana and me, to appraise your performance. I gave you high scores. You are intelligent and professional. I wrote that you could contribute more to the company if you were placed in an advanced position. I added that the company was cheating itself because you have so much more to offer." Heather stopped.

"Well?"

Heather pretended to be torn by the words that would follow. "Stephanie, you must promise not to say anything. *Please*."

"I promise."

Heather cleared her throat. "Montana said that you weren't ready. She wrote that she had seen recent improvements, but your performance was just mediocre. I was flabbergasted. I could not believe what I was reading. It was hard to understand how she could write that with everything you do at work."

"How do you know what Montana wrote?"

Heather smiled slyly as if she held a secret. "While I was in Paul's office, his assistant, Lisa, asked him to step out for a moment. I know

I shouldn't have, but I looked. When Paul came back, I felt so bad because Montana wrote such horrid things about you. I told Paul that I felt you should get the maximum raise and Paul agreed." Heather waited for Stephanie to digest everything she said.

"I can't believe that!"

"I know. It's awful. I wouldn't have believed it either if I hadn't seen it with my own eyes," Heather said concerned. She reached across the table and patted Stephanie's hand. "I'm so sorry."

"Thanks for telling me, Heather," Stephanie said calmly, but she was boiling inside.

"Tell me about Montana," Heather said.

"There's really nothing to tell."

"Everyone has a secret and someone always knows. I'm sure you know plenty about Montana."

"I don't know anything about Montana that would be considered a secret."

Reluctantly, Heather realized Stephanie was telling the truth. "I don't mean to pry, I just want to be friends with Montana that's all. I think she's a good person. Sometimes I think she needs help and doesn't know how to ask for it or is too proud to ask. Maybe the best way to be friends with her is to become friends with you."

"Why are you so interested in becoming friends with Montana and me? You've never even acknowledged me until recently."

"I've just been through a lot. There have been so many personal things going on in my life. I'm really sorry if it made me seem unapproachable."

"I really don't need any friends." Stephanie was becoming increasingly uneasy.

"Oh, come on now, we could all use another friend. I can be a really good friend. I know I could use one. I'm not really good with

people, and I have a hard time meeting new ones. That's why I've
kept to myself. I'm normally a loner, but I get so lonely by myself,"
Heather said, forcing tears in her eyes.

Stephanie sat in deep thought for some time torn between
reaching out to someone in need and wondering if Heather's
intentions were as honorable as she professed.

"Stephanie," Heather said, interrupting her thoughts, "do you
think you could find it in your heart to try to be my friend? At least
think about it?"

"I'll think about it, Heather, but I can't promise anything. I've got
a lot going on in my life, too."

"I understand, but at least you'll think about it. Thanks." Heather
ordered a bottle of Merlot and didn't flinch when the server
mentioned the sixty-dollar price tag.

They ate lunch while Heather continued to plant seeds of doubt
in Stephanie's mind. Stephanie seemed to absorb what she said, but
she did not want to come on too strong. *It has to be a natural
progression, nothing forced,* Heather thought. As Heather drove back to
work, Stephanie leaned back and closed her eyes. Heather looked at
Stephanie's legs and admired her athletic build. The darkness of her
skin glistened under the sunlight begging to be touched. The thought
of putting her hand up Stephanie's dress crossed her mind. *Better
wait until the right moment presents itself,* she thought.

"I'm really glad you had lunch with me, Stephanie. It was so
good to have someone to talk to. Thank you."

"You're welcome. Thanks for asking me."

"We should do it again, but maybe we can make it dinner. I know
this really nice place we could go."

Stephanie didn't answer. She sprayed breath freshener in her
mouth and checked her appearance.

"You look fine. You didn't do anything to get messed up." *This time,* Heather thought. "So what about dinner?" Heather asked again as they were in the elevator.

"We'll see."

They got off the elevator. "Thanks again for going to lunch with me," Heather said.

"Thanks for asking."

They parted ways and went to their respective stations.

"Very good. I am pleased," Satan told Heather once she returned to her office.

"This is fun. I like it."

"The best is yet to come."

"So how was lunch?" Montana asked when she saw Stephanie later.

"Oh, uh, it was fine."

"So you're hanging out with Heather now?"

"Heather's okay. I think you have her pegged wrong," Stephanie said defensively.

"No, I don't, but you better make sure you know whose bed you're sleeping in," Montana warned. "Be careful, Stephanie."

"You are always so uptight. Sometimes, you have to let loose. Not everyone is out to ruin you like some people."

Montana didn't understand what she was talking about, but this was neither the time nor the place to discuss it. Stephanie was not listening anyway. Whatever happened at lunch was starting to create a wall between them. The only way Montana could reach her now was to pray for her protection.

◈ ◈ ◈ ◈ ◈

"Man, I'm glad it's Friday," Heather said to Stephanie.

"Me, too."

"You want to get together tonight?" Heather asked.

"Well, my boyfriend and I were planning to go out."

"Why don't the four of us get together?"

"You've got a boyfriend?" Stephanie asked surprised.

"Let's just say, I've got a friend who takes care of me when I need it," Heather said and winked.

Stephanie laughed. "I hear you, girl."

"So I'll call you later and let you know where. Then afterward we can all go to my house for a little dessert."

Stephanie hesitated for a moment. She was about to tell Heather no when the thought came to her that she should accept. "Okay, that sounds good."

Not as good as it's going to be, Heather thought.

Once Heather arrived home, she looked for Greg Hogan's number, the cable technician who had come to her house one day. He tried to hide it, but she could tell he wanted her. After repairing the cable, she invited him to have a drink and a little sexual tryst. She didn't want him, but thought he might come in handy one day.

Heather and Greg met Stephanie and Michael at Pacific & Vine. They ate dinner, talking the entire time. Heather slipped off her shoe and placed her foot between Michael's legs massaging him with her toes. He looked at her shocked, but too pleased to resist, and she winked in return.

"I can't wait for you to taste my dessert. Only special people get it," she said discreetly directing her comment to Michael. "I can't wait either."

Men are so stupid. Whatever it takes to get the job done, I'm willing to do. The end always justifies the means, no matter what the cost is to someone else, Heather thought. When they got to her apartment, Heather placed a CD in the player, whispered into Greg's ear, and walked into the kitchen.

"Michael, would you help me, please?" Heather asked.

"Do you mind?" he asked Stephanie who shook her head. "Sure," Michael said, standing. He told Stephanie he would be back.

Heather had never been intimate with a black man before, and if what people said was true about the size of their members, she might have to consider being a switch hitter again. It was the price of pleasure.

Michael was six feet tall and sturdy like a rock. His waist was small, but in proportion to the muscles that rippled across his chest. He was a large man, but not threatening and his commanding presence made him appear taller than he actually was. When Michael walked into the kitchen, Heather was sitting on top of the table. Her legs were spread open to reveal that she was not wearing underwear. She slowly stood, lifted her dress, and took it off, letting him know how the gods had smiled on him. Moving toward him, she got on her knees, and unzipped his pants.

She had never seen such a large penis. An orgasm slid out of her as she admired the size of it and hungrily accepted it into her mouth. She had not done this before, but the throbbing of his massiveness excited her. He pulled her to the table and she positioned herself so he could have access either way he wanted. She wrestled and fought with him to make him use force when he took her.

"You're a freak, aren't you?" It was more a statement than a question.

"I just love having sex any way I can, as much as I can," Heather said. She tried unsuccessfully to stifle her screams, but regained enough composure to loudly say, "Greg, would you turn up the music, I can't hear it in here." *I can't afford to screw up my plan,* she thought.

"Have you ever done this?" Greg asked Stephanie as he showed her the cocaine he had pulled out of his pocket.

"No, and I don't plan on doing it now," Stephanie said. "I wonder what's taking Michael so long?" She stood up and called him. Waiting a moment, she started walking toward the door.

"Hey Stephanie," Greg yelled loudly, "don't leave me in here alone?"

Heather overheard him. Quickly rearranging her clothes, she smoothed her hair and walked out looking a bit worn.

"Are you okay? What happened?" Stephanie asked.

"Oh, I'm fine. My hair is so soft, it doesn't take much to turn it into a tousled mess. Trying to get the stems out of those strawberries was so hard. I've never seen anything like it."

"What was hard?" Michael asked as he joined them later.

"The strawberry stems you helped me pull out," Heather said, smiling slyly.

"Yeah, it *was* hard, but once you got it going, it was much easier to work with."

Heather burst out laughing. She couldn't help it. "Oh, excuse me, I had a little Black Russian in the kitchen. It must have gone straight to my head."

"It must have," Stephanie said a little miffed, although she was not sure why.

Heather looked at Greg and saw the cocaine. "I didn't realize it was snowing."

"Enough to build a snowman. Have as much as you want."

"Of course," Heather replied.

"Look, this is not my kind of party. Michael, I'm ready to go," Stephanie said.

"Well, I'm not ready. Every time I try to have a little fun, you always try to spoil it. You are so uptight. This is a new day, baby. You need to get with it before you get left behind."

"If this is what a new day is all about then I want to get left behind. This is the kind of thing that brings our people down. I thought you stopped using drugs?"

"I stopped using them around you. All I ever heard was how horrible they are, the harm they cause, this is what the white man brings into our neighborhoods, and how it destroys black families. Who wants to hear that crap?"

"Michael, this is not the place to discuss this. This is not how problems are worked out."

"I don't have a problem. In fact, everything seems to be wide open."

"I can't stay here. I'm leaving. Are you coming with me?"

"I'm not going anywhere."

Stephanie got up and looked at all of them with disgust resonating from her eyes. "This is so pathetic," Stephanie said, walking toward the door.

Heather sensing the need for immediate intercession got up and joined her. "Stephanie, look this is not what it seems. I don't like coke either, but Greg's got a habit. I would rather he do it here where I know he's safe than to be out in the street. I do it because I love him. Maybe it will keep us together. I can't lose him. I would do anything." Heather put her face in her hands. When she looked up, her eyes were filled with water.

"Stephanie, I'm not strong like you, but I want to be. Will you help me?"

Stephanie looked at her and for some reason felt compassion. She put her arm on Heather's shoulder. "Heather, you seem strong, but I will do whatever I can to help you, but I really do need to get out of here. It's obvious Michael and I don't need to occupy the same space right now. Can I use your phone to call a cab?"

"No, but you can take these." Heather reached for her car keys and tossed them to her.

"I can't take your car, Heather. You just got it and I really don't want to be responsible. If anything happened, I couldn't pay for the repairs."

"That's why I have insurance. Anyway, it is too late for you to be roaming the streets by yourself. It would make me feel so much better."

"Heather, I don't know what to say. I have been horrible to you at work and here you are trusting me and doing things for me that my own family wouldn't even do."

"That's what friends are for. At least, that's what I hope we become. You weren't mean, just a little standoffish. I guess you become that way when you don't know whom to trust. But you can trust me. I only want the best for you and that is what a friend is all about."

Stephanie felt ashamed. "Thank you so much. I'm glad you asked me to come. I would have never seen this side of you. Thanks for wanting to be my friend."

Stephanie looked at Michael, partially out of disgust, but mostly out of love. "I wish you nothing but the best. It's a shame you can't see your own worth, but I can and it hurts. I don't think I need to see you again."

"I *know* I don't want to see you. You're a drag."

Stephanie looked at him and shook her head.

"I'll make sure he gets home. My brother was like him, I know exactly how to handle him. He'll be home before you know it," Heather said.

"I don't care if he gets home or not. He's not my concern anymore. He's a big boy—at least he thinks he is."

"I'm so sorry, Stephanie. You deserve someone better than him."

"Yeah, I thought I had better *in* him."

Heather walked over to her purse and pulled out her wallet. She handed Stephanie a credit card. "Here, take this. I know the stores are closed now, but when I'm mad, angry, or depressed, shopping always helps me. Why don't you go shopping on me tomorrow? After all, if it hadn't been for Greg and me, none of this would have happened."

Stephanie shook her head.

"Please, Stephanie. It'll make me feel better. I grew up never knowing how to love someone. My parents showed their love with money. It's all I know, and it's the only thing I know to do."

"I can't do that, Heather. It's not your fault."

"I insist. I feel so responsible. I just hope my buying you a few things will help to make up for this. I am sorry. I really like you, and you are becoming a good friend. I'm so afraid this has ruined it all. I need a friend so badly, but no one wants to spend time with me."

"Heather, I'm sure we can be friends, but I don't do drugs, okay?"

"Okay, but it would really make me feel a lot better if you let me buy you a few things," Heather said a little more insistently.

Lust and want snaked its way into Stephanie's mind. "Well, if spending money on someone makes you feel better . . . it will make me feel great!" Stephanie accepted the card and relinquished her soul. An uneasy feeling tugged at her, as if she had just signed her name in blood. Heather held Stephanie's hand between hers, sealing the deal.

"Thank you, Stephanie. I will always be here for you. I promise. I'll get Greg to take Michael home. And Stephanie?"

"Yes."

"Get whatever you want." Heather hugged her a little too long.

"Thanks, Heather."

"No problem."

Heather closed the door and rearranged her face. "Gentlemen, let the party begin." She pulled her dress over her head and spread her legs. Greg placed his hand between them, but all Heather wanted was Michael.

"You can do that now, but I want Michael again. I'll get to you when I'm done. Michael, come here," Heather cooed.

"You called?"

She cupped her hands around the bulge in his pants. "Mm, this is so huge and magnificent. I want it hard, really hard."

Heather took turns with both of them until they were exhausted, but she was still unfulfilled. Rushing them out the door, she did not like to have discarded remnants linger too long after the fun was over and she had tired of their usefulness to her.

After they left, Heather looked at her watch. It was 4:00 in the morning, but she did not care. Jez might be asleep, but she would drop anything just to be close to Heather.

"Hello."

"Hey, it's me. I want you to come by later this morning. I've really missed you and I need you. I really need you," Heather said.

"Do you want me to come now?

"No. Why don't you make it in about two hours? I need to freshen up a bit okay?"

"I'll be there at six. I can't wait to see you, Heather."

"I can't wait, either."

Heather hung up and started laughing. *This is the best of both worlds. Once I pull Stephanie completely into my web, she will do as I say and everything will be perfect. It may take a few tries, but eventually she will accept her purpose,* Heather thought as she smiled. *The fun is just beginning.*

CHAPTER SIXTEEN

"Sweet and sour walk hand in hand."
Efik Proverb

"Hi, Anne," Montana said as she entered the office of Rivers and Associates.

"Hi, Montana. I haven't seen you in a while. You look like you've been finally getting some rest. Actually on second thought, maybe it's just the look of love."

"What are you talking about?"

"Don't play dumb with me. You and Garrett can't fool an old lady. Something is in the air, and it's not the pollution. He's acting like a teenage boy with his first crush. He leaves early and he's singing. He only sings when he's happy and lately, that's all the time. You must be having one whirlwind romance and you should enjoy every minute of it."

Montana stood speechless. She didn't know what to say, but she could feel her cheeks reddening. Clearing her throat, she said softly, "Uh, we're just friends."

"Yeah, and I've got some beachfront property in Arkansas. Go on in. He's expecting you." Anne smiled as she looked at Montana's face, which was radiant with love.

Montana closed the door behind her. "Hi there, handsome."

Garrett smiled. "I've got to go now. I'll talk to you later." His eyes ingested her whole and he quickly disconnected the call.

"Hi, gorgeous." Garrett rose like a great conqueror ready to accept his reward for victory as he rounded his desk to embrace Montana.

Encircling him in the confines of her arms, she held on tightly until she had received enough comfort to propel her forward. Looking into eyes of desire that mirrored the contents of her own, she kissed him gently. "What do you feel like eating?"

"Are you on the menu?"

"Only yours."

"Why don't we try the Fish Market?"

"Sounds good. I haven't eaten there in a while. I like the food, but you have to wait so long since they don't take reservations."

"Sometimes they do. After you, my dear." Garrett closed his office and they walked to the lobby. "See you later, Anne. I guess I'll be back," Garrett said with mischief in his eyes.

Montana blushed and looked away.

"Everything shows on her face. She can't hide anything," Garrett remarked.

"That's the sign of an honest person," Anne replied.

"Thank you, Anne. It's nice to be admired for your qualities," Montana said.

"Oh, I admire your qualities. Boy, do I admire them," Garrett said, teasing.

"Get out of here before you two smoke up my office."

Montana playfully hit him on the arm. "You are so bad."

Garrett shrugged. "What? I do admire your qualities."

"You know what I mean."

"Anne knows we're in love. Actually, I think everyone knows judging from the way people have been looking at us."

Several minutes later, Montana pulled into valet parking at the restaurant. The attendant hurried over to open her door assisting her out of the vehicle. They walked up to the hostess. "Good afternoon, Mr. Rivers. How many in your party?"

"Two. How are you, Lori?"

"Fine, thank you."

"Right this way, please," she said. Lori led them to their table and placed menus in front of each respective seat as Garrett pulled the chair out for Montana.

"Hello, Mr. Rivers?" Montana repeated, surprised at Garrett's notoriety.

"You know it's not like that. In my line of business, having connections is important. There's no better time to close a deal than after a fantastic meal. It makes people relax, which brings to mind what has been going on with you at work? You told me a little, but it sounded so strange, I probably need to hear it again and this time with details."

"You remember me telling you about Heather?"

Garrett nodded.

"She has done a complete turnabout. That girl used to live to make my life miserable. Every opportunity she had to make me look bad or to say something ugly, she jumped at it. Now, she acts so sweet and considerate. She is even quoting scriptures."

"So what's the problem?"

"I don't know, but something's not right. You can tell when someone is sincere about his or her walk with God. With her, it seems to be just an act. How does she know *every* scripture in the Bible? I prefer the old Heather to this supposedly new-and-improved one. At least with the old one, I knew where she was coming from. This one scares me. She is so believable. Every time I give her the benefit of the doubt, something pulls at my spirit. I was talking to her the other day and I could have sworn she was making love to me right there."

"See how beautiful you are. You're pulling from both sides."

Montana glared at him. "I know you're trying to make me relax about this, but I'm telling you, something is really wrong here. I can't say it's evil, because I do see some light."

"Baby, don't let the light fool you, it is not always an indication of good. You must be careful, okay? I know you and when you get your mind fixed on something. You will walk boldly up to Heather without consulting God, and I just want you to be out of harm's way. And you need to remember that Satan can quote the Bible verbatim, but he can't interpret it because he doesn't have the Holy Spirit to translate it."

"I know, love." She held his hand. "It just makes me so mad when I think she could be pimping God like that. I know I'm not supposed to judge her, but that's exactly what I'm doing. If there is any good in her, I hope my prejudice doesn't keep me from seeing it."

"It will all be revealed to you at the right place and time. You have to put your faith in God, not in Heather's actions. I think that's enough talk about Ms. Heather. It's time to concentrate on us. We haven't had a lot of time together lately."

"How did the deal go in Chicago?"

"Surprisingly, they resolved all of the company's concerns and addressed our issues. We are more than satisfied with the arrangement. They signed the contract, no questions asked. Now, that's scary. This is a *big* account. Rivers getting this account means the difference between us living comfortably to our living a lifestyle of luxury and being able to really help those who don't have. When the stock splits, we will become multimillionaires overnight."

"I am so proud of you. You worked so hard on that account. I think the move you made is a smart one. The emphasis in technology will be in the home. Residential demand and the company's stock are going to skyrocket."

"I only regret it has taken so much time away from you and Chesne. Did she get my letter and presents?"

"Yes. She used to read that letter repeatedly. The dress is big, but it should fit her perfectly next year. By the way, what are you doing buying her such expensive presents. A dress, shoes, and purse? We almost had a fight because she wanted to sleep in it. Where is she ever going to wear a fancy dress like that?"

"You never know what formal occasion may present itself in a princess' life. So who won the fight?"

"Well let's just say we reached a truce."

"Well, hello Garrett," a young woman said, interrupting their conversation.

"Uh, hello there, M-Ms. Chambers," Garrett stuttered. The woman smiled a little too friendly. "Montana, I'd like you to meet Ms. Chambers."

"Hello."

"Hi. So you're Montana," the woman said curtly shaking her hand like a cold, dead fish.

Montana fought the urge to wipe the slime off her hand. She looked at Garrett for an explanation as to how this stranger knew of her and she was more than a little perturbed that she had not been given the same courtesy.

"I'll see you, later." Ms. Chambers said confidently.

"Yeah, I'll call you." Garrett smiled sheepishly as she walked away.

"So, how do you have the pleasure of knowing Ms. Chambers?"

"I don't really know her. She's a client. I don't know any more about her than that."

Montana knew he was lying, but she couldn't prove it nor did she want to dig any deeper at the present time. She had learned through experience that all things are eventually uncovered no matter how well they are hidden. A familiar memory twisted her stomach and she felt as if she were going to be sick.

"Alright, Garrett. I believe you. But, I don't need to remind you how much I detest lying or how much this would erode my trust in you if I found out otherwise, right?"

"I'm not lying."

But you're not telling the whole truth either, are you? Montana asked silently even though she knew she had not always done so herself.

Garrett muddled through lunch with as much charm as he could summon. He did everything he could to keep the mood light. He hated to lie to Montana, but sometimes it just couldn't be helped. They finished lunch in strained silence and walked out.

The valet finally brought the car, which provided some distraction from the icicles aimed at him from Montana's eyes. Garrett had just closed the door for Montana when his cell phone rang.

"I meant to turn this thing off. Rivers speaking." Dead silence. Garrett immediately went into a comatose state, incapable of speech or involuntary eye movement.

Montana could not ascertain if he was breathing until she heard faint, ragged breaths.

"How did you get this number? Don't call me on this phone again. Any business we have to conduct can be done in my office." The person on the other end must have apologized because Garrett said, "I can understand that mistakes happen, but you know the importance of this. Don't make this mistake again. I would appreciate your discretion. Very well. Good-bye." Garrett angrily hung up the phone. This time he made sure he turned it off.

"What was that about?"

"It was Ms. Chambers." Garrett waited for the storm to attack him mercilessly.

"What is she doing calling you and why is she calling on your cell phone? How did she get the number?"

"I don't know why she's calling me. She's a client, but our business is almost over. I don't know how she got this number." Garrett was honest in his answers, but that did not give Montana any relief.

"Whenever you get a chance, we need to talk. Not now, but when we aren't rushed. There are a few things that I would like to straighten out."

Garrett could have relaxed more had Montana gone into a rage, but her quiet calm was much too unpredictable. You could never determine where, when, or how it would strike. But he knew Montana and she would strike and catch him off guard.

Montana pulled up to his office and Garrett got out of the car. Closing the door, he turned and placed his hands on the ledge. Garrett looked like a small boy who was in trouble despite telling the truth. "Will I see you later?"

"Sure. Chesne has ballet tonight so it may be this weekend."

Garrett looked discouraged. "That's two days away, baby."

"It'll give you a chance to miss me."

"I already do. I love you."

"I love you, too."

Feeling disoriented to the brink of exhaustion, she drove back to work. The drive was similar to virtual reality as she drove on the Indy 500 with dilated eyes. "What in the world is happening? First the assault on Chesne, then Heather, Stephanie, and now Garrett. Is my whole world crumbling before my eyes? The only foundation I know that can withstand anything is God, and I have to trust in that. I will be anxious for nothing. I will seek His face. When the wicked, even mine enemies and my foes, came upon me to eat up my flesh, they stumbled and fell. Wait on the Lord, be of good courage, and He shall strengthen thine heart; wait, I say on the Lord."

Montana quoted every scripture she could think of to encourage herself and keep her mind focused on God. It was more important now than ever that she observed with her spiritual eyes. From the flesh to the spirit, it was coming at her from all angles.

Montana was listening to 97.5 FM on the radio when she heard "The 23rd Psalm" and started singing. As she sang, her spirit rose a little higher and helped her make it through the day.

It was eight in the morning when Montana suddenly woke up. She was supposed to be at work, but with all the traumatic events of late, being at work on time was the last of her concerns. "I'm not going to fight it anymore. Working for someone else has never been for me. I'm going to start my own business when the time is right." Montana got up.

"Chesne, baby, you need to get up. We're late."

Montana and Chesne were ready within an hour.

"We've never been ready that fast. Have we, Mommy?"

"No, baby." A wave of fear coursed through Montana's body making her tremble. She knew something was waiting around the corner, it was only of question of timing and content.

Either I need to be at work on time or I need to be ready for the battle I must endure. Actually, the way things have been going, it's probably both, she thought.

Montana dropped Chesne off at school who had adjusted amazingly well after the incident with Collier. Her friends had been wonderful and became Chesne's personal guardian angels. Michael and Gabriel were always first to the rescue and guarded her as if she were a priceless treasure that everyone wanted to steal. Her best friend, Kayla played the big sister who made sure Chesne had everything she needed.

Garrett had been a tremendous help with Chesne. He was there at her disposal, able to reinforce that there were truly strong, positive, responsible, caring black males. Chesne and Garrett grew closer and became friends who immensely enjoyed each other's company.

There is no way I could ever thank him enough. Chesne never spoke about it, but I am sure more wounds were healed than just those inflicted on her from Collier. I think Garrett was able to smooth the scars and fill a void that only a father's love can, Montana thought.

After Chesne's attack, Ms. Flynn had talked to the children about molestation and how important it is to talk to someone. Loren Reed, an employee of protective services was invited to speak with the children about their bodies and proper touching. She asked each class to write down any questions they had. Anonymity helped the children get answers to questions they may not have asked ordinarily. Parents attended the meetings as well since studies had shown that children were more relaxed in discussing these issues when their parents were actively involved.

There was a flood of questions from the kids. It was difficult for Montana to hear and heartbreaking to realize how frequently molestation actually occurred in homes of otherwise decent people. The last update Montana received about Collier was that he had been sent to a military school after he was caught stealing his mother's jewelry. After that, Mrs. Yadrow changed the lock on the door and made sure he did not get a key. Montana felt sympathy for them and sent up a silent prayer.

Somehow, Montana arrived at work only a few minutes late. Walking past the break room, she saw Stephanie and Heather talking, actually whispering about something. *God only knows what that child is up to now. And to think Stephanie let herself get pulled in. Lord, please protect Stephanie. Be her covering so that the snares of the devil will not overcome her. I know she has to choose I just hope she continues to choose You. I sure would hate to see her get hurt, but then sometimes that is exactly what it takes. I commit her into Your hands, Father.*

Montana looked at the stack of papers on her desk and suddenly was exhausted. She opened up her e-mail and was surprised to see sixty-seven messages. *Was I out yesterday? How do these things accumulate?* Montana wondered.

There was a presentation she had to give in three days and had not even started it. With all the research that needed to be done, it would be a miracle if she were able to complete it by then.

Suddenly filled with inspiration, she created the presentation mentally. She would not do the same old dog and pony show, but would create a new program, a greatness program. It would empower employees to perform duties outside the scope of their present job and provide the client with superior service. They would constantly look for ways to invent and reinvent the tried and true. They would create the ninety-nine-cent solution that could save the company thousands and still provide financial rewards to the employees, giving them the freedom to direct their own career paths. A project team would be organized to create online classes, electronic reference manuals, coaching materials, and workshops to assist any employee in upward mobility by becoming an internal entrepreneur.

She was grateful for God's gifts. They always arrived at the right time, order, and place.

After the presentation, Paul walked up to Montana to congratulate her once again for her phenomenal performance.

"Thank you so much, Paul. I always try to do the best I can."

"And it shows. I can't tell you how grateful I am to have you on my team. To show you how much that means to me, why don't you give me a list of the things you want in your new position and I'll approve it. At this rate, there is nothing that we would not give you."

Montana was dumbstruck. Before she knew it, she was hugging Paul until she realized where she was and apologized for such an open display.

"Thank you. I can't tell you how much this means."

"I can't tell you how much you mean so I guess we're even. Just have it on my desk and your wishes are granted."

Montana walked away feeling that she had finally captured the brass ring and best of all, it was a delivery directly from heaven.

CHAPTER SEVENTEEN

"If you carry the egg basket, do not dance."
Ambede Proverb

Stephanie and Heather were quickly becoming the best of friends. Heather had not been successful in blackmailing Stephanie in order to ruin Montana, but she had an alternate plan that was guaranteed to work. This was the final triumph Satan was looking for and Heather was confident her reward would exceed her highest expectations. If what she had received thus far was any indication, she was definitely pleased.

Heather imagined her new life of affluence and the unlimited supply of money and the things she would possess—designer clothes, luxury cars, spectacular house, and sex that would fulfill her most uninhibited desires. Through acceptance of his gifts, she unconsciously solidified her allegiance to the devil as he manipulated her like a disposable pawn in his destructive game. Even if she knew of his entrapments, Heather would have freely exchanged her intangible soul for material gain.

To initiate her plan, Heather decided to take Stephanie shopping after hearing her say that she needed more clothes and was tired of constantly wearing the same things. She frequently complained that she never had any money left after helping her family. Stephanie was hungry and there was no better way to manipulate someone than by satisfying that hunger.

You can only wear pinstripes and checks so long, Heather thought mocking Stephanie.

The following weekend, Heather called Stephanie. "Hey, you want to go shopping with me?"

"I don't have any money to go shopping."

"I don't either. I thought we could window-shop and hang out. You never know what might happen."

"What are you doing now?" Stephanie asked.

"Just opening my mail. What is this, I didn't . . . oh, my. I don't believe it."

"Believe what?"

"I just got a platinum credit card with a $75,000 credit limit."

"A what?"

"A $75,000 credit limit. Get dressed. We're going shopping and anything else you want to do."

"I can't."

"You have no choice. If you don't, I'll pick everything out for you. And you know what I like." Heather was a flamboyant dresser and used every opportunity to show her cleavage and legs. She was country and cheap sex wrapped in designer sackcloth.

"No, that won't work."

"Then you'd better come."

"Thanks so much, Heather. I don't know what I would do without you."

"Thank your lucky stars you won't have a chance to find out. I'll pick you up at eleven."

"Okay. I'll be waiting."

"I knew you would come through. You could have made it a $250,000 credit limit. Just remember that the next time. You need me and I expect to get paid," Heather announced to Satan. She stopped as if she were listening. "Yes, I know I'm having fun, but that's beside the point. You keep your end of the bargain, and I'll keep mine."

Heather picked Stephanie up a little before eleven. They browsed through every exclusive clothing, shoe, and jewelry store in Atlanta. By the time Stephanie was finished with her selections, she had a fabulous new wardrobe.

While shopping at Neiman's, Heather gave the salesperson her credit card for the $25,000 purchase. The woman stared at the two women oddly and in return, Heather looked at the saleslady's nametag, which read BRITTANY TAYLOR.

Reading her mind, Heather mentally responded, *Not yet, but we're going to be soon. Would you like to join us?*

Brittany looked as if she had seen a ghost. She was so flabbergasted that she forgot to swipe the card and started stuffing the merchandise in shopping bags. Heather walked over to Brittany discreetly licking her ear and whispered, "I'll be back to lick *you* later. You won't believe how good I can make you feel." She screamed and ran away.

"What's wrong with her?" Stephanie asked.

"I don't know. I just told her that I could see her nipples."

"You told her what?"

"I told her I could see her nipples and it was turning me on." Heather laughed.

Stephanie looked at Heather not sure if she was joking, but as she felt the weight of the bags pulling on her arms, she realized she could not afford to say too much of anything. After all, she had a fantastic new wardrobe and that was worth more than anything Heather could do.

"I wonder what Montana will say when she sees you on Monday. Everything you have is equal to or better than what she wears," Heather said.

"She will probably tell me how nice I look."

Heather looked at her, surprised. "She's not your friend. I have been a friend to you. I have done things for you that no one else did. I deserve to have your loyalty."

Stephanie shrugged. "You do, but that's just how she is. I have never seen her hold any resentment against someone who had more than she did or disdain for those who didn't."

"Aren't you ever going to learn? Don't you remember what she said about you?"

"I remember what you told me. It's just hard to believe that about her. I'm not saying it's not true. It's just so out of character for her. Every time I begin to believe what you said happened, something tugs at my heart."

Heather decided not to push the issue. Willing or not, Stephanie was going to betray Montana, and she could hardly wait.

"I understand. It's hard to believe anything bad about someone when you really like her. Eventually, everything will be exposed, but until then, I'm starving. Are you hungry?"

"Yes. All this shopping has drained me."

"And for more than just food." Heather mentally undressed a handsome, finely dressed man walking in the mall. Stephanie looked at her amazed.

"Do you think you can put your eyeballs back into your head?"

"Oh, I didn't know I was that obvious."

"Let's put it this way, if he had been sixteen, you would be charged with statutory rape."

"At this point, that doesn't sound like a bad deal," Heather said.

"Where do you want to eat?"

"There's a place in here called The Pub. Their food is pretty good."

"Okay, let's go," Stephanie said.

When they arrived, it was crowded and they decided to order drinks and appetizers at the bar instead. Heather asked the server to safeguard their packages until they left.

Heather looked around watching everyone engaged in conversation. "I want to do something tonight."

"Like what?"

"We could ask some of my friends over. I think you'll like them. They are really cool people."

"I can't stay out too late, but I'll come over for a while."

"That's great! I was hoping you would come." Heather smiled, realizing that is how the evening would end.

The drinks were bitterly strong and by the time they were ready to leave, the two women were incapable of walking a straight line. They repeatedly laughed, talked, and stumbled on their way to the car.

When they walked into Heather's apartment, she told Stephanie to make herself comfortable. She picked up the phone and made a couple of calls, then changed and walked into the kitchen.

"My friends should be here in a few minutes. Do you want something to drink?"

"Sure. Whatever you've got."

"You like margaritas? I make a mean one."

"Okay. You need any help in there?"

"No. I'll be out in a minute." She pulled out a bottle and put it in her pocket. She brought out the pitcher and four glasses. "Why don't you put on some music while I pour the drinks," Heather said.

"Okay."

When Stephanie walked over to the CD player, Heather dropped Roofies into Stephanie's glass. "I don't have that many new CDs, but I have few old ones you might like."

"Thanks." Stephanie looked through the CDs and chose an ancient George Benson.

Heather stirred the drinks thoroughly. *I hope this stuff works as well as they claim it does,* she thought. She made sure Stephanie got her specially prepared drink. Heather sipped on hers while two-stepping to George Benson. "That sounds good."

Stephanie looked at her and smiled, taking a sip of her concoction. "This is really good. What kind of tequila did you use?"

"It's not the tequila, I added a little secret ingredient to it. I thought you might like it. You do like it, don't you?"

"Yeah, it's really good. You'll have to give me the recipe."

The doorbell rang. "That must be my friends." Heather stood to answer the door.

"Hi, Jez, David. Come on in. I'd like you to meet a really good friend of mine. Stephanie, this is Jez and David."

"Nice to meet you," Stephanie said.

"You guys want a drink?"

"She makes a slamming margarita," Stephanie said.

"I'm a straight Scotch man myself," David replied.

"I drink anything with alcohol," Jez said, laughing.

Heather poured the drinks. "I'll bring the appetizers out in a minute."

"My, aren't we the little Ms. Homemaker tonight," Jez said with jealousy lacing her voice. She could not remember a time when Heather showed her the simplest kindness.

Heather gave her a look of caution, but Jez ignored it.

"So Stephanie, how long have you lived in Atlanta?" David asked.

"All my life. I'm a native."

"Really? I've live here for fifteen years and I've never met anyone from Atlanta," Jez said.

"I've always liked it here. Everyone is from somewhere else." Stephanie started feeling terribly warm. "Is it getting hot in here?"

"No, I'm comfortable," David said.

"Me, too," Heather said, putting the appetizers down.

Stephanie grabbed a paper off the table and started fanning her face. She stood to walk and swayed slightly falling back into her seat.

"You okay?" Jez asked.

"I guess."

David pulled out some Ecstasy. After Heather took it, she turned to Stephanie.

"Want some?"

"You know I don't do drugs."

"Come on. It just helps you relax and makes you feel on top of the world."

"I feel like I'm already on top of the world. At least, it's spinning like I am."

"This will help, Steph, I promise," Heather said. "Here, take it." Heather handed it to her like a mother concerned for her sick child. Stephanie hesitated, but did as she was told. "That's a good girl. Feeling better?" Stephanie nodded weakly.

Jez and David began their own intimate activity. Finishing with Jez, he tried to entice Heather, but she was too engrossed in Stephanie. After thirty minutes, Heather grew tired of trying. Jez moved toward Heather and they joined in mutual pleasure.

Heather saw Stephanie stir and said to Jez, "I think you can move in now."

Stephanie raised her head. "Where am I?"

"You're at my house. You feeling any better?"

"A little. I feel like a wound up ball of yarn."

"Maybe it'll help if I massage you. I'm an excellent masseuse," Jez said.

"I can vouch for that. She does things to your body that are unbelievable," Heather said.

"You're going to need to take off your blouse." Jez helped Stephanie remove it and gently rubbed her neck. "Doesn't that feel better?"

Jez massaged Stephanie's shoulders and felt her relax. Moans emitted from her throat as she felt her body melt from Jez's touch. "Um, that feels good."

Kissing her on the neck, Jez said, "Stephanie, baby, I'm going to need to take off your bra, okay?"

"Okay."

"That's a good girl." Jez took off her bra and started to rub her swollen breasts.

"Wait, you're not supposed to, I'm not a ... um ... that feels wonderful." Stephanie said, squirming and asking for more with her body as Jez aroused her. Removing Stephanie's skirt, Jez experienced her own excitement from the manual manipulation. She positioned Stephanie and began her assent to sexual satisfaction and their descent to hell.

Heather insisted that David leave, but when he vehemently refused, she grabbed an andiron and struck him with it. He looked bewildered, quickly scurrying to get dressed as Heather's eyes turned into cold black marbles. She was about to hit him again when he dashed through the door.

Quickly returning to her previous demeanor, Heather saw Jez pleasing herself. Jez did not like Heather dedicating so much time to Stephanie, but she was under Heather's influence leaving her no choice if she wanted to remain in her life.

Inhaling Stephanie's intoxicating scent, Heather was stimulated as she strapped on her apparatus.

Satan watched with pleasure. He was delighted and decided to give Heather a few surprises.

As Heather snapped the apparatus into place, she saw that it had somehow become real and was naturally attached to her. She touched it and felt pleasure move through her body. Heather could feel her muscles contracting. Never having this sensation before, she felt as though she was transformed and filled with power. When she looked down, she saw her penis.

She had the ability and control to bring Stephanie to the apex of ecstasy as she moved in rhythm with her, immensely enjoying the exchange as she screamed out. Heather released herself feeling a euphoria that was unbelievable.

Heather's hand slowly moved down Stephanie's flat, velvet stomach as she squirmed under her touch. Kissing Stephanie, she timed the sequence of her motions with absolute precision.

Stephanie's orgasms continued to flow freely, and Heather mounted her again. She was grateful her master was able to do such wondrous things and she thanked him as she erupted.

"It's such a shame you won't remember any of this. We'll get together again. I'll make sure of it." Looking up at the blinking light on the camera, Heather winked as she climaxed again.

CHAPTER EIGHTEEN

"The bridge is repaired only when someone falls in the water."
Somali Proverb

eather walked into the office confident she now possessed the deed to the world and nothing could have made her happier. She remembered her mother talking about whores and lesbians, but did not feel she was either. A whore or lesbian was inwardly ashamed, but she was not. In fact, it had been her pleasure to experience and enjoy both sexes for this was her calling. He told her so and he had not misled her yet. The way she looked at it, it was her way of bringing peace—or rather a piece—to the world.

Instead of turning toward her office, she walked toward the receptionist's station. "Hi, Stephanie."

"Hey."

"No reason to act shy now. If anything, you should be proud. Your performance was wonderful the other night. I must say you certainly do know how to use your tongue. You are an amazing lover and you taste magnificent."

"What are you talking about? You have lost your mind. I think you've been taking a few too many of those drugs you try to push on me. What has gotten into you?"

Heather ignored her remarks. "I want you to come over tonight and meet another friend."

"I don't know what you're talking about, but whatever is going on, I am not going near your house. You must be having a bad trip or something 'cause you have gone over the edge. I don't know why you're saying such ridiculous and hurtful things. I am not even going to justify your remarks with a comment. You need help, Heather."

"I think you'll change your mind. Anyway, tomorrow's a holiday. I thought you and I could have a wonderfully erotic evening with my friend. By the way, did I tell you that Michael and I are lovers now?"

"What? When?" Stephanie glared at her. She was caught in a huge web that was spinning haphazardly out of control, and she could feel the spider move viciously toward her. She didn't know what was going on, but it was better to not say any more until she did.

"Are you offended? You weren't offended when you were with Jez or when I took your breast into my mouth. You weren't even offended when you licked me dry. In fact, you seemed to like it all. I even have pictures.

"Like I said, Stephanie, come over tonight, alright? You won't like what happens if you don't. Imagine what your employer would say if he knew the lifestyle that you are leading. How would you feel having your life exposed in the paper complete with pictures for all to see? So it's tonight then, okay? I've got something indescribably delicious for you to taste." Heather walked away proudly.

Stephanie shook her head. "She must be crazy. I didn't do anything. I couldn't have. Or did I? Wouldn't I remember? I'm not a lesbian. I couldn't have done any of those things. We went shopping, to her house, met some of her friends and she dropped me off. That's all that happened." Stephanie shook her head sure that Heather was certainly losing it.

Montana caught a glimpse of Heather as she past her office. "Hey, Heather. How are you?"

"I couldn't be better." Heather looked at Montana lustfully. Thoughts of her legs spread wide open thrilled her and she became moist. Soon, very soon, she would have Montana, and she was worth any price. She could feel the intense throbbing between her legs as if she had swallowed her heart.

"Well, I've got to go." Heather walked to her work area. She was glad everybody in her department was gone for the day. She took off her underwear, threw her legs on her desk and took matters into her own hands as she thought of Montana. *I don't know if I want to destroy you or make you my slave.* Heather mulled it over in her mind and the thrill of each possibility made her feel powerful.

Montana did not want to talk to Heather, but she needed to look into her eyes, and what she saw confirmed her worst fears. Heather's soul was definitely darker. Whatever she was doing was working quickly.

Montana called Stephanie. "Hey, girl!"

"Hi, Montana."

"I haven't had a chance to talk with you lately. Between work and my life, I'm moving at the speed of light."

"Yeah, I know. It's okay," Stephanie said, still bewildered.

"Are you okay?"

"I'm fine."

"You sound stressed. Listen, if you ever want to talk or need help with anything, I'm here for you, Steph."

"I know, but some things you just have to work through on your own."

"I know about that, but if you need a friend, a true friend, I'm here."

"Alright, thanks."

"Stephanie?"

"Yeah?"

"You know you can go to God with anything. He loves you."

"So they say." Stephanie hung up.

Montana was worried. In the time she had known Stephanie, she had not heard her deny her faith in God or sound so despondent. Picking up the phone, she called Garrett.

"I told you, Mr. Rivers is not here." Montana heard Anne say to someone as she picked up the phone to answer it.

"Rivers and Associates. This is Anne."

"Hi, Anne."

"Oh, hello, Montana. It's good to hear your voice. Hold on for me, will you?" After a few minutes, Anne returned to the phone. "I'm sorry about that."

"I guess some people just don't get the message. Would you ask Garrett to call me please?"

"He's right here. Hold on."

That's strange, Montana thought. *Why would Anne tell someone he's not there when he is?*

"This is Garrett."

"Hi." Montana was relieved to hear his voice.

"Well, hello there. How are you doing? I sure do miss you."

"I'm fine and I miss you, too. Would you like to have lunch today?" Montana asked.

"Sure, what time?"

"About one o'clock. I'll pick you up. I need to get out of here."

"Heather again?"

"Yeah."

"Are you okay?"

"I'm fine. It's not me. I'll tell you about it at lunch."

"Okay, I'll see you then. I love you, baby."

"I love you, too." Montana needed the strength of his arms around her.

It was only ten in the morning and though her day had barely started, she was as tired as if she had worked a double shift. Having lunch with Garrett would give her soul comfort through the power of their love.

Montana walked to the lobby. As she approached Stephanie's desk, she said, "Stephanie, I won't be back today. If anyone needs me just send them to my voice mail. Oh, by the way, I meant to ask you if anyone from Chesne's school called a few weeks ago."

"Not that I can remember. Heather relieved me a few times. Maybe she answered the phone."

"That explains everything."

"What happened?"

"Nothing, just her stupidity could have made a disastrous situation catastrophic."

"Montana, Heather is going through a lot right now. You need to be more understanding."

"Oh, so now you're defending *her*?"

"Well, someone has to. You are always on her case. We all mess up now and then. We're not all like you!"

"And what is that supposed to mean? I have done nothing but try to help you, Stephanie, but you've changed. Or maybe I have. I just can't believe that you are now putting yourself in the same category as Heather. It's wonderful to have friends, Steph, but like I said before, you need to be careful. Her spirit is not clean."

"Not everyone can be as faithful and perfect as you, Ms. St. Claire. We all have done something we're ashamed of or can't get ourselves out of. I can take care of myself. I don't need you to come to my rescue."

"No, you're right, you don't need me, but you sure need God. Does He need to rescue you from something? I think I already know the answer to that." Montana looked at Stephanie with compassion and walked toward Paul's office.

Montana saw Heather coming out of Paul's office and walked past her as if she were invisible. She wore the look of a woman on a mission and charged toward Stephanie.

Paul was on the phone when Montana peeped into his office. Pulling a pad from her purse, she scribbled a note stating she was leaving and placed it on his desk. He nodded and waved good-bye. When she turned to walk out, she saw Stephanie and Heather huddled together like football players discussing a covert play.

"Good-bye, ladies." She heard a strained response as they returned to whatever was so important.

Montana drove into the parking lot of Garrett's office and pulled into a thirty-minute space. It was a beautiful day and she did not feel like shopping or reading, and instead decided to meet Garrett a little earlier than planned. Maybe she could even talk him into hanging out with her. That would certainly uplift her spirit. An overwhelming feeling of joy consumed her and she was unexplainably happy.

"Hi, Anne. How are you?"

"Hi. I'm fine."

Montana noticed the wrinkles on Anne's forehead and a look of fear that seemed to have frozen her usually animated face. "Are you okay?"

"Yes, Yes, I'm fine. Of course I am. What could possibly be wrong?" Anne was trying hard to convince Montana, but she could not even convince herself.

Montana did not believe her. As her stomach tumbled over, she mistook it for hunger. "I came to surprise Garrett."

"He's on the phone," Anne said.

Montana had already started toward his office. Anne tried to stop her, but before she could say another word, Montana was walking down the hall. She heard Anne call her. "I won't disturb him, I promise. I'll be quiet as a mouse."

Montana silently opened the door and saw Delores Chambers and Garrett kissing. Garrett's grasp on her forearms seemed unusually tight.

"Excuse me."

Garrett broke the embrace, looking as if he had been caught with his pants down.

"I came to surprise you and once again, I get surprised. So she's a business client? I wonder what kind of business you're actually conducting. History has a cruel way of repeating itself, doesn't it, Garrett?" Tears flooded Montana's eyes. "I guess you know what to do, right?" Montana ran out tripping over her heart, leaving all hopes of a life with Garrett behind.

"Let's see how she handles that. Timing is so important. A wrong word or action sets into motion a totally different set of responses. How does it feel to have the love of your life in someone else's arms again? You can't get away from me. You are mine. You are my destiny," Satan said.

"You're tougher than I thought. I just knew if someone vile touched your precious little girl it would send you over the edge. You got angry, and I could sense your taste for blood, but you kept clinging to God as if He was really going to come down and help you. Why would you love someone that you can't get anything from until you die? That is so stupid. You need to have it now while you are living. Look at all my converts. They have material wealth that even Rockefeller would envy.

"I like you though, you challenge me. When I get you, and I will get you, we will control the world. You are my ultimate test. You cling to Him as if your life depends upon it, but I'll show you a better way. You won't ever have to worry about people running over you again. You will have to adjust to the special piece of lakefront property that I have. The screams of agony and pain are another matter though. I don't know why they cry out for Him when they die. They knew what they were getting into. Well, maybe I neglected to tell them that part, but that's their fault, not mine. I can't help it if they didn't read the fine print. You'll get used to it though. I have. When you rule a kingdom, there is always a price to pay, especially when your subjects are fools."

CHAPTER NINETEEN

"God does not ask you to withstand more than is possible."
Amara Proverb

ontana walked down the stairs into the kitchen to get something to drink. Scottie, as usual, was by her side. Times of distress made her grateful he was there. He never demanded anything, yet at the same time, he was a constant reminder that she was not alone.

She walked into the tranquil place that was decorated with a butterscotch leather sofa, an overstuffed eggplant-and-caramel chair with ottoman. Moss green and eggplant-striped pillows were placed on the sofa and chair. There was a feeling of warmth in the room that provided comfort, reassurance, or whatever your need was at the time. The light filtered softly through the blinds and bronze sheers creating honey- and cream-colored stripes on the walls of the room. The ceiling fan made the air comfortably cool as the fragrance from the Lampe Berger sent whiffs of tropical flowers throughout.

It was quiet without Chesne, deathly quiet. The image of Chesne leaving flashed through her mind. Chesne had vehemently protested leaving her mom, and Montana did not want her to go but she had to let her. She fought the urge to scream "don't leave, please don't leave me alone, I need someone who truly loves me here," but Montana knew in her present state, she was not good for Chesne. She put on her happiest "don't worry" face and told Chesne how much fun she would have.

Tears filled Chesne's eyes as she said, "If you need me, please call. I'll be back before you know it." Montana fought to restrain the tears that threatened to tear down the door of emotion that she had locked. She needed to keep it under control so she could send her child off to Washington, D.C. with Noelle for the summer. It was not the child's place to worry about the parent, but the other way around.

Chesne and Montana hugged each other tightly as they shared a tearful good-bye.

✧ ✧ ✧ ✧ ✧

The tranquil place normally made her relaxed and calm, but today it did nothing to remove the cloak of darkness that seemed to be closing in on her. Montana tried to meditate to get in touch with her inner self, but every attempt was futile. She felt completely drained, as if someone had entered her being in the darkness of the night and stolen her soul.

Possessing none of the energy that was characteristic of her, she was exhausted and forlorn to the point that lifting a finger required effort that was absent in her. Sighing heavily, Montana let her head fall on the back of the chair. She closed her eyes trying to feel God, who now seemed so far away. Tears escaped from her lids and created salt-water streams that ran lazily down her cheeks. The toll of life and the traumatic events she had experienced lately etched weariness on her face.

If only Mama were here. She would know exactly what to do to help me through this, she thought. The reality of never being able to talk to her mother again and not being able to hear her voice hit hard. Montana choked back the emotion that seemed ready to burst at the seams. She could not lose control; there was no time to break down.

Just when you think you've got it all figured out and everything is on track, something always comes along to knock you down. You don't drown because you fall in the water; you drown because you stay there, she thought.

Times like these meant she was closer to God than Satan wanted her to be. It also meant Satan had peeked into her future and seen God's wondrous works in her life. He was coming to steal, kill, and destroy and would stop at nothing to get what he wanted. It was what he lived for—to watch people create their own road to hell, with a little urging from him, of course.

Montana had seen evidence of Satan's work in her mother's life, but through God's grace, Grace had overcome. Grace made sure Montana knew and loved God. It was the only weapon against Satan who pursued Grace all of her life, but then Grace died and went home to live with God. This made Satan furious, and he vowed to possess her children and her children's children, but Satan knew only what God allowed him to know. Montana and Chesne were degrees of Grace because they were Grace's lineage, and with God's love, they both were able to move from one degree of grace to another in their walk with God.

Satan hovered over Montana, watching. The sight of her aroused him. He was amazed at how seductive children of God could be. Innocence was a definite turn-on. Eve had the same effect on him.

Montana was the woman he wanted and was meant to have. Chesne being a part of the package just made it even more attractive. He shook his head, remembering when he tried to violate her by possessing Collier. The feeling Chesne gave him mirrored her mother's.

"All that little snotty wimp did was to turn the other cheek and forgive him. Every time she got angry and the embers would start to catch fire, she would do something to defuse them. She's going to be more trouble than she is worth, just like her mother is trying to be. I underestimated her once and once is one time too many. She will lose this time and I will own them both."

The lesson Grace taught Montana about faith and obedience being what God loves found fertile soil within her and grew roots until she became one of the elite few who would play an essential role in ministering to people about Christ. Montana had taught that same lesson to Chesne, and Satan was on a mission to stop it permanently. Once he converted Montana, Chesne would naturally follow.

Montana sighed resignedly. She felt so alone, so discarded.

Oh Gracious Father, please forgive me. I know You love me beyond reason, beyond measure. I am so grateful for that, but I yearn desperately for the arms of my Mama. I miss her so much. I know in my spirit, You are all I will ever need, but as a human I need touch and I am so empty without my mother's arms. I hope You are not angry with me. I pray this desire has not cast me away from You.

Please let this cup pass me by. I don't know if I have the strength. I almost lost my precious Chesne, now I've lost Garrett, and I feel as if I'm losing my life or it's losing me. I have never prayed for anything material. I have only prayed that I do Your will and that You protect those I love. Was that so much to ask? You know I am in tremendous pain right now, and I don't feel that You're doing anything. Are You even listening to me? Do I matter to You anymore? What do I need to do to move beyond this? All I know to do is to hold on to You, and I ask that You not let me go.

Montana was completely drained. She had said all that was in her heart, but she still did not feel it was enough.

"I love you. Come to me. Feel the warmth of my embrace. Feel the urgency in my loins for you," Satan whispered as he crossed over and caressed her breast. "Once you have me, you will never want another."

Scottie began to bark incessantly. Montana jumped as if something evil had just moved through her.

"What the . . .?" The smell of decayed flesh permeated the room. "Where is that smell coming from? What is going on?" She was gravely frightened.

Her heart raced. She was not sure what to think, so she did the only thing she knew, she prayed. *God, please protect me. Surround me with Your white protective light so that no evil can touch or harm those I love or me, but if I must die then let me die for You.*

"That little bitch. She knows she wants me. Why else would I feel her arousal? Why won't she just admit it? I know what to do the next time. She felt me." Satan was satisfied with that for now.

✢ ✢ ✢ ✢ ✢

Not knowing what her next steps should be, she retreated within herself to join with her spirit. The emptiness in Montana expanded to encompass her being. She knew what she had to do and walked to her desk. It was time to end this. She was so tired of fighting. Slowly, pulling out a paper and pen, she began to write.

CHAPTER TWENTY

"A united family eats from the same plate."
Kiganda Proverb

Dear Mama,
It's been such a long time since I've talked to you and it seems strange talking to you this way. It makes it even more apparent that you're no longer with me, and it leaves me with such a haunting feeling.

I miss you more than I ever thought possible. Though Chesne never says anything, I know losing you affects her more than she lets on. I miss seeing you and your smile, but most of all I miss talking to you and hearing your voice. That seems to be the hardest for me now—remembering your voice. I miss the treasure I lost in your invaluable wisdom. I regret we did not have a chance to say good-bye. It was as if the floor crumbled beneath us, and before we could react, the sliver of a moment we had was gone. I wish we had been able to talk about things that I have so many questions about now.

Do you know how much I love you? I am so thankful that you were my mom and loved me beyond comprehension. Do you know how grateful I am for the sacrifices you made in your life, so I could have happiness in mine? Did I love you enough in return?

I cannot help but feel that we were cheated. For a quite a while, I was furious with God, but then I realized my fury would only put me farther from Him and you. So I stopped screaming and started crying. Though no one sees my tears that often now, the ones I cry inside have formed a river.

I do not know what to do with my life without you. All my life included you. We were as intertwined as Siamese twins. How do you explain to one twin that when you were separated, the other was not strong enough to survive?

Well, Satan is holding on to my coattail now. It has been almost three years since you passed and his attacks on me seem to have increased since you left. I know it's a battle I can win, but it sure would make me feel better if you were here. I know how to put on the armor of God, I just don't know if it still fits. I love God with my whole heart, and I have tried to get back to where I was, but I feel slightly removed somehow. I know it is not God who has moved, but I. Somehow, I know I will get through it. It's always harder at the beginning when you aren't sure of your steps. I miss you, Mama.

Mama, please pray for me. Please continue to ask God to protect us. I feel as if I must walk into the pits of hell and fight. I'm not sure if I will return unharmed, but that's the only way I think Satan will finally leave me alone and then I can go about my Father's business.

Wait a minute! That's it! That's my answer to all of this. I am here to take care of my Father's business. Nothing else matters.

This is proof that everything in our lives is already planned; we just have to be obedient to the will of God and watch the pieces effortlessly fall into place. God is an awesome wonder! Even beyond the grave, I feel your guidance and love. Thank You, God. Thank you, Mama. I love you with everything I am and will ever be.

As always,
M

CHAPTER TWENTY-ONE

"Not even the five fingers of our hands are alike."
Afghan Proverb

*M*ontana walked upstairs and slipped on a pair of black linen pants and a sleeveless ivory silk sweater. She was tired of feeling sorry for herself. Truthfully, she was scared to death of what lay ahead, but she knew she had to see her destiny through.

Lord, I am really fearful, but I must be of good courage. Being courageous means standing in the presence of fear despite all that I see. Please continue to encourage me so that I may be strengthened by Your word. You have not called me to do something I am not capable of, and You would not send me where I am not protected. This destiny You have trusted me with is what You require of me. For all the things You have given me, this is my gift to You.

Montana was determined not to let anything prevent her from doing God's will. If she completely trusted God, which she did, there was no room for doubt or failure.

Lord, I am not foolish. I know that Satan should not be feared, but I think when any of us are confronted with evil head-on, we become fleshly

and our hearts fail us for fear. Please order my steps and direct me in the
way that You would have me to go.

Satan overheard Montana talking to God. "Who do you think
you are? You are a simple woman. Do you really want to step into
this uncharted territory? There are serpents at every turn. You have
no idea what you're getting yourself into. Surely, God would not
send you on such an arduous task. If He really did choose you for
this task, you are favored. To have that honor is enough. You cannot
let yourself be persecuted at His expense. If God is not a respecter of
persons, why does He only work through men? Look at who He's
used—Moses, Noah, Abraham, Elijah, David, and His son. You must
have misinterpreted what He meant. He wouldn't use a woman.
How can you fight this battle alone? Remember how He left Jesus on
the cross as His own son cried out for mercy? What kind of parent
would do that to his own child?" he asked.

Montana was beginning to doubt God and her ability. *God rarely*
chooses a woman. Why would God choose me? Did God really say what I
think He said? Who am I? I can't do this. Even if I tried, I might not
understand which way God wants me to go. Do I understand Him all the
time now? This can't be what I'm supposed to do. He can't force me, that's
why He gave me free will.
A magnificent light filled the room and struck her causing her to
freeze in place. Suddenly the smell of flowers created an intoxicating
fragrance. "What in the . . .?" The light became brighter until it
possessed the intensity of the sun, yet was gentle to the eyes.

Montana shook her head in disbelief as she saw what appeared to be a giant mass of light, and the purest form of love she had ever seen. She started to kneel when it stopped her.

"No, I am not to be worshipped. I am an angel of God. He sent me to tell you that He loves you. Do not be afraid. There will be a battle that you must endure, but you will endure it and win. Remember, you are the salt of the earth. Salt is not a passive element. It initiates action. When it is placed on ice, the ice melts. So, too, will people who are in your presence. You will melt the ice away from their hearts and warm them with the love of God. When salt is poured into water, it blends with it. You will help people to blend their life with God, and any area that is sore or festered will be burned by God's strength in you and be restored. Be strong and believe in the Lord," the angel said and left.

"Am I losing my mind?" In her heart, Montana knew she wasn't. She had difficulty grasping what she had seen, but there was no doubt that she had seen it. Falling to her knees, Montana gave into the epiphany of the moment and thanked God for it.

She wanted to call someone. Wanted to tell what she had seen, but who would believe her? Almost immediately she knew that this journey was best kept quiet. Then she heard the voice of God say, *"Place the seed of My Word in your mouth and sow it so that it may reap the fruit of My harvest."*

Montana drove to Chattahoochee River Park and strolled alongside the lake. She watched the ducks swim leisurely following the leader. A couple of ducks were playing and waddling in and out of the water. This silence was what she craved and she earnestly needed to hear from God. It was still difficult to fully digest all that had happened.

Walking to a secluded spot under some shade trees, she sat down on the bench. People were in canoes rowing across the lake and some were fishing. Children played energetically on the playground and the sound of laughter echoed across the lake pulling at her heart. She missed Chesne. "I am so glad she's not here right now," she said aloud.

"Excuse me, what did you say?" an old woman said, appearing instantly. She used a cane that violently shook every time it was placed on the ground. Moans emitted from her throat as she put one foot in front of the other making it difficult to determine if the cane propelled her or if the moans abated her steps.

Montana got up to help her. "Did you want to sit down?"

"Yes."

Montana helped her walk toward the bench and was instantly uncomfortable. *What could this old lady possibly do to me?*

The force the old woman placed on Montana's arm startled her and she could feel the imprint of newly formed bruises that would be on her arm tomorrow. She believed this woman could help *her* to the bench.

"What's wrong, honey?" the woman asked.

"Oh, nothing important. Here you go." Montana barely helped her to sit.

"Beautiful day isn't it?" the old lady asked.

"Yes, it is. Another one of God's beautiful creations."

"I heard it's supposed to rain."

"I love the rain. It reminds me of God's abundance."

"Do you always talk about God this much? Most people who do generally aren't sincere."

Montana knew she did not care for this woman and now she understood why. Feeling the love of her companion angel, she looked into the woman's eyes into a black soul. *Satan, I know who you are. If you think you can beat God, bring it on,* she thought. "You are entitled to your opinion. I am not here to convince you, but if you would like to know God as I do, I will be more than happy to pray with you. Do you believe in Him? If you are lost, He will help you find your way to Him. All you have to do is ask. Do you want to pray?"

"Oh, I believe in Him, but everything is not cold or hot as He says. There is a lot of lukewarm. I live in lukewarm."

"There is no lukewarm, according to God. There are no contradictions in the Bible. It either is or is not. God will turn away from those who are lukewarm and spew them out of His mouth. I know you don't want that."

"I have already been disregarded. He dishonored me when I showed Him who I was," the woman said in a raspy, heinous voice.

"Then you didn't show Him the spirit He created. Perhaps what you showed Him was the spirit you corrupted and made in the image of arrogance, pride, and greed."

"I showed Him what I was and He couldn't take it!"

"No, you showed Him what pride made you become. You exalted yourself above Him. You thought you should rule instead of Him. Heaven is not a democracy. God created you. How could you possibly think you could overthrow Him?"

"You can't believe everything about anything. If you've never tried the other side, how do you know God is the best?"

"I know because He came from Heaven and incarnated himself as Jesus as proof of His love for me. Jesus paid the price for a debt He did not owe and a debt I could not pay. God has no hidden agenda. There are no tricks up His sleeve or clauses regarding my soul that are written in small print. I would rather die believing and loving God than to live believing and loving Satan. To do that is not living at all. By the way, you never answered my question, do you want to pray?"

"I don't need you to pray for me. You had better worry about yourself. You have no idea what you're getting yourself into," the old woman said.

"Yes, I do. I know exactly what I'm getting myself into, the rhythm of God's heart. Have a blessed day." Montana smiled and walked away.

"Okay, that wasn't bad, but it was only a test to wet my feet. Through God's grace, I didn't flinch or fumble, I knew exactly what to say and when. Thank You, God for encouraging me," Montana said.

Montana drove around enjoying the wind that blew through her hair and the cleansing effect it seemed to have as she felt the uncleanness of evil being blown away. Driving past the discount movie theater that was usually packed with kids during the summer, she saw *Mulan* displayed on the marquee. *A girl fights on her father's behalf. That seems appropriate,* Montana thought as she glanced at the empty parking lot and pulled in.

Montana bought popcorn and a Pepsi at the concession stand and walked into the theater. The movie had already started and it was pitch black upon entering so she waited for her eyes to adjust before moving. When she was finally able to see, she noticed she was the only adult in the theater without a child.

Montana had watched about a half-hour of the movie when she felt blackness looming loosely around her at first, then quickly closing in. She could feel her lungs collapsing as they were deprived of air. It seemed as though she was dying and the life within her was being sucked out. *You can't panic. You must remain calm.* Putting the popcorn and drink down, she tried in a vain effort to compose herself. Just then something tightened around her throat like a noose, but when she touched her neck, there was nothing there. Getting up quickly, but quietly, she walked out. Grabbing the first bench she could find, she held her head in her hands. *What is wrong with me? I feel like I'm going crazy.* Tears flowed gently down her cheeks.

She heard someone walk up to her. Another test was not what she needed at the moment. Montana was afraid to look up, but forced herself to anyway. When she did, she looked into eyes so pale she could almost see through them.

"Why are you crying?" a little boy asked.

"I just got, I just got . . ." Montana stammered.

He interrupted. "God loves you, you know. He said to tell you, 'I am patient and long-suffering. There is nothing you need that I will not provide. There is nothing you can do to make me stop loving you. I am with you always.' " The little boy smiled, patting her hand gently then ran off to catch up with his mother.

"Okay, I get the message, press on," Montana said. The day had been filled with great things that depleted her energy causing her body to crave rest. She decided to head home in case Chesne called.

Opening the door, she turned off the alarm and saw Scottie was there to greet her, happy to give her all the love he had. "You're such a sweet boy." Scottie tilted his head in understanding.

"You want to go outside?" She put her purse down and took him out. He saw the neighbor's cat across the street and started barking and spinning around. "You are so silly. How are you going to get through the fence?" She struggled to bring him into the house as he turned and barked jerking the leash.

Montana checked the messages. There were three from Garrett, but not one from Chesne since the day before. Picking up the receiver, she called Chesne and left a message. "She must be having fun. I'm glad she's able to spend some quality time with Noelle." The weight of the day knotted the muscles along her shoulders as she ascended the stairs.

She felt anxious and decided to take a bath pouring in the lavender and rosemary bath gel. The hot water heated the fragrance and the delicious aroma filled the room. It relaxed her immediately. Undressing, she slid into the water and let it envelop her body as she watched the water ebb and flow taking on the form of her body. She leaned back into the pillow at the end of the tub. Any other time, she would have turned on the Jacuzzi, but silence was what she needed, not the roar and vibration of a motor in its futile attempt to relax her.

"Montana?"

"Yes," she replied hesitantly.

"You are not where you are supposed to be in Me."

"I am about my Father's business. I will go where He leads me."

"I am your Father. You are not listening to Me. You must conquer the flesh and the carnal thoughts of men. Satan has used hate to put a wedge between you and your neighbor who you are commanded to love, but you don't."

"I don't hate anyone."

"Yes, you do."

"Who?"

"White people."

"I don't hate them and I don't dislike *all* white people."

"I have written 'For by one Spirit are we all baptized into one body, whether we be Jews or Gentiles, whether we be bond or free; and have been all made to drink into one Spirit.' You hear the whisper just as they do. To hate one of them is to hate Me. I created all of you."

"But there are some black people I don't like, either."

Silence.

"I'm sorry."

"Your responsibility is not to judge someone based on something as temporal as the color of his or her skin. Do you honestly think that white people are guilty simply because they are white? I painted you all with the same brush. You are much smarter than that. You are doing to them what they have done to you."

"But there is so much hurt. When I think of all the tragedies they caused, all the inhumane treatment, it just makes me cry."

"What about those who helped like the Quakers and Abolitionists who risked their lives because they believed that all people are equal?"

"But they are different."

"How? Are they not still white?"

"Yes, but their hearts are different."

"Then you should look at the sincerity of one's heart instead of the hue of one's skin. Once you begin to see, then you will change."

"And how will I see?"

"You must look beyond someone's color into their soul where the two of you are one and made of Me."

"That's easier said than done."

"It was not easy for Me to sacrifice My Son, but I did because I love you. His sacrifice gave you life. That is My ultimate gift of love. The question now is what are you going to do with this gift?"

Tears ran down Montana's face, and she was ashamed. "I am so sorry, Father. I have been wrong for so long. I thought I walked with You, but part of me walked with him. Please forgive me. I thought I was fighting the good fight, but it was only for a select few. I repent from my ways and turn away from my iniquities."

"I am so proud of you, daughter. I don't expect you to be perfect of your own volition, but you are made perfect through Me."

The hypocrisy Montana had practiced for years leaped off the pages in the book of her life and replayed themselves. It was hard to admit the ugliness she saw in herself, and she hated what she saw.

"I have forgiven people in my personal life, but not those who oppressed my people. I now forgive them and release them unto You, Heavenly Father. I ask that they also forgive me. I can no longer harbor hatred and expect to find favor with You nor can I profess my love for You and not practice it with all of mankind."

Montana suddenly wanted to go out and talk to every white person she met.

"That is not what you need to do," she heard Him say. "Go talk to your neighbor Olivia. She hides many feelings from you. She holds painful memories of her childhood close to her. Listen and see the hate that spews out. Look at its ugliness. When she is finished, talk to her as I have to you. To embrace Me, you must embrace your neighbor and love your neighbor more than you love yourself."

Montana was not sure what to say to Olivia. She knew that Olivia's past had been a painful one. Olivia had told Montana that her grandmother used to tell stories of her great-grandmother in Louisiana. One story in particular she remembered vividly. Her great-grandparents, Elijah and Martie, had been slaves on the Beaumonde Plantation. They were mulattos with an appearance more like someone white, but they were a proud people. Instead of their skin permitting them access into the house, their defiance placed them in the field. Elijah had been taken tragically from their lives and was beaten to death for protecting his family. One day, the mule died and the crops could not be plowed, so Andre Beaumonde, the master of the plantation, placed the straps around Martie's shoulders and forced her to pull the plow through the fields until he bought another mule three months later. As Olivia relayed the story, tears then hate transformed her face.

She continued on about the day that he repeatedly raped Martie who became pregnant with his child. He returned night after night forcing himself on her until one day when Olivia's great-uncle, Henry was old enough, he killed Andre and they ran away fearing for their lives. But before leaving, Martie cursed the land and the people who lived there. Legend had it that soon after their flight, the fields became barren incapable of producing food or revenue. Slowly, the members of the family died from one mysterious disease after another until no one could remember the days of the plantation's fruitfulness only its famine.

Montana recalled Olivia's unsteady hands and how easily they turned into iron fists as she squeezed them tightly trying to hold everything in. She could tell it was too much for Olivia to bear, but she was at a loss as to how to help her and decided to just listen without judgment or advice.

Montana's thoughts returned to the tasks at hand. The last thing she wanted to do was to put on clothes and talk. She just wanted to stay prayerful and think upon the things that had happened today.

"If you're tired, God will understand. You're going through a lot right now. You need time to get it together. Just turn on some music and relax. This is the first time you've had a chance to simply be since Chesne left," the devil whispered.

"Get thee behind me, Satan. There is no rest for those who love the Lord. When I am tired, He will restore my energy. When I am troubled, He will calm my mind. When He instructs me, He will supply all that I need along the journey."

Montana threw on some jeans, an old Bob Marley T-shirt and slipped on her shoes, telling Scottie she would be right back. She walked over to Olivia's and knocked on the door. It took her a while to answer. So long in fact, Montana turned to walk away, but before she did, Olivia opened the door.

"Hey, baby. To what do I owe this pleasure?"

"I just need to talk."

"Well come on in, so do I."

The two friends talked into the wee hours of the morning experiencing a roller coaster of emotions. Tears, laughter, and anger interspersed through the conversation. Montana told Olivia about her conversation with God and what she had been directed to say. It took Olivia a while to bring to the surface all the hate and hurt that was deeply embedded within her. She did not want to release it, but the Holy Spirit moved through and among them. Once the journey was complete, all that remained was peace. The burden she had carried all her life was finally removed.

"I feel as if I've lost fifty pounds. I feel so free. Thank you, baby. It is amazing that you can see the ugliness in other people and point your finger, but when you look at the finger pointing back to you, the ugliness you see is much harder to swallow. All these years, I have been bitter and held on to the remnants of hatred because of the injustices we have endured. It seems that the shackles of our mind bind us in ways we don't even know. Now that they are removed, I can truly live and that is exactly what I am going to do. This truth has been revealed a little late in my life, but in God's order, it is right on time."

"Don't thank me. I am only the messenger. Thank God." Montana glanced at her watch and saw it was 3:15 in the morning. "Oh, my goodness, I didn't realize it was this late. I'm so sorry to have kept you up, but I needed to. My work for now is done. I'm going to go home and get restored for the next phase.

"Thank you, Olivia, for being open enough to want to hear and see. That took a lot of faith and courage. It's not always easy to look at yourself through a magnifying glass. I know."

"I'm so glad you came by."

"Me, too. Have I ever told you I love you?" Montana asked.

"Yes, but not today. I love you, too, sweetie. If I ever had a daughter, she would be you." When Montana looked at Olivia, it seemed as if years had been erased from her face. She was radiant.

God is truly magnificent. He is repairing and rebuilding lives to carve a path for the resurrection of His people, she thought.

"Good night, baby."

"Good night."

"I'll check on you tomorrow. Please come by or call if you need anything," Olivia said.

"I will, and thanks for being like a mom to me."

"The pleasure is mine." Olivia watched to make certain she made it home safely.

Montana walked toward her house and though it was completely dark, all Montana saw was light.

Chapter Twenty-Two

"What is hanging up, cannot be reached sitting down."
Amhara Proverb

*G*arrett had a hard time concentrating on anything of simple substance. Since Montana was no longer in his life, he had not been the same. It surprised him that he was incapable of pulling himself out of the pit that had now become his home as he wallowed in his own self-induced sludge.

He wanted relief and needed to renew his mind so he could think clearly. Once he did that, he could decide what his next steps would be. Garrett had not slept peacefully since Montana walked into his office and caught him with Delores Chambers. He could have killed Delores for pulling a stunt like that.

Never once had his eyes or mind strayed and this time, he had done everything right with Montana. He had overcome infidelity and yet it was the very thing that had reared its head and pushed Montana away again, this time possibly forever, but he was innocent. How could he prove that?

Garrett was not interested in Delores at all and apologized to her if he somehow led her on, but he also told her how angry he was with her actions. On numerous occasions, he told her that Montana would always be the only woman he would ever love and the only one he wanted to spend the rest of his life with. It was incredible that he did not see the signs of illicit desire that he used to read so well. He had not used the ploys of a player since he accepted God into his life and they had gotten rusty over the years. Once he was reunited with Montana, there was no need to think of them. Now here he was—a rusty old player who had been played.

Sleep was a rare commodity these days and one that he definitely needed more stock in. He was exhausted and it was an effort just to make it through a four-hour day much less an eight-hour one.

"A joint would help get you through this. It would help you relax and chill for a minute. It won't hurt. It would just be one blunt and that would be it. Just one," Satan whispered.

Since he had changed his life, Garrett had lost contact with his drug connections. He looked through his Palm Pilot. There was nothing there.

"Just as well, I don't need to start this," Garrett said to himself.

"You aren't starting anything. You're just smoking one joint. It doesn't lead to becoming an addict. Man, it's just a blunt. You should be able to handle that, if you're a man that is. After all, didn't God put it here? He wouldn't have placed it in the ground if it wasn't meant for your pleasure and consumption," Satan continued.

Getting some chronic shouldn't be that hard. I deserve to let loose every once in a while. I can handle this. Nobody gives a damn about me anyway, Garrett thought. He looked at his watch and saw it was 2:30. He pushed the intercom button.

"Anne, I'm leaving for the day. If anyone calls, refer them to Eric Bishop."

"Okay."

Anne walked into his office. "Garrett, this is none of my business, but you ought to call Montana to explain what . . ."

Garrett cut her off. "You're right. It's none of your business. When it *was* your business, you couldn't keep Montana out of my office. You knew what was going on."

Anne was shocked and hurt. "I tried to stop Montana, but she wouldn't take no for an answer. How was I to know that something *else* was happening in your office? I thought your business was finished."

Garrett was angry. "That is quite enough, Anne. You really need to keep your thoughts to yourself. Perhaps if you paid more attention to your own life instead of mine, you might be able to get a man."

Tears formed in Anne's eyes. She tried to say something, but her voice betrayed her. As she fought back the tears, she gained strength and finally managed to speak. "You've suddenly turned horribly ugly, and sadly I must say it now suits you." She turned around and walked out.

Garrett heard the door close loudly. Thinking, she had left for good, he got up to check, but her purse was still there. He quietly walked back into his office and left the door slightly ajar.

A few minutes later Garrett's intercom buzzed and Anne said, "I'm making arrangements for my replacement. I'll be gone by the end of the week." She ended the conversation without giving Garrett an opportunity to respond.

Garrett started to get up to tell Anne he was sorry for what he said and that he did not want her to go, but he could not. He knew that once words were spoken, they were out there and could never be taken back. *Even if I ask for forgiveness, she might forgive me, but she would never forget. I couldn't look into those eyes and be reminded of the hurt that I intentionally caused her. She was only looking out for me as always*, he thought. He felt worse than ever.

Garrett drove over to Simpson Road. No one was open for business. There was no one in the usual hot spots on Metropolitan, Sylvan, and Bankhead. He was just about to go home when he saw some activity up the street. Garrett slowly pulled up and motioned to a guy, signaling for a dime bag. They exchanged packages so quickly that to the untrained eye it looked like a handshake.

You still haven't lost the touch, Garrett thought, almost proud of himself. He drove to a nearby park and rolled a blunt. Lighting it, he inhaled deeply. It had been a while. He was feeling good, but he needed more, something stronger.

Returning to the previous spot, he bought a few ounces of cocaine. Things looked a little too dangerous for him to stick around so he drove home to cook the feast he had just purchased. He was almost buzzed from the thought of his first hit.

Garrett walked into the house and deactivated the alarm kicking off his shoes as he entered the family room. He turned the radio to 91.9 and started looking for a container. There was not a pipe anywhere in the house, then he remembered an old opium pipe he had brought back from Laos some years ago.

The sensation from the drug hit him immediately as it coursed through his bloodstream in two paths, one aimed straight for his brain, and the other shot straight for his heart. *God, why did I give this up? I must have been crazy,* he mused.

He had forgotten how hyperactive crack made him and decided to walk out onto the deck. Looking down at his prized garden, he saw weeds beginning to overtake his roses and calla lilies. The lilies reminded him of Montana.

Climbing down the stairs he walked into his greenhouse to get the hoe, pruning shears, and some weed killer. Garrett started digging up the weeds, and as he reached another section of the garden, he stepped back on the pruning shears. Trying to avoid tripping over them, he moved too quickly. Losing his footing, he landed with a thud as he hit has head hard on the ground just missing the stone walkway.

Everything became black as Garrett moved at the speed of light through some sort of tunnel. He saw blurred images but could not make them out. Coming to an abrupt halt, he saw people he knew from his past. These people spoke to him, but he could not understand what they were saying. He was moved and placed at a dead end with one path to the left and the other to the right. On the left side people were beckoning to him—old smoking buddies and one-night stands. On the right, were his grandparents and a few aunts and uncles. The smell of someone smoking crack appealed to him. Those on the right called out to him though they did not utter a word, he felt their love and his shame. He was moving to the left when he was whisked away again. This time he was in a room of extremely bright, but not blinding light.

It was filled with peace and a powerful atmosphere of love. People, if he could call them that, were singing. It was the most ethereal sound he had ever heard. He was shown a place with beautiful blue skies made of sapphires that shimmered against the light. Garrett saw waterfalls that were dotted with diamonds and the most exotic flowers with precious gems as petals. The entire place smelled like spring, but better. Everyone moved effortlessly and communicated without spoken words in complete understanding. There was laughter, joy, and peace throughout.

He was taken to the top of the highest mountain where the mist of the clouds met the pinnacle of the mountain and formed an indigo barrier between him and what lay beyond. The barrier was transparent enough to see through, but not clear enough to identify what was behind it. It was reminiscent of a veil. Garrett heard his name. When he walked toward the voice, he was suddenly behind the veil and in the presence of Jesus who spoke with Garrett about his life. He told him that he had given him one last opportunity to live with Him eternally, but he declined it. Jesus read from the Book of Life, but did not find his name. Garrett's eyes became dead pools as he heard Jesus say that no matter how much He loved him, He had no choice but to let him go. He had shown him mercy and grace, but Garrett continued to chose the wicked one. "It is to him that I now send you," Jesus said.

Garrett cried out. He told Jesus he wanted to stay, to live with him eternally. He pleaded for mercy.

"I knew you not," Jesus said as tears slid down His face. He turned and walked away.

Garrett screamed as he was grabbed and dragged into a pit. The creatures' sharp claws pierced his flesh. The pit became darker as he traveled deeper into it. He scratched and clawed at anything to keep from being taken deeper into the blackness. As he scratched, his nails and flesh were torn. He screamed in agony, but his screams blended with those of others. It was so dark; he felt blind. All he could feel were the sharp nails of the beasts that grabbed him. Slowly, it became a little lighter, and he could finally see shadows. It was unbearably hot and his skin felt as if it was melting. He could hear his blood boiling as he got closer to the floor of the pit. The heat was inescapable. He heard desperate, desolate cries. Cries of pain and torment, eternal despair, and hopelessness. Garrett felt such compassion and repulsion for these people.

Hands reached out from everywhere—even from holes in the walls. As he looked, he noticed that the walls were made of people pieced together like a jigsaw puzzle trying to grab him and tear his flesh. Garrett heard the sound of gnashing teeth moving back and forth until there was silence. Then all he could hear were gums rubbing against themselves and the sound of flesh against flesh until there was nothing left except the slow, mechanical grinding of bone.

Constant chaos was the environment these occupants inhabited. Beings were huddled in corners drooling and nibbling on their fingers until the blood freely flowed. Appalled, he watched them devour their own flesh. Still others were swatting at imaginary insects that flew around the dung they played with. A group of obviously violent people cursed and fought each other using the bones of previous victims as weapons. The walls were black and wet like lava. Smells turned his stomach as what had an odor of tar mixed with feces, vomit and decaying flesh formed the squashy carpet on which he now stood. He saw that the skin on some people was torn and hanging, and on others pestilence rotted their flesh, and they were being eaten away by thousands of hairy worms. Eyes hung out of sockets and tongues were rendered useless as their occupants chewed on them.

Residents of this God-forbidden place wanted things they could not have and were slowly going mad because they could not have it. They wanted alcohol, food, drugs, and sex. They seemed to have an unquenchable thirst that was akin to being stranded on an island surrounded by the ocean, but having no water to drink.

There was absolute anarchy everywhere and in the middle of it all was Satan who at first glance was beautiful. When Garrett looked at him again, he had transformed into a grotesque beast. Satan stood proud, laughing at the agony of his inhabitants. He seemed to enjoy watching these souls in torment.

"I don't belong here," Garrett said.

Satan gestured for Garrett to be brought over. The claws dug into Garrett's flesh again, and he winced from the pain as he was hurled at Satan's feet. "It took you a minute, but I see you made it to your final destination. Welcome to your eternal resting place. Make yourself comfortable, you'll be with me for a long time." Satan started laughing hysterically.

"Oh God, please forgive me. Do not forsake me. I repent. I will never again turn away from You. I will respect, honor, and obey You. I am weak, but in You, I am strong. I will seek Your face all the days of my life," Garrett pleaded. He cried unashamedly tearing his clothes to show his sadness and shame.

Garrett slowly regained consciousness. His body was drenched in sweat. When he realized where he was, he jumped up and ran into the house. He grabbed a giant trash bag and threw away the drugs, pipe, paraphernalia, and all the liquor in the cabinet. He fell to his knees and cried out, "Thank You, Father. Great is Your mercy and grace. I thank You for my life, and I will worship You for the rest of my life. I will let Your words abide in me, as I will abide in You. Please forgive me. Cleanse me with the purity of the precious blood of Jesus." Within the twinkling of an eye, he was forgiven.

Jesus reached down to take Garrett's spirit back and placed it where it would not be lost again. The heavens were filled with songs of gladness.

CHAPTER TWENTY-THREE

"A friend is like a source of water during a long voyage."
Nilotic Proverb

Montana was up before her alarm went off. She needed to be prepared for the war against principalities, which she felt would be fought at work. To fully comprehend the instructions of God, she prayed for divine guidance, strength, and wisdom.

With Chesne in D.C., Montana had an opportunity to analyze the situation that would surely present itself soon. The only safety she had to worry about was her own and even that she was not concerned about. There was no doubt in her heart that she was protected and so was Chesne.

Montana became quiet as the Holy Spirit filled her and gave her the knowledge she needed to proceed. After praying, she felt more focused and the love of God poured over her warming her spirit. There was something to be said about the power of prayer.

Slowly she rose wiping the tears from her face. She opened the shower door and stepped in, feeling renewed as the water cleansed her inner being as well.

"You know, you're going to be alone for the rest of your life. The one man you loved doesn't love you. He betrayed you. He was just stringing you along. Most men would envy his position, but what did he do? He used you. You are every man's fantasy, yet he made you look like a fool," Satan whispered.

"Get behind me, Satan. You will not deter me from my mission. You are not a hindrance to me. My destiny was written long before I was born, and it will be fulfilled. You are a fool if you think you will be victorious. Not only do you not know what God is going to do, but you also forgot one extremely important lesson: God will never let you steal the show."

"You can smile now, but you won't be smiling long."

"I will continue to smile as long as God loves me. You're trying to possess my soul, but the only soul you will see is the sole on the bottom of my shoe when I crush you through the power of Jesus Christ."

Montana decided to skip coffee. She did not need anything to alter her mind or her being and quickly took Scottie for a walk.

"I don't have time to play this morning, sweetie, but I'll see you this evening."

She jumped in the car and started her drive to work. Traffic was lighter than usual and when she got to her office a half-hour later, the parking lot was virtually empty.

Grabbing her purse and briefcase, she locked the car, and walked into the lobby where she saw the security guard. "Good morning, Everett. How are you doing today?"

"I am abundantly blessed. Listen, I never thanked you for your support and guidance when I was at my crossroad. You helped me to truly accept Jesus into my life. I may still have problems, but I have such peace now. It is true that it is a peace that surpasses understanding. Thank you. You are my angel on Earth. If I can ever do anything for you, please let me know."

"You're welcome, but I didn't do anything. I was merely the instrument. It is God who you should praise. He was waiting for you with open arms. You walked toward Him, and that was all He needed. As for me, the only thing I need is prayer. If you do that, it is more than enough."

"I will pray for you, but whatever it is you're going through, something tells me that you already have the victory."

"Thanks, Everett. I needed to hear that. I'll see you later."

"Have a blessed day." He waved good-bye.

Montana walked toward the open elevator. When she got off, the office was dark. She looked at the clock and it was 7:30. Stephanie was normally already at work by this time. At least she used to be.

She unlocked the office door and placed her purse and briefcase on Stephanie's desk. Pulling out a pad to write a note to Paul, Montana changed her mind and decided to leave a voice mail message instead.

Turning the light on in her office, she put her things in place. Montana opened her drawer and saw an unfamiliar box. "What in the world is this?" She picked up a pen and lifted the lid. Inside was something wrapped in tissue paper. Moving the paper to the side as carefully as she could, she jumped when she saw the chicken foot resting on the bottom. She instinctively knew no one but Heather would do something like this. She was not sure what Heather was trying to pull, but it was not going to work.

As a child, she used to hear her great-grandmother talk about roots. She heard stories about magic and spells that involved chicken

parts, oils, candles, and blood. Montana's great-great-grandmother
was a well-known shaman. People came from all over to see her.

She grabbed a napkin and wrapped it around the box. She
walked out of her office toward the break room and placed it in the
trashcan. She did not believe in it, but she also did not want anything
sacrilegious in her presence. Even so, thoughts of voodoo tried to
penetrate the fertile soil of her mind. *I will always direct my thoughts to
the Most High God. There is no room in my mind or my heart for the works
of the devil. God is my rock and my refuge. My enemies crumble in the
presence of God and His children.* The thoughts shriveled up and were
cast off.

✧ ✧ ✧ ✧ ✧

*"She is becoming stronger. I know she wants to take her pain out on
someone, but I can't seem to find the right bait,"* the devil said. *"Let me just
think about this for a moment. I can't lose now, I'm much too close."*

✧ ✧ ✧ ✧ ✧

As she walked out of the break room, she saw Stephanie. "Good
morning, Steph."

"Oh hey, Montana." Stephanie seemed preoccupied.

"Are you okay?"

"Yeah, I'm okay. I just have some things to work out."

"Let me know if you need anything. I'll be more than happy to
help if I can."

"Okay."

Montana watched Stephanie walk toward the lobby. "Hey,
Stephanie?"

"Yeah?"

"I just want you to know that I love you and I am here for you no matter what."

Stephanie walked up to Montana and hugged her tightly. Montana could feel Stephanie's internal tremors. Whatever she was working out thrust her body into chronic turmoil. Tears rushed from Stephanie's eyes to Montana's shoulder, and she seemed overwhelmed with pain.

"Oh, Stephanie, honey, what is it?"

"I can't talk about it now, not here."

"Okay, I won't push."

"Please pray for me. I need help."

"I will. I do everyday, but I'll send up a special one."

"Thanks. I'll talk to you later."

Montana was worried, but she had to stay focused. She could not, would not let anything prevent her from completing God's assignment.

Once Montana returned to her office, she offered a prayer for Stephanie. *The time is near,* Montana thought. She picked up the phone and dialed Paul's extension. To her surprise, he picked up.

"Hi, Paul. It's almost time for performance appraisals and I was wondering if you had a chance to review the assessments I gave you a few weeks ago. I would like to meet with you to discuss them. I'm available this afternoon. What does your schedule look like?"

"I can meet you say around two o'clock?"

"Perfect. I'll see you then," Montana said.

"Okay, good-bye."

She pulled out the appraisal forms and started writing. Stephanie's was easy. She was always an exemplary performer. Heather was another story altogether.

Something suddenly struck Montana. She called Stephanie. "I would like to have lunch with you, but I don't want it to be known. If you would rather not, I understand. I realize you're at a crossroad right now and we don't talk like we used to."

"No. I really want to have lunch with you. I miss how we used to laugh and act silly. I miss your goodness."

Montana was about to respond when she sensed something. "Don't say anything. Can you go at 12:30? Just say yes or no."

"Yes."

"Okay, I'll meet you outside. Wait for me at the turnabout and I'll pick you up there. Is Mrs. Greenberg there?"

Stephanie hesitated puzzled, then said, "No, she's out this week."

"Well, I'll call back later. Hang up."

"If I speak with her, I'll let her know you called. Okay. Good-bye." Just as Stephanie hung up the phone, Heather came around the corner. Stephanie was glad that somehow Montana knew Heather was near.

✦ ✦ ✦ ✦ ✦

"Who were you talking to?"

"Someone called for Mrs. Greenberg."

"Oh. I wanted to have a little tryst this afternoon, but I've decided to go shopping instead. I would ask you to go, but I need time alone to think." Heather hoped when she did not invite Stephanie that she would beg to come, but Stephanie seemed unmoved. Heather had thought her blackmail plans would have worked by now, but Stephanie did not seem to care.

Stephanie had to resolve the mess she had gotten herself into, but did not want to agitate Heather until she knew exactly what to do. "I know how it is when things are on your mind. Don't worry about it. We can go shopping some other time."

Heather decided to try something else at the urging of the whisper in her ear. "Oh, I meant to tell you. Don't tell anybody, but I won the Grand Lotto last night! Can you believe it? Even with taxes, I should get at least $105 million. Isn't that great? I can't wait to get my hands on all that money. When I think about the power and influence I will have, it just makes me want to cum. People will do anything to be associated with me, and that's exactly how I want it. People are so greedy. They would sell their soul just to get their hands on a little money. And I'm willing to buy. Money is such an aphrodisiac, but not as good as you." She licked her lips and winked. "I'm on top of the world!" Heather walked away.

Heather smiled as she walked by Paul's office and peeped in. "Hi, Paulie."

"Hello, Heather. Good to see you. Come on in."

"Can't right now, but I'm sure I'll see you a little later." Heather had been flirting with Paul for the past month or so. She wanted to make sure that if she needed his help in dealing with Montana, he was willing. Men were so easy to control.

Heather couldn't wait to start spending the money from the Grand Lotto. Satan told her it was hers once she got Montana to reject God.

With the money, she would have more power than she knew what to do with. Sex was fine, but sex without power was just sex, and she needed more. But the more sex she had, the more perverted it needed to be to satisfy her. She would make it a point to talk to him about any ideas he might have to increase her pleasure. After all, she knew watching her, aroused him.

Heather looked up the hall and saw Montana watering her plants. She wondered if Montana had found her present. She did not know if it did anything, but that is what he told her to do.

"Now, that's a flower I would *really* like to cultivate. Nothing kinky. Just good old-fashion sex." Heather fantasized about Montana as she watched her bend over slightly. The shape of her behind was a perfect peach. It was round, nicely plump and ripe for the picking. Heather could only image what pleasure awaited her with Montana. Walking toward Montana's office, Heather was drawn by the smell of her perfume. It was intoxicating and made her drunk with longing.

"Well, hello there," Heather said, smiling.

"Good morning," Montana said perfectly calm. Heather walked up to her leaving less than a foot between them.

"You know, we should get together. I would love to show you my favorite spot. *My G-spot that is,* Heather thought. Driven to touch Montana, she pretended to brush some lint off Montana's sweater and moved her hand close to her breast. Montana moved back casually as she felt her spirit drained by Heather's touch. Heather smiled in bewilderment still feeling Montana even though her hand was removed. The touch of her skin was like liquid satin. She was amazed that a touch could move her that way.

"Oh sure, that would be great! Why not this week?" Montana asked.

"Really? Okay sure. When?"

"Well, why don't you come over to my house around seven on Sunday?"

"Okay, I'll see you Sunday evening. I'll get your address later." *Finally,* she thought.

"Oh, no, I meant seven in the morning. I thought we could get together and go to church."

"Oh, no. I don't do church," Heather said angrily.

"And I don't do anything except church."

Heather huffed and stormed out of her office. "That bitch. I'm going to make her suffer. The gloves are off."

"No, you will not harm her in any way. Do you understand?" Satan said.

"Why? She means nothing to you. I'm the one who told you about her."

"You're a stupid one. You have obviously misjudged yourself. I knew about her before she was born. I just made you think you were bringing her to me. I've wanted and waited to be with her for years. At last, she will be mine," he said.

"Be yours? What do you mean?"

"Instead of questions, you need to concentrate on how you will deliver your end of the bargain. The clock is ticking. You've got three days," he said and was gone.

✦ ✦ ✦ ✦ ✦

Heather saw Montana walk toward the bathroom around noon and thought it might be her chance.

She quietly opened the door and locked it, waiting for Montana to come out of the stall. As soon as Montana cleared the door, Heather jumped in front of her. Montana was amazed at her level of calmness. Any other time, she would have jumped out of her skin.

"So what are you doing?" Heather asked as her nostrils were seduced by Montana's scent.

"I'm going to wash my hands."

"No need to worry about that. You're going to have dirty hands for the rest of your life."

"Heather, I don't have time for your sick games. Move."

"Okay." Heather stepped back.

She watched Montana walk to the sink, bending slightly to reach under the spigot and admired her behind, breasts, and hips. While Montana's hands were still wet, Heather walked up behind her and stood close, leaving no room for Montana to move. The intensity of Montana overwhelmed her, and she released herself. She wrapped her arms around Montana trying to cup her breasts as the feeling caused her body to shake with pleasure unknown. But Montana saw Heather coming behind her and anticipated she would do something wicked. She didn't move, but turned the water on a little more. "Oh, you might need this. Heavenly Father, I ask that you bless this water and make it holy." Montana reached under the faucet, filling her cupped hands. "Your spirit needs to be washed clean. In the name of Jesus . . ." Montana twisted around toward her.

Heather backed away deathly frightened.

"In the name of Jesus Christ, I rebuke thee Satan." Montana threw her hands up as the water landed on Heather. Montana continued to refill her hands. Every spot the water touched on Heather's skin turned bright red and left second-degree burn marks.

"Stop that!" Heather screamed as she backed away more.

"Oh, come on. You wanted to get close to me."

"Not like this. You've marked me."

"No, you marked yourself."

The bathroom filled with the light of Montana's companion angel. Heather saw the angel and looked as if she had seen death. She tried to run out of the bathroom, but forgot she had locked the door. Heather fumbled with it until she released the lock. In an effort to escape quickly, she hit herself so hard in the head with the door she thought she was going to black out. The watermarks were searing her skin.

"Now that's what I call an exit." Montana started laughing.

Going back to her office, she made copies of Stephanie's performance appraisals. For some reason, she felt compelled to give them to her.

"Thank You, Father, for Your help and direction. I am so blessed to have Your love and presence in my life. I love you."

She thought of the look on Heather's face. Smiling at Satan's foolishness, she grabbed her purse and walked toward the lobby nodding to Stephanie as she walked out to meet her for lunch.

Chapter Twenty-Four

"One piece of green wood is enough to stop the others from burning."
Nilotic Proverb

"So how have you been, Stephanie?" Montana asked after Stephanie placed her order.

"I've been trying to make it. I don't know if I told you, but Michael and I broke up."

"You did? I thought you guys were doing really well."

"We were, but he could never stop using drugs and I don't need that kind of drama in my life."

"I can understand. Must be going around, Garrett and I broke up too."

"No! That can't be. You guys were so picture perfect."

"I guess sometimes the picture isn't always what it seems."

Stephanie nodded and fiddled with her fingers. "Aren't you hungry?"

"Yes, but my hunger is not for bread."

"Montana, what do you think of me?"

"I think right now you are going through some things, but you're a wonderful person. You're kind and compassionate, intelligent, and ambitious. I know you as a faithful Christian. I pray that you continue your journey with God and fulfill the plans He has for you and the ones you have for yourself. I hope that answers your question."

"You still think that of me?"

"Yes. Why wouldn't I?"

"Well for starters, I've been hanging out with Heather, and she's not exactly your favorite person."

"Who you hang with is your business, Steph. It doesn't change you, and it doesn't affect my relationship with you. Or does it?"

There was a long, uncomfortable silence. "Montana, I don't know how to ask this, but why did you give me such a poor review earlier this year?"

"I didn't! I talked to Paul about your preliminary appraisal, but I gave you all fours. I told Paul that I felt you were an excellent employee who took pride in her job and that you deserved the maximum raise when it was time for your formal appraisal. Here, these are copies of your preliminary and formal appraisals. I can't explain why I needed to bring them, I only knew that I did."

Stephanie took the papers from Montana's hand, but did not read them. She knew Montana had spoken the truth. "I am sorry. I betrayed you."

"How did you betray me? I can't lie and say it doesn't hurt because it does, but we all make mistakes. Who am I not to forgive you? I think you betrayed yourself more than me."

Stephanie nodded in agreement.

Montana paused. "I know the answer before I ask, but what made you think I gave you such a poor rating?"

"Heather told me she went to bat for me because you were trying to get rid of me."

"Stephanie, I'm not going to try to convince you who's telling the truth; you have to determine that on your own, but Heather was the one bad-mouthing you and it was all because you were my friend. Remember when she did the presentation for one of our clients?"

"Yes."

"How do you think she got that project?"

"I just assumed Paul was giving her a chance."

"He may have been. All I know is she went to Paul behind my back and told him that I was trying to start my own business by stealing Lafayette's clients. Thank God, Paul didn't believe it. When that didn't work, I guess she decided to go after you. I'm so sorry, Stephanie. I guess I wasn't really a good friend if you believed that I would do something like that behind your back. In the past, haven't I come to you directly whenever there was a problem?"

Stephanie nodded.

"Then why would I go behind your back now? The things that I discussed with you were personal issues not professional ones and would not have had a negative impact on your appraisal. Either way, you would have gotten the same rating and a substantial raise." Montana felt empathy for Stephanie. *It must be a terrible feeling not knowing if someone is leading you to the water or the swamp,* she thought.

Stephanie hung her head. Heather had lured her and she was surprised at how easy it was for her to be led astray. "Montana, I think I'm in trouble. I'm not sure, but I think Heather has some damaging information about me. She keeps insinuating that I better do what she wants otherwise I'll regret it."

"What did you do?"

"I don't know. I don't remember doing anything, but I lost a big block of time somewhere."

Montana looked puzzled.

"I remember being at Heather's house with some of her friends and we were just talking and drinking. Later when I opened my eyes, her friends were gone. It seemed as if I was asleep, but I'm not sure. It felt like one of those dreams you have that seem real when you wake up. I felt different, like I was touched or something, but I can't remember for the life of me." Tears spilled from her eyes.

"Stephanie, I don't know what to tell you except that the devil has no new tricks, just new faces, and Heather's playing a starring role in his script now. You are not a quitter. You fight to win, and that's what you need to do now. You can only lose if you let her win. A job can be replaced, your reputation and dignity can't."

"But she was so nice. She even bought things for me, expensive things. She treated me so good."

"Yeah, but at what price? Good to you has never equated to good for you. You mentioned she was trying to blackmail you. What is she asking you to do?"

"Help her to destroy you." She looked up sheepishly. "Can you forgive me?"

"Forgiveness is yours even if you didn't ask, Stephanie. We've all done some horrible things to others of which we are ashamed. I'm not worried about my destruction and you shouldn't be either. That is not God's plan. I wouldn't worry too much about Heather either. Like you said, she's not after you, she's after me. To her, I am a constant reminder of everything she's not. I am also the one preventing her from getting whatever Satan promised her, *if* he lives up to it."

"But, Montana, she's still trying to use me to get to you."

"You must take care of you. Everything will happen as it should. I can't tell you what to do, but you must decide which master you will serve and at what price."

"I never meant for any of this to happen. I don't want you to be hurt and I don't want to be the accomplice who helped it to come about."

"Nothing will happen to me that is not already written. I'll be fine. I have angels camped around me.

"I guess it's time to get back, but I want to tell you this before we go, God will always protect you and when He hears your prayers, He has already answered them. It may not be the answer you want, but it is always the answer you need," Montana said.

"Thank you so much for listening to me. I needed to talk to you more than I knew."

"You're welcome. I'm always here for you, but you must talk to God and obey Him. He's the only one who can rescue you. Satan and Heather are too strong for you now. God will give you the strength and protection you need to get through this. He will lead you to the place where grace and mercy sit waiting for your arrival."

✦ ✦ ✦ ✦ ✦

Montana had just walked into her office when the phone rang. "Guess this is it." She slowly walked over to her desk and picked up the receiver on the fourth ring.

"Hello."

"Montana, I need you to come to my office now!" Paul shouted into the phone.

"You mean would I mind coming to your office?" Montana corrected.

"Yeah, would you? Please," Paul said, straining to control his voice.

"Sure I can come now."

Montana replaced the receiver in its cradle and got the appraisals even though she knew she would not need them.

She walked into Paul's office and saw Heather sitting there wearing a look of victory on her face that said, "I've got you exactly where I want you now." She looked relaxed as she leaned back into the chair without a care in the world.

Montana sat down, placing the appraisals on Paul's desk. Her heart raced wildly until she thought about Jesus as He humbly stood in front of Pontius Pilate, neither denying nor affirming who He was or the charges set against him. Jesus willingly accepted his impending sentence and just as He had to endure so would she. Montana was not sure what was coming, but she knew it would be something out of left field that would appear to be true.

"Uh," Paul said and cleared his throat, "Montana, some things have just been brought to my attention. I must say I am terribly surprised and under normal circumstances, I would not give weight to accusations made against you. However, due to the severity of these charges and the position in which it places Lafayette Drake, I am legally obligated to discuss them with you and determine what happened." Paul shifted in his chair as he nervously glanced at Heather.

Here it comes, Montana thought.

"I'm sure you know why Heather is here."

"No, Paul. I can't say that I do. Why don't you enlighten me?"

"Heather states . . ."

"Heather alleges," Montana corrected.

"Yes, of course. Heather alleges that you have been making sexual advances toward her. She is extremely offended and finds your behavior reprehensible, as do I. She also says—uh, alleges—that you have threatened her with the loss of her job if she told anyone.

"Montana, I must say this does not sound like you at all. What do you have to say for yourself? These are extreme charges and though I do not want to, they must be dealt with fairly and swiftly."

Montana silently sat in the chair remaining calm and reserved. Her face was void of emotion.

"Did you hear me?" Paul asked.

"Yes."

"Well?"

"Well, what?" Montana asked.

"What do you have to say?"

"Nothing."

"Nothing? How can you sit here and not address these issues? Am I to believe that what Heather says is true?"

"You can believe whatever you wish, Paul. I am not here to convince you. What you want to believe is your decision."

"Aren't you *even* going to defend yourself?"

"The truth stands on its own. There is nothing to defend. I am a child of God and anointed with His righteousness."

"Fool. Belief in God is for the weak," Heather said, trying to agitate Montana.

"The strong person is one who admits her weaknesses and rises above them despite the obstacles. However, I would say that fool is a better description of you. For it is written, 'He that hides hatred with lying lips and he that utters a slander is a fool. The lips of the righteous feed many, but fools die for want of wisdom.' You have allowed yourself to become like the one you serve. You have renounced the Christ within you and chosen darkness and confusion to reign supreme in your life. It is too late for him, but you still have an opportunity to change your course and turn away from the evil one. You are like a tare that grows with the wheat in a vain attempt to choke the living Christ out of the good harvest."

"Look," Paul said, "this is not about God. I don't know what's going on between you two, but if you don't offer me something, anything to the contrary, I'll have to launch a full-scale investigation into the charges and force you to take an administrative leave until this mess is straightened out."

"Paul, do what you have to. If there's nothing further." Montana pushed back her chair, stood, and walked out. She could barely stand and headed for the conference room to gain her composure since it was closer than her office. She overheard Paul shouting at Heather.

"Heather, where are you going? What the *hell* is happening?" Paul asked, exasperated, after she left his office.

Montana heard footsteps trailing behind her. Heather grabbed her arm, but the power of God coursed through her hand like lightning and she quickly snatched it back from the pain that shot through it. "With all your intelligence, surely, you can't be ignorant enough to believe in God. Anything that is real and that matters, you can see," Heather said.

"Can you see the wind? Yet you can feel it when it touches your skin or when it asks a blade of grass to join it in a dance of celebration. So, too, is the love and existence of God. It is not something you see, but something that is deeply felt within the core of your spirit and once felt, you are never the same. Can you see love? No, but you can feel it as it warms your heart and deepens your life with sparkles of color. Anything in the entire cradle of humanity that is significant, you will never be able to see. It must be felt because it requires a witness to attest to its magnificent power."

"It doesn't have to be like this," Heather said, touching Montana's arm.

Montana pulled away and looked into eyes where demons live.

"I have $105 million and it is all yours."

"What would it profit me to gain the whole world and lose my soul? I would rather die lying on a bed of rocks, the victim of persecution, disease, and mutilation than to live one night in a mansion built by Satan."

"I don't want your soul. I just want to be your friend."

"Ah, my friend. So that's the new word for it these days. No wonder I don't have any."

"Let me show you something."

Montana looked around, and she was suddenly at Maxim's in Paris, dressed in the latest haute couture from one of Italy's hottest designers, wearing the most exquisite jewelry she had ever seen. There were two exotic-looking and remarkably handsome men on each side giving her their unyielding attention. She ate selectively of the plate placed before her that was undoubtedly filled with the finest cuisine. International high rollers who possessed and flaunted apparent affluence surrounded her. They all seemed enchanted by Montana's presence.

"What you've shown me is a beautiful restaurant with beautiful people. The jewels are exquisite, and I'm sure the food being served is wonderful, but to be surrounded by people of affluence does not fulfill my spirit. My eternal home is built with jewels that make these seem paltry by comparison. Jesus fed five thousand people from two fish and five loaves of bread, what more would He do for me so that I would not be fed by the hands of Satan?"

Heather was becoming enraged. Nothing seemed to entice Montana—not money or material things. Suddenly, a wicked smile crossed her face.

Heather took Montana to a dark and remote place. There was a cabin bordered on one side by the mountains and on the other a rolling river. The sunset painted the sky with muted shades of violet, cerulean, and persimmon. She was led into the front room of the cabin. The smell of burning wood filled the air, enticing her senses. Montana and Garrett lay in the middle of the floor on a faux fur rug. They were talking, laughing, and loving. Montana's heart pounded fiercely as it ached to be united with Garrett again. They touched each other gently, lovingly as they embraced and relished every moment of splendid pleasure. Garrett's hand touched Montana's swollen belly and he sang a lullaby to the unborn child she carried. Montana's heart cracked. It was as if it had broken and shattered into a billion pieces never to be whole again.

"The loss of the love of your life doesn't make it much of a life," Heather said, realizing she had finally touched a nerve.

Montana was quiet wrestling internally with an invisible foe. "If I never love another person again in my life, I have had more love than most people ever have. The One who created me loves me, and I am abundantly blessed. Jesus is my comforter. He will never leave me nor forsake me. He loves me as I am for all that I am."

"I can give you untold wealth, riches, and of course Garrett. It is yours. All you have to do is kneel before me and serve the one I do."

"I cannot kneel to something that is beneath me. Satan is my footstool. I am the head, and he is the tail. In the Name of Jesus, I rebuke thee Satan. I have resisted you and now you must flee."

Heather became dizzy appearing to awaken from a hypnotic state, shaking her head for clarity. "Why do you believe in God?"

"Because I have seen His wondrous works and He loves me unconditionally despite my faults. In serving God, I have found that a true Christian is like a drop of water in a pond. The ripples created by that drop, which is the light of Jesus, will eventually affect everyone it touches. Have you asked Satan if he believes in God?"

"No."

"Why?"

"It never occurred to me."

"The reason it never occurred to you is because he didn't want it to. Satan believes in God because he has seen Him and knows His great power and capacity for love. Does it not seem foolish to rise up against someone whom you cannot beat, no matter how hard you try? That is why your master is the king of fools. He was kicked out of heaven with a third of the angels for attempting to exalt himself over God. It is an impossible feat, but he didn't know that until it was too late. Satan forgot that the reason he possessed the power he had was because God had given it to him. Do you know why he wants me?"

"Yes. Well, I'm not really sure."

"There are two reasons actually. The first is that he wants me so he can recapture what he lost in the beginning. To him I am his second chance. The other reason is God gave me a magnificent gift that could change the world and the power of that gift frightens Satan."

Heather looked confused. "Second chance for what?"

"When Adam and Eve were in the Garden, Satan disguised as a serpent, tempted and deceived Eve and she ate of the fruit—well it wasn't actually fruit, but that's another lesson—that she was forbidden to eat. Once she did, Satan was sure God would cast her out and away from Him forever. He wanted Eve because she was one of God's original creations and was without sin, which made her powerful and Satan wanted that power. In Satan's mind, I am Eve."

"That's not true."

"Yes, it is."

"No, it can't be. He told me I was the one. He wouldn't lie to me. He wouldn't deceive me. He loves me."

"You would not be the first one he lied to. Satan is a master of deception. He loves no one but himself. Satan is pulling your strings just like the wizard in *The Wizard of Oz* who maintained his illusion by magnifying himself to be worshipped by the people. He uses fear, lies and deception, but once you've humbled yourself before him, he exploits all of your weaknesses to keep you groveling in the depths of decay. He's a master deceiver, but only if you relinquish your will. What does Satan give you that makes him worthy of serving?"

"He gives me money."

"But at what cost? Are you sure he is not pulling your strings as craftily as the wizard? Is it truly free? Okay, what else besides money?"

"Love."

"Love! Is that what you call love? Well, who do you love?"

"I don't know."

"There is no one you love?" Montana was startled and saddened by Heather's answer. "Does he give you peace?"

Heather was silent.

"When he is in your midst, do you feel a loving, kind, gentle presence all around you? Does he leave a light that fills your heart, mind, and soul? Or does he leave you confused with more unanswered questions? Does he give you anything without some condition being attached to it? Let me tell you a story I heard.

"A minister was standing at the pulpit one Sunday morning with a rusted, dented bird cage beside him with the door slightly ajar. He told a story about a young boy who had two beautiful sparrows. He asked the boy if he enjoyed the birds and the boy replied no. The minister then asked what he was going to do with them. The boy answered that he was going to use and abuse them, deceive them, and ultimately destroy them. The minister asked the boy how much he would sell the birds for. The boy said you don't want to buy these stupid birds, they will betray you, make false promises, call on you for everything they need or want, not love you as you love them, and they will cause you nothing but grief. The minister asked once again, how much do you want for them? The boy said two dollars. The minister paid him the two dollars and set the birds free.

"Satan is no different than the little boy. He will use, abuse, deceive, and destroy us. Just as the minister paid the price for the birds' freedom so has Jesus Christ paid the ultimate price for ours for no other reason than he loves us unconditionally."

Montana could see the life that had been drained out of Heather slowly returning as color filled her cheeks.

"Have you ever read the Bible?" Montana asked.

"Bits and pieces when I was a child, but I was always afraid of God. I was told He was an angry, punishing God and I would burn in hell no matter what I did because I was not anyone He would want."

"God wants every one of His children to gather unto Him. He created us and breathed a part of Himself into us. He loves us so much that He gave His only begotten Son to die for our sins so that we may be free. He is full of grace, mercy, and love."

"Jesus doesn't love me, He couldn't. He didn't die for me. No one did anything for me?"

"Jesus did. Would you like to know if Jesus loves you? Would you like to see?" Montana was not sure where this thought originated from, but she was obedient to speak what she was told.

Heather looked at Montana. Her eyes filled with tears that threatened to fall. She nodded, and the tears flowed freely.

Within minutes, the room filled with light and an impression of great magnificence manifested.

"Ask Him," Montana said as she gazed upon Him with love that overflowed in her heart but showed in her tears.

"Ask Him what?"

"Ask Him how much He loves you."

Heather, moved by the feeling and Spirit that surrounded her, did as she was told.

"How much do you love me?" Heather asked with the trembling voice of a child.

Jesus extended his arms toward her holding out His nail-scarred hands.

Chapter Twenty-Five

"The wind does not break a tree that bends."
Sukuma Proverb

*M*ontana knelt down to pray. *Thank You so much, Father, for delivering me. Thank You for Your protection and Your love. You gave Your angels charge over me. They held me within their wings so no stone would harm my foot. You found favor in me. You are the reason I am all that I am. Your grace and mercy have been the most precious gifts to me. If I had ten thousand tongues I could never thank You or praise you enough.* She wept in her silence.

God revealed that He was pleased that Montana had been a faithful and obedient steward. She felt blessed beyond anything she had ever experienced, and beyond any comprehension she could express. She did not know what would happen to Heather, but she prayed for the recovery of Heather's soul.

Though Montana was grateful her battle was over, the apprehension had been worse than the actual event, but she learned a lot about herself and God. She knew with unfailing certainty that God loved her. She had seen proof of it. God did not prevent trials and tribulation from occurring, but He brought her through the storms making her stronger, more determined and with greater wisdom. Despite the drama, God held her hand as she endured it all and when she could no longer stand on her own, He carried her.

Soon after Heather was shown Jesus' hands, she called Paul. "I need to meet with you. It's important." She walked into Paul's office a few minutes later and he immediately noticed how different she looked, almost innocent.

"I wanted to meet with you to correct the wrong I have done. Montana never made sexual advances toward me. I wanted to hurt her so badly, it didn't matter what it cost. I know you don't understand why I did what I did, but I offer my heartfelt apologies to you and the company. I am submitting my two weeks notice. Again, I am so sorry."

Disgusted with her unethical behavior and the position she intentionally placed the company, his compassion for her soured. "Have you apologized to Montana?"

"No, not really."

"I'm calling her into my office and I want you to apologize. Not only is it imperative, but you owe it to her."

"You're right."

Montana sat across from Heather soon after Paul called her. As she looked at Heather, Montana could not really describe what she felt. There was such a mix of feelings that it sent her emotional barometer into overdrive causing her to feel nothing.

"Montana," Heather said nervously, "I want to sincerely apologize to you for the harm I have intentionally inflicted on your life and the unnecessary stress my actions have caused you. I ask that in time, you find it in your heart to forgive me."

"I accept your apology and I do forgive you. I hope this doesn't come out the wrong way, but you had no power to harm me. I was always protected."

"It must be wonderful to live as you do. I know I wasn't exactly the easiest or nicest person to be around, but I'm hoping that will change," Heather said.

Paul was ashamed and confused, but realized he didn't want or need to know more.

"Montana, I'm sorry. I did believe you, but I had to protect the company. I hope that I didn't offend you. Everything you have ever shown me has been above reproach, but I had to ask."

"I understand."

"Heather, I hope you find the help you need," Paul advised.

"Thank you. I will."

Heather stood and extended her hand to Montana who shook it. Heather then extended the same to Paul. Turning to Montana she said, "Thank you for showing me the way."

"You're welcome." Montana turned to leave.

Heather nodded at Paul and followed loosely behind Montana. It was time to resolve things with Stephanie, no matter how frightened Heather was of the outcome. "Stephanie, could I talk to you for a minute?"

Stephanie hesitated.

"I promise it won't be long. I just need to clear up a few things. I mean no harm. I need to apologize."

Stephanie was wary of Heather's intentions, but her eyes looked sincere. "Okay, Heather, but don't let this be some—"

"I'm not trying to do anything, honest."

"Okay."

Stephanie placed the switchboard on automatic and walked with Heather to the break room.

"Stephanie, I have to apologize. I was not the most honest or honorable person with you. I did any and everything I could to trick you. I know it's hard to understand, but it wasn't personal. I was just using you to get to Montana, but I have done the most harm to you."

"What did I ever do to you, Heather?"

"Nothing. You were there and convenient. All I could see was what I wanted, and I didn't care who was hurt in the process. There are many things I must confess to you, and they will be difficult for you to hear. If you can't or won't forgive me, I wouldn't blame you."

Heather took a couple of deep breaths, then continued. "Remember the night that you and Michael went out with me and my friend?"

Stephanie nodded.

"Well, while Michael and I were in the kitchen, I had sex with him and when you left, I had sex with him and Greg. I knew Michael was your man, but it didn't matter, I was out to get Montana and anything that was in the way, I rolled over."

Stephanie was fuming. "You scheming, betraying, selfish, whoring bitch!"

"I know, but unfortunately, you haven't heard the worse," Heather said calmly.

"I don't need to hear anymore!"

"Yes, you do. You need to hear it as much as I need to get this off my chest. The night you came over to my house, my friend Jez and I had sex with you. I put some Roofies, the date rape drug, in your drink. Later, we gave you Ecstasy. That's why you didn't remember anything."

Stephanie fell against the wall. "How could you do such a horrible thing? It's not possible! I am not a lesbian."

"You didn't know what you were doing. It's not your fault."

"Oh, I know it's not my fault." Stephanie punched Heather so hard in the face, her head vibrated from the impact. "Don't you ever come near me again! I will kill you and save them the trouble of locking you up! Anybody who could do what you did has no heart. People mean nothing to you." Anger grabbed Stephanie's fist and she hit Heather again with all the strength she could muster, knocking Heather to her knees.

Stephanie saw Heather walk away deflated, but she could not summon any pity or compassion for her, she fell into the chair as her anger made her cry. She needed to make sense of what she had heard, but she did not understand how something so horrible could happen, or if she could ever accept the fact that it did. Ashamed, she realized Heather did not do anything to her that she had not allowed.

"Oh, God, please help me. I don't know what to do." Stephanie walked to Paul's office and told him she didn't feel well and was leaving for the day.

Heather angrily walked to her office, confused and sure at the same time. She needed to take another first step and that started with Jez. Picking up the phone, she told her it was over between them. Jez was hysterical begging, promising anything to prevent Heather from leaving. All Heather could do was hang up. She hoped God would be with her as Montana said. Heather did not believe she had a choice before and now felt her life might be salvageable after all.

The manifestation of her thoughts and self-perception had led her on a path of destruction, but if she could just hold on to God, she might be able to stay on the right track. Never in her wildest dreams had she thought there was a loving, forgiving God who cared about her, but once convicted by the Holy Spirit, her acceptance of Jesus paved the way to her salvation. It would not be easy. Satan was not finished with her, and she would have a fight on her hands that made the one with Montana seem like child's play.

Montana was excited about Chesne coming home and wished someone were there to share it with her. It would take some time, but she would become accustomed to living without Garrett. Growing old alone never appealed to her, but she did not think she could handle being in another relationship.

Frequently, she analyzed her relationship with Garrett to determine if she had done anything to cause it to unravel, but it only created more questions. Were her expectations too high? Was she not enough? Or were men naturally callous and dishonest in their quest to conquer?

Whatever the reason, she was not going to put her life on hold, but would live it fully despite her current situation. She had God and Chesne and there was nothing else she required at the moment.

Montana baked a cake and hung a banner on the wall in the foyer, anxiously waiting to welcome her daughter home. It was important to Montana that she did not suffocate Chesne by making her fill the void that Garrett's absence left.

As much as she knew God lived in her, a part of her heart still yearned for Garrett. Montana prayed for strength and for the removal of desire in her heart.

Looking out the window, she saw Noelle pulling into the driveway and felt like a child seeing snow for the first time. It was difficult to contain her excitement.

Montana noticed how much Chesne had grown once she exited. Noelle walked to the back of the SUV, lifted the door, and pulled out five suitcases.

What in the world did they bring back? I guess D. C. has not had a retail boom like this in years. I'm surprised they didn't get the keys to the city, she thought and smiled. Montana fought the urge to run to meet them, wanting Chesne to come in and see the welcome she had planned for her.

The doorbell rang and within seconds, the door was flung open. "Hi, sweetie." Montana eagerly hugged her.

"Hi, Mommy! I missed you."

"Not as much as I missed you. Boy, I'm glad you're back!"

Chesne had not noticed the surprise welcome and Montana forgot all about it as they hugged each other cocooning themselves momentarily in their private world.

"Oh, this is beautiful," Noelle said. There was a purple-and-white banner that read WELCOME HOME, CHESNE AND NOELLE. There were purple, white, and silver balloons of all shapes on each side. To the right of the table was a beautiful white cake decorated with purple flowers and the same words as the banner.

"Oh, Mommy, this is wonderful."

"We can eat the cake later. Are you hungry?" Montana asked.

"No," they both said.

"Well, come on. Tell me about your trip." They walked into the tranquil place.

"We went to the Washington Monument and the zoo. I went to a meeting at the White House. I think they were trying to pass a bill or something. We went to Mrs. Howard's house, Noelle's aunt, for a cookout. One Saturday, we had a picnic lunch at the park. We went to the National Museum of African Art and looked at the artwork and sculptures. We went to a play at Studio Theatre. We went to the Kennedy Center to watch some dancers, to the movies, to dinner, and we did a little shopping." Chesne was tired all over again.

"My goodness, it sounds as if you were on the go the entire time. How was the session at the White House?"

"It was boring. The men kept raising their voices and they weren't nice to each other either."

"Well, since you only did a *little* shopping, may I ask why there are five suitcases when you only took three?"

"Noelle's mom, Mrs. Nichols, took us shopping a few times. I told her I didn't need anything, but she asked me to show her stuff I liked then she wanted me to try them on so she could see how I looked. When I was finished, she bought them all. I told her I didn't need them, but I'm only a kid, how can I stop a grown-up? She wouldn't take no for an answer. And well," Chesne continued smiling, "I didn't want to disappoint her."

"I just bet you didn't. I'm going to owe her my next three paychecks."

"You know better than that! Mama would beat you with a noodle if you tried to pay her back. When have you ever known my mother to accept money from you or me?" Noelle asked.

"Never."

"Let Mama have fun. It's her way. You know how she feels about Chesne. And between you and me, if you told her not to, it would hurt her. She would feel she wasn't a part of Chesne's life. You know how she treats you when you're around?"

"Yeah. Every time I turned around, she was trying to feed or buy me something. I gained five pounds the last time I was there. I thought I was going to burst, but I will say the lady can *burn!*"

"You got that right," Noelle agreed.

"So show me what you got, Chesne," Montana said.

"Do you want me to try them on, too?"

"Of course! What good is seeing your new clothes if I can't tell how beautiful they will look on you?"

Chesne smiled and blushed, willing to oblige her mother. As Chesne tried on the clothes, Montana was amazed at how mature she appeared. *I'm losing my baby*, Montana thought.

In all, Chesne had nine new outfits with matching accessories, shoes, and a beautiful white-gold necklace with a diamond-studded cross. Chesne handed Montana the necklace to fasten around her neck.

"The clothes are beautiful. You have exquisite taste," Montana said.

"Yes, I know," Chesne said, smiling.

Noelle and Montana looked at each other and started laughing. "Get upstairs, girl! You are a trip. You need to send Mrs. Nichols a letter thanking her for her kindness and generosity."

"I am. Right after I hang up my clothes. I don't want them to get messed up." Chesne happily trotted up the stairs.

"Who does that sound like?" Noelle asked.

"You."

"Yeah, right."

"So what's been going on? You look tired, yet renewed like you just unloaded a heavy burden or something," Noelle said.

"I did. You know the saying: "truth is stranger than fiction"? When I tell you, I don't know if you'll believe it. What are you doing for lunch tomorrow?"

"Nothing. I'm off," Noelle said.

"Great! Me, too. Let's have lunch at Copeland's. I'll tell you all about it then. I also have a proposition for you that I've been mulling over, but we can talk about that then. I don't want to ruin your homecoming."

"Girl, I'm so glad to be home. I love my mother, but if she babied me one more time, I was going to scream. She means well, she just gets lonely sometimes. I know I need to enjoy every minute with her that I can," Noelle said.

"You know, I know."

"Yeah. How are you doing? I've never known you to take any time off from work. You okay?

"I'm better than I can tell you. We'll talk. Are you sure you aren't hungry?"

"I'm fine. We ate before we left, and Mom packed snacks and sandwiches."

"So did *you* have a good time? How is your mom? I never had a chance to talk to her while you were there. How's she doing without your dad?"

"Yes, I had a good time. It's funny. No matter how old you get, you will always be your Mama's baby. I complain, but I wouldn't change it for anything in the world. It's hard for her without Pop. She is doing so much volunteering that she stays busier now than when she worked. I was amazed at the number of older well-to-do black women there are. Cultivating tropical flowers is her passion now. She had my nephew, Kenny, to build her a greenhouse. She has some beautiful flowers. You would love her calla lilies. I told her they were your favorite so don't be surprised if she finds a way to ship them to you. You know I am really blessed to have my Mama. I don't know where I would be without her." Noelle paused. "I don't know if I've ever told you, but I don't know what I would do without you, either. Having you as a true friend means so much to me. I am really grateful to have you."

"It's easy being a friend when it's someone like you."

"Okay, enough sentiment by the mutual admiration society. Look, I would never butt into your business, but have you tried to talk to Garrett?"

Montana glared at her.

"Okay, that's my answer, but you need to make sure what you saw is the way it is. I don't think you should automatically jump to conclusions. He deserves a chance; both of you deserve a chance. I know he did some horrible things in the past, but let the dead bury the dead. How do you know it was not *her* doing? You can't put anything past women today."

"I know, but right now I can't even look at him, and trust, well . . . I can't do it right now. I'm scared and I can't handle getting hurt again. This time I'm letting God tell me if and when. Until then, I'm not doing anything."

"Okay. I've butted in enough for one night, but I'm not through with this. Just think, wouldn't it be a shame if it was all a horrible misunderstanding?"

"What, his lips were looking for a place to rest and just bumped into hers?" Montana waved her hand. "Never mind. I'll see you tomorrow."

Montana watched Noelle get in her SUV a few minutes later and contemplated her words.

⊕ ⊕ ⊕ ⊕ ⊕

The next day, Montana was seated at a table near the window mulling over ideas when she saw Noelle walk into Copeland's.

"Hey, Noelle."

"Hi, sorry I'm late."

"No worry. I was just looking over the menu getting hungry. I'm starving."

"Me, too. I've been craving their crab and corn bisque since we talked. So why are you taking time off from work?" Noelle asked after the server took their order.

"While you and Chesne were in D.C., I had to go to war with Satan and his number one recruit, Heather."

"What!"

"Well, you know the things that have happened—Chesne, work, and Garrett. Those were all ploys to deflect my attention from God and onto my personal dilemmas. I was supposed to get so tangled up in pity that I would start questioning God's actions and eventually doubt Him. Well, when that didn't work, I guess that bug decided to take a more direct approach and what better person to use than Heather? He used Heather to blackmail Stephanie so I would be double-teamed, but it didn't even get to that."

"I can't believe this!"

Montana recanted the events that had happened to her as Noelle vacillated between astonishment and anger.

"You mean you didn't slap that devil's advocate upside her head? I would have thrown that bit—uh, that girl, out the window of the thirty-second floor."

"And that's exactly what Satan would have wanted. It didn't get ugly or anything unless you count Heather." Montana smiled. "No, I'm just kidding. Heather tried to tempt me, but the scary part is that I resisted everything until she tempted me with Garrett. I hesitated because my heart ached so. I wanted him so badly, but I know that Satan is a liar and even if I did what he wanted, I would never get what he promised. I know that God has power over everything and I still hesitated. I am so ashamed."

"Girl, when you love someone, you love him. Your heart wants what it wants," Noelle said.

"Yeah, I know." Montana looked down trying to gather the strength she needed to continue. Her eyes were moist when she looked up.

Noelle wanted to console her but she knew touching her or responding would initiate the tears that Montana was trying desperately to fight back.

Her voice was unsteady when she continued. "It was so awesome, Noelle. Just to be in the presence of Jesus. I have never felt such pure, complete, unrestricted love. He is beautiful. He was all spirit, just an essence and an inner knowing that it was Him."

Noelle sat on the edge of her seat hanging onto Montana's every word. "Girl, chills just ran through my whole body. I would have given anything to have seen that."

"The thing is people like us, don't need to see Him to believe, but Heather did. He gave her a special guest appearance. Remember the story about the shepherd who had 100 sheep and lost one and how that shepherd did everything just to find that one lost sheep?"

Noelle nodded.

"Heather is the lost sheep. I just hope that moment changes her life. I know it did mine," Montana said.

"Me, too, without a doubt. You know you are really something. After all the hell she put you through, you still wanted to help her."

"It wasn't my work, but God's, I had no choice. I have never experienced anything like that in my life. It was true epiphany. I can only imagine how Moses must have felt after God parted the Red Sea. Anyway after that, I realized I had served my time at Lafayette Drake and it was time to move on. I'm taking some time off to decide what I'm going to do with the rest of my life. That's when you crossed my mind. You know how we've always talked about starting our own business?"

"Yeah, it's been my dream."

"What do you think about starting it now?"

Noelle sat thoughtfully for a minute, the wheels in her head spinning in full motion. "Yeah. Why not? I'm tired of having to defend anyone and everyone by the letter of the law instead of by the law of the Spirit. It gets harder and harder to represent guilty people who are grateful that the law allows them an escape. Our own business, uh? Sounds like a dream come true to me."

"Now we just have to think of the kind of business we want. I've thought about interior design, an outreach program, a restaurant, a clothing store, or a gift shop. We could do anything. We both have the same interests and are quick studies. What do you think would be a good business?" Montana asked.

"I opt for a clothing store that is also an outreach program. We can teach them practical business skills like management, accounting, customer relations, and minister to them at the same time. We could recruit the fashion design students who are enrolled at the Atlanta School of the Arts and close to graduation. They could design their own unique line of clothing that we can sell exclusively in our store," Noelle said.

Noelle was getting excited. "We could offer a fresh perspective to the fashion industry and provide the latest in style and design. We would not only be able to cater to the younger generation, but ours as well. I know this guy and all he designs are clothes from the 1930s and '40s. The clothes are sexy, sophisticated, and beautiful, but he has no outlet. We could be that outlet. Everybody has to start somewhere."

Montana caught the fever. "That is an awesome idea!"

"Sounds like we have a lot of work to do, but we can do it," Noelle said.

"Are you sure you want to do this?"

"Yes. I've got a pretty good-size nest egg for emergencies. I wouldn't need to use all of it anyway. I still won't have to touch my retirement fund. This does qualify as an emergency, you know. It's about making the most of my life while I have a chance."

"Goodness, how much have you got? Don't answer that question, it's not my business. I forgot how much attorneys make." Montana reached into her briefcase. "I wrote out some preliminary information that we need to find out. Now that we have decided on a clothing store, we need to research the market, find our target customers, look at space, and a ton of other stuff. If we decide to buy property, it will require more overhead expenses, but the rewards may be greater financially. I'll type up the business plan once we have the details. I should have it in a few weeks. We can go over it then."

"How did I know you would be prepared?" Noelle asked.

"Well, partner, it will be a pleasure doing business with you. Oh, what are we going to call it?" Montana asked.

"Noelle St. Claire."

"I like the way you think."

The innovative entrepreneurs lifted their glasses in a toast. "Partners," they chorused as their glasses touched. They grinned like Cheshire cats basking in the sun.

"Excuse me, ladies," a man said, walking up to them. "I couldn't help but overhear your conversation. My name is Patrick Peters. I am a venture capitalist." He handed each of them a business card. "Starting your own business is an exciting endeavor. I'd like to meet with you and discuss how I can help to make your dreams a reality.

Do you mind if I join you for a cup of coffee to explain the process and determine if this might be something you're interested in?"

"Sure a cup of latte would be nice, but I won't be able to stay the entire time," Noelle said. "Perhaps you can finish explaining it to my friend here, then we can get together later to discuss it."

"I don't believe I got your names," Patrick said.

"This is Montana, and I'm Noelle."

Patrick gave them an overview of venture capital as well as the pros and cons. Even though he was talking to both of them, his eyes never left Noelle.

"Excuse me, I don't remember your name," Patrick said.

"Montana."

"Well, Montana, I can provide you and Noelle with more detailed information about venture capital and a list of clients. You are welcome to call any of them for a reference."

"That would be great. Perhaps you can give them to Noelle."

"I'm kind of tied up the rest of this week, but I guess I can rearrange a few appointments to go over things with you," Noelle said.

"Thank you for your time, Mr. Peters. I really must go," Montana said.

Montana was irritated and she had to leave before she lost control. She did not like people who pushed themselves on her without invitation. Moving back from the table, she rose from her chair. Patrick stood and extended his hand to help her up.

"It has been a pleasure," he said as he held Montana's hand. "Are you leaving, too?" he asked Noelle when he saw her rising.

"Yes, I am, but it was nice meeting you."

Patrick walked to Noelle's side and helped her with her chair. He held her hand a little longer than required.

He definitely has eyes for Noelle, Montana thought. *Even if he is obnoxiously rude.*

"It has been my pleasure meeting you," he said to Noelle.

Noelle and Montana bade him good-bye as they walked to the door.

"Seems you reeled in another one," Noelle said.

"*Me?* He was looking at you. You kept trying to push him on me so much that you didn't even notice. I know you're concerned about me, but I don't want nor need another relationship now. Okay? I need to work out the end of my relationship with Garrett on my own and in my own way," Montana said as she glanced over at Noelle.

"Okay, I'll let you do it. Even if you are wrong."

"Thank you so much for your confidence in me."

"You're welcome. I know it's hard to live up to *my* perfection."

"Puh-lease," Montana said, rolling her eyes and laughing.

CHAPTER TWENTY-SIX

"When a lion roars, he does not catch game."
Acholi Proverb

"What did you think you were doing?" Satan asked.

"I was doing what you asked me to do," Heather said.

"I asked you to bring her to me, instead it seems *she* brought you to *Him*."

"I tempted her with the things you told me to. Everything I tried, she rebuked. If you couldn't tempt Jesus, how did you think I could tempt her? She has no interest in you. You repulse her."

"Shut up! You are an idiot. You don't know what you're talking about."

"Actually I think you're the idiot. How could you possibly think you could overthrow God? He created you, stupid. And another thing, why do you want her? You told me you wanted me. Why is everything you promise either a lie or has some string attached to it? Don't you love me?"

"You don't ask the questions. You don't have enough intelligence to question me."

"And evidently you don't either. You just use people until there's nothing left, and then you throw them away. You don't care about me, you never did."

"You didn't want to be cared for. All you wanted was to live out your sexual fantasies. I gave you every fantasy you wanted and more."

"Through my thoughts, you gave me every desire you had and I modified my will to satisfy your wants. Would you die for me?" Heather asked angrily.

"I'm already dead. You used me as an excuse to do what you wanted. I'm not the one to blame."

"I was your puppet, but you have no power without me. I gave you power because I allowed you to influence me. I'm tired of pleading ignorance and asking for forgiveness later. I'm done with you!"

"Listen, you worthless bitch, you don't run things around here. I do. The reason I want Montana is because unlike you, when she loves, she loves completely. She is committed all the way and the closest thing to innocence I've ever seen. Yes, I want her. Who in their right mind wouldn't?"

"So you just lied to me?"

"That's one of my best traits. What do you have to offer someone? You are used goods. I couldn't even give you away."

"Jesus wants me."

"Don't you ever use that name around me. I will not allow it."

"You have a severely inflated opinion of yourself. Yes, you are handsome, beautiful in fact, but when I think of all the things I've done, I am ashamed."

"Shame is for fools. If you enjoy what you do, and you did, there is no reason to be ashamed. How could you doubt that I love you? Of course, I love you. I love you with all my soul," Satan said.

"But you have no soul. Whatever is left is already damned."

"Good point," he said, laughing. "I have given you more than anyone in your life because you are important to me. People respect you. You walk into stores and all the salespeople know you by name. When you walk into a restaurant without a reservation, they change everything around to accommodate you. You have more money than you will ever need. You know with money comes power. You are on the road to fame."

"Then why do I feel like I'm on the road to hell?"

"You're already in hell, my dear. That feeling of spiritual joy you have now is temporary. It is a false image and will wear off eventually. It always does. You think you're special because He appeared to you? He's a master illusionist. You must forget all about Him. He will do nothing but let you down. When you really need Him, He won't be anywhere around."

"I can't forget Him. When I reached out to touch Him, I had such a wonderful feeling. One unlike any I've ever had with you or anyone else in my life. Jesus made me feel special, loved and I was changed. He didn't want anything from me, but to believe in Him. You believe in Him, don't you? Jesus said he would never ask or expect anything of me that I was not capable of doing. All I had to do was accept Him as my Lord and Savior."

"But you didn't. That shows He has no power," Satan said.

"But He does and I did accept Him. I still feel His presence and love."

"You will do what I have commanded. You cannot get away. Your soul belongs to me and before you do something I'll regret, I'll take what belongs to me."

"No, my soul belongs to God. You deceived me. You lied to me. I don't want to have anything to do with you anymore. I'm going to walk with Jesus. He will take me as I am."

"You will wither away and die before you can get to Him. I promise you that! You have nothing to offer."

"Jesus!" she shouted at the top of her lungs.

As quickly as Satan had come, he was gone.

"I don't know who he thinks he is. Montana was right. He's just like the *Wizard of Oz*. All hype no hope. Ouch." She grabbed her stomach.

Heather was suddenly gravely tired. She walked to her bedroom to lie down. The pain in her stomach became unbearable. She needed something to make it go away, but on the way to the bathroom, the pain made her double over.

"Oh, somebody help me!" The intensity of the pain caused her to faint.

"Too late for someone to help you now. I told you not to mess with me. I have been here since the beginning of time. I'm too big of a turd to excrete. You can't destroy me, and you will not betray me. Those who did lived to regret it," Satan said.

He looked down at her. "Let's see how you like this? No power, huh?" He laughed and slithered off.

When Heather finally came to, she was grateful the pain was gone. "I don't know what that was, but I'm glad it's over now." She walked to the sink and turned on the water.

She cupped water in her hands and splashed it on her face. It burned. She looked in the mirror and her entire face was covered with oozing lesions. "What is this?"

She looked at her arms; the lesions were there. Unbuttoning her blouse, she saw they were on her chest as well. In disbelief, she began to scream.

When her voice would no longer permit her to scream, she cried until there was nothing left. She called work and told Stephanie she would not be in because she was ill. Another day passed and she did not go to work. Three days later, she continued to stay inside living the nightmare.

Paul called Heather's house to see how she was doing. He told her that even though she only had a week left to work, she needed a doctor's excuse.

"I can't go to the doctor. I can't let anyone see me like this."

"Heather, policy is policy. I can't make an exception for you unless of course you are willing to do a little extracurricular activity. I still remember that day you were in my office. You don't have to resign. You know what you can do?"

"Gee, thanks Paul for being so understanding." She slammed the phone down.

Heather could not talk to anyone about what was happening to her, but she knew she would have to talk to someone eventually. When Stephanie called later that day, she was relieved to have someone to share her burden with.

"I don't know what's wrong with me. It all started with these really severe stomach pains and I passed out. When I woke up these oozing boils were all over my body. I look horrible. I am so ugly."

Stephanie fought the urge to say what was really on her mind and instead asked, "Have you been to a doctor?" Stephanie was not sure why she cared about Heather after all she'd done, but God had rescued her, and she needed to do the same for Heather even though she was tormented by it every minute.

"No, I don't want anyone to see me like this. It'll clear up."

"You need to see a doctor. It's not going to just go away!"

"I'll be fine, Stephanie. Don't worry about it."

✥ ✥ ✥ ✥ ✥

Montana drove as fast as she could to Heather's house after getting a message from Stephanie that Heather was sick. She rushed up the stairs and rang the doorbell, but there was no answer. She knocked on the door.

"Heather, I know you're in there. Open the door!"

The door slowly cracked open. It was pitch black. *Lord, please don't let this be a trap,* she thought as she walked in.

"Heather, where are you?" Montana noticed a repulsive smell in the apartment. Heather walked out of the kitchen into dim view of Montana.

Montana moved toward her seeing pus running out of open sores that appeared to be all over Heather's body. The horrid smell grew stronger the closer Montana got. She wanted to vomit, but fought the urge. "Oh my God!" she gasped as Heather moved into brighter light. "I've got to get you to a doctor!"

"No."

"You cannot stay locked up forever. You've got to find out what this is. How will you get better if you don't do anything to get rid of it?"

Heather begrudgingly agreed.

Montana rushed her to Grady Hospital's emergency room. The doctors looked at Heather and immediately admitted her. Blood was drawn and tests were conducted so the doctors could diagnose Heather's ailment. Montana stayed with Heather until she was comfortably situated in her room.

"Why are you helping me?" Heather asked calmly as the sedatives she had taken started to work.

"Because you need it. Here's my cell phone number if you need me. I'll be by tomorrow to check on you." Montana walked to the door.

Oh my Lord, what is wrong with her? It looks like what Job had in the Bible. Was that leprosy? Montana said a silent prayer for Heather's healing as she closed the door.

She returned Heather's call later that evening. "Hi, Heather. What's going on?"

"You've got to come here right away! It's terrible!"

Montana sighed. "I'm on my way." *Lord, I'm not complaining but I sure will be glad when this is over so I can resume my life without so much drama,* she thought.

Montana turned off the radio and drove in silence. She enjoyed this time of year when the leaves painted a rich background against the sky. The changes in the color of leaves from golden butterscotch to brick red were so dramatic. She loved watching them fall creating a patchwork path as they rustled under her feet. It made her think of fireplaces and quiet, intimate moments with Garrett. This was not the time to reflect upon her long list of sorrows and regrets. She turned into the hospital entrance and parked close to the building. Taking the elevator to Heather's floor, she walked into her room.

"Montana, you've got to help me," Heather pleaded.

"Calm down, Heather. What's going on?"

"The doctors asked if I knew that I had sickle cell trait. Then they asked if someone in my family had sickle cell anemia. I told them no, but I did get tired sometimes. Do you know those doctors looked at me as if I was stupid? They said it was a disease that only affects African-Americans. I told them I wasn't black, my parents are white. They looked at me as if I was crazy."

"Well, Heather, if you are black, it's not the end of the world."

"It is for me. There is no one black in my family."

"That you know of," Montana said.

"I am not black! This has got to be some kind of awful mistake. This is the worst day of my life. Do I look black to you?"

"Heather, there are quite a number of blacks who look just like you, but in case you forgot, Jesus showed Himself to you. He loves you no matter who you are. I forgive your ignorance and stupidity, but insulting me by acting as if being black is a curse is not the answer to your problem nor is it an incentive for me to help you. Being black is not awful, but being a coward is." Montana opened the door.

"You can't just leave me like this. I need you," Heather screamed.

Montana shook her head and stormed out of the room.

✧ ✧ ✧ ✧ ✧

Heather cried into the wee hours of the night and when she couldn't cry anymore, her body trembled from fear.

"I can't believe this is happening to me. First, these sores and now I'm black. If this is what living is all about then I may as well be dead."

✧ ✧ ✧ ✧ ✧

"You're right. You can't live like this. It would be better to die than be black. Your life is over. It will never be the same. You will be disrespected, oppressed, ridiculed, and hated. No good can come from being black," Satan taunted. *"Look at you. You look like death walking on a stick. You are repulsive, ugly, and you stink. No one will ever want you, especially once they know you're black. You will live your life alone. You will never have anything or be anyone."*

Heather had crawled through the quagmire of depression before, but this was the worst it had ever been. She tried to find some good from this situation, but everywhere she turned, Satan whispered and she concluded that he was right.

This was not living and if it was, this life would not amount to much. She scraped her arm on the table next to her until the metal frame caused a deep gash across her wrist. It was painful, horribly painful, but she did not want to leave anything to chance. Turning over, she scraped the other one until the flesh yielded. It took an extended effort to rip it open as the pain radiated through her arm, but the flow of blood brought a warm release.

The thick red liquid oozed out of her body and she felt lighter, happier. This was the right choice and she was glad he had helped her to make it. The room spun slowly as scenes from her life replayed themselves in her head. Her breathing slowed and ceased.

"Heather, look I'm sorry. I . . ." Montana said as she walked into Heather's room and stopped, shocked by what she saw.

Heather was lying in her bed barely alive. Blood was splattered everywhere, the dense fluid dripped heavily onto the floor.

"Nurse! Nurse!" Montana yelled.

✛ ✛ ✛ ✛ ✛

Satan was disgusted. He did not know what to do. Everything he had planned failed. *"I can't depend upon anyone except myself."* He moved the toothpick around in his mouth stirring his thoughts. He had to come up with another plan, but whatever it was, it would have to catch them off guard.

"You can't touch them," God said.

"What do you mean? I'm not done yet?"

"You are for now."

"As you command." Satan bowed. "We'll just see about that," he said silently.

CHAPTER TWENTY-SEVEN

"Love is like a rice plant; transplanted, it can grow elsewhere."
Madagascar Proverb

Heather recovered from her self-inflicted wounds and was forced to enter counseling. She was in restraints and on suicide watch. It scared her to think how close she was to death by the tricks of Satan. She was more determined than ever to change her life and walk with God. Satan still tried to whisper to her, but every day she gained more strength and was able to resist his influence.

One day while Montana visited Heather, she asked her if she knew of someone who could baptize her while she was in the hospital. Montana told her that she would ask her pastor when she went to Bible study.

Later that week, Heather was excited to hear that Pastor Brooks agreed to baptize her and would be there the next night. After the baptism, Heather became a new person as she was filled with the spirit of God.

The doctors could not determine what disease she had or its origin, but as quickly as it came, it disappeared. Earlier, her blood had shown signs of gross contamination. The serum specialists could not analyze what it was and tried to coerce Heather in taking more tests to understand this mysterious disease. Heather politely told them that her body was not available for scientific exploration. Soon, Heather's vital signs returned to normal and so did her blood tests.

Once Heather was released, she called her mom, Lillian Maitland, and told her what she found out. "Why didn't you ever tell me?" she asked.

Her mother did not or could not answer. She broke down in tears. "I always meant to tell you. I just never knew how. Your father and I really loved each other, and we wanted to get married, but my family wouldn't allow it. They treated me horribly for loving a black man. I needed my family, so I married a boy they approved of.

"I always hoped I would see him again, but I never did. I know a mother should love her children the same, but I loved you more than the others. I loved your father, and I grew to hate your stepfather, but he could always make a dollar and we needed his financial support. I felt I had to be with him and because of that, I could never show you how much I really loved you.

"Every time I wanted to do something special for you that I hadn't done for the other children, he would berate me and call me names. Do you remember when we were going to the park for a picnic, just the two of us?"

"No."

"Well, when your stepfather found out, he almost beat me to death. He had no mercy on me and told me I was worse than nothing. He said if I ever tried to do anything like that again he would kill me. I had no way of supporting all of you on my own so I had to stay. In order to keep food in everyone's mouth, I had to take what he gave. I had to be harder on you than the others because whenever you got in trouble, he would say something ugly about you being a half-breed or me being a traitor and another fight would start. I love you and I am so proud of you."

"You're proud of me?"

"Of course I am. You are my baby, my angel. You always have been. Please forgive me, baby. I didn't know how to give you the love you needed. I knew you were hurting, and I couldn't do anything to soothe your pain. I'm so sorry, sweetie. Can you ever forgive me? Do you think you could come home so we can work things out? I would love to see you."

Emotions attacked Heather from all sides, but she decided to move back home. Her hands had already caused too much hurt to others. More than anything she wanted to sit down with her mom and resolve the issues that were responsible for the destruction they brought to her life. Granted the partnership with the devil was her own doing, but in all fairness her lack of self-esteem and self-love were rooted in her childhood. This formed a destructive mirror image that almost ended her life.

Before Heather left to go home, she went to see Montana.

"I just wanted to come by before I left to say thank you so much. I will never forget what you've done for me." Heather extended her hand. They said their good-byes, parting with as much inner peace as possible.

Montana was tired. All she wanted to do was sleep. She did not return Patrick Peters' call. Stephanie told her that he had called the same day she learned about Heather's illness. Part of her wanted to for Noelle, but the bigger part of her thought only of Garrett. It would take time, a lot of time, to accept being without Garrett, but she could do it. She had no choice.

Guilt attacked her conscious for willingly accepting offers from anyone, everyone to take Chesne, but she was forced to push it aside if she was to complete her mission that was a part of God's will. In the end, Chesne would be the benefactor and have a deeper understanding of how important it was to obey God even when your heart contradicts what you are told.

Olivia insisted that Chesne come over to spend the night with her niece, Jordan, since her sister, Barbara, had come to visit. Jordan and Chesne got along fine even though Jordan was a couple of years older. Olivia was not sure of everything that had happened in Montana's life, but looking at her, Montana looked aged beyond her years. If she did not allow her body to restore itself, she would collapse.

The doorbell rang as she descended the stairs to watch a Lifetime movie. At first, she thought it was a salesman until she looked out her window, and saw the Porsche Targa parked in her driveway.

"Who is it?"

"Patrick, Patrick Peters."

What is he doing here? A wave of fear catapulted through her body. *How did he know where I lived?*

"Mr. Peters, thank you for coming by, but I don't really feel up to entertaining a guest right now."

"I understand, but that's not why I came by. I tried to call you at work to let you know that you left your credit card at the restaurant. I just thought I would bring it to you personally."

"Oh, my goodness, I'm sorry." She opened the door. He looked rather dapper in a burgundy silk v-neck sweater and a pair of crisp khaki pants.

"Thank you for bringing this by, but how did you know where I lived?" She felt the hairs on the back of her neck stand at attention.

"I called the credit card company and told them what happened and that I was trying to return your credit card. The rep admired my honesty and said she wasn't supposed to give out cardholders' information, but in this case she would make an exception."

"I'm surprised they are willing to risk being sued." *I can't believe they would divulge knowledge about me to anyone without my permission. There are laws against this especially with identity theft being so prevalent. I'll have to call them about this. I don't appreciate information about me being given to strangers,* she thought. Montana kept her distance.

"Yes, I understand. I apologize if I've imposed. Anyway, here's your card. I just wanted to make sure you had it." He turned to go.

"Wait, I apologize. I'm not acting grateful, am I?"

"No, I would act the same way. Better to be safe than not."

"I've been running so much that I hardly have time to breathe, much less think. Why don't you come on in?"

"Are you sure? I don't want to intrude."

"It's a little late for that. Come on in."

He was hesitant. He should have just mailed the card to her, but he had to see her again. He stepped inside.

"Would you like something to drink?" *Please don't say alcohol,* she said silently.

"Yes, I'll take water with a twist of lime, if you've got it."

"Sure coming right up." Montana got his water and poured a Pepsi for herself.

"Here you go," she said as she handed him the glass. Patrick sat on the sofa as she positioned herself on the antique chair adjacent to it.

"You have exquisite taste."

"More taste than money, I'm afraid, but thank you."

"Your artwork is incredible." He stood to admire her pieces.

"Once your business gets started, you will have no worries about money."

"How do you figure that?"

"I have a feeling any business you start will be phenomenally successful. Did you decide what kind of business you were going to open?"

"Yes. Why?"

He was taken aback.

"I don't mean to be rude. I just don't like my ideas out there. I know it's silly, but I think if you keep talking about it, anyone in the universe can pick up on it."

"I understand. There's something special about a vision you give birth to."

She nodded in agreement. Her stomach growled softly. "Excuse me. I just realized I haven't eaten all day." It growled again. She grabbed her stomach as if clutching it would somehow stop the noise.

"Are you hungry?"

"No, my stomach just growls for no reason."

"I guess that was a little obvious, huh?" Patrick asked.

"Yes."

"Do you want to go out to get something to eat? He looked at his watch. "There are probably a lot of places still serving lunch. Maybe you could ask Noelle to join us. I would love to see her again."

I knew he liked Noelle. It was all over his face when he mentioned her name, Montana thought.

"I'll just get something later, but why don't you ask Noelle yourself?"

"Uh, no, that's okay."

"What's wrong?"

"Nothing."

Montana didn't know what was wrong, but she was going to make sure that neither she nor Noelle walked in water as they touched what could turn out to be a charged situation.

"Look, why don't we just order something in if you want. We could call Take-Out Anywhere. I've got their number memorized. All I seem to do is work. Eating on the run has become my way of life. It makes for a clean house, but it gets old quick," he said.

"Okay." Still unsure why she had not politely kicked him out of her house.

Patrick placed the ordered and they chatted as they waited for the food to come.

She sat back in the chair and tucked her legs under her, closely watching the man across from her.

"I didn't mean to bombard you and Noelle the other day. I must confess that I didn't come over just to return your card. I know I'm taking a chance, but I felt a connection with Noelle. Maybe I'm wrong, but I felt that she sensed the same thing with me. I wanted to see her again, but the only way that could possibly happen was to see you first. I promise my intentions are honorable. Imagine my surprise when I realized you left your credit card. It was like kismet."

"I don't understand. If you are attracted to Noelle, why are you over here?"

"I came because I was hoping you would put in a good word for me with Noelle," he said hesitantly. "I am desperately shy, especially with women I'm attracted to. My friends used to tease me about being a virgin until I started kicking their butts. I've always been a big guy, so needless to say they didn't tease me for long."

"You're shy?"

"Yeah. I'm a lot better than I used to be, but it comes out more when I see a woman like Noelle."

"I never would have guessed it."

"Most people assume because I am attractive and successful that I am a player. Women hate you, but are drawn to you and men envy you. It's so hard being me," he said, smiling.

Montana laughed. She liked that he could laugh at himself and felt it was an important trait.

Montana admired the person Patrick showed her, but she was taking cautious infinitely small steps. Noelle's best interest was her first concern.

What happens if Noelle is only interested in him as a friend? Well, that's her choice. I personally think she would be making a mistake, but it is her life, Montana thought.

Patrick shifted uneasily on the sofa. He was getting cold feet. "You know this was not a good idea after all. I never should have done this. I'm sorry to disturb you." He stood to leave.

"Oh nonsense. Now that I think about it, Noelle could use some help forming the financial structure of the business. I'm sure she would find your help vastly beneficial."

"Thank you so much. I won't forget your kindness."

"Don't thank me yet. What happens is up to Noelle."

The phone rang and Montana excused herself walking into the kitchen discreetly watching Patrick.

"Hello."

"Hey. What you doing?" Noelle asked.

"You won't believe who's here?"

"Garrett?"

"No, Patrick."

"Patrick. Patrick who?"

"Patrick Peters, the guy from Copeland's."

"Oh, *that* Patrick. Well, call me tomorrow. I've got some kids for you to meet."

"Already?"

"I don't let any dust gather under these feet. Plus, I didn't want the excitement to die down. We'll talk tomorrow."

"Okay, but Noelle, Patrick is interested in *you*." Montana hung up and laughed.

"What did you say?" Noelle asked when she called back.

"I said Patrick is interested in you. Why don't you come over now?"

"No, I don't want to know anymore right now, but call me in the morning, first thing," Noelle said almost excited.

"As I drink my coffee."

CHAPTER TWENTY-EIGHT

"Even without drumbeats, banana leaves dance."
Ekonda Proverb

ontana called Noelle the next morning and asked her if she could come over around noon so they could talk about Patrick and the business. Montana didn't tell her that Patrick would be coming, too.

Montana greeted Noelle with flour coating one hand and a paper towel in the other.

"You're cooking?" Noelle asked.

"You don't have to seem so surprised. I cook for Chesne."

"Yeah, but she's not here. So why are you cooking?"

"Well I thought it would be good excuse to eat a wonderful meal. I've made lump meat crab cakes, parmesan potatoes and a spinach salad with my special croutons. I also made a strawberry cake."

"What can I help you with?"

"Do you mind setting the dining room table? You know where everything is."

"Sure, no problem. I hope this business stuff doesn't take long. I haven't had your crab cakes in ages. They used to be so good," Noelle said.

"They're better now. I've revised the recipe a bit."

"Well excuse me Emeril of Historic West End."

The timer in the kitchen chimed. "I've got to check on the crab cakes."

While Montana was in the kitchen, the doorbell rang.

"Hey, somebody's at the door. You want me to get it?"

"No, just let them stand outside ringing the doorbell all day."

"Smart butt. You know sometimes I hate you."

"Yeah, me, too."

Montana heard Noelle gasp as she opened the door and quickly closed it back. She knew Noelle was shocked to see Patrick standing outside. She chuckled to herself.

Noelle ran into the kitchen a few seconds later. "Guess who's outside?"

"Someone wanting to come in?"

"Stop! This isn't the time for your smart mouth. Patrick's out there."

"Oh, is he?"

"You seem awfully calm about this. Did you know he was coming?"

"I may have."

"I could kill you! You could have told me."

"And if I had, you wouldn't have come. You would've made up some kind of excuse. He's still standing outside. You gonna let him in or what?"

"Oh, I forgot!" Noelle said, covering her mouth. "I won't forget this."

"No, you won't and you'll thank me for it."

Montana heard Noelle muttering to herself as she opened the door. She could only imagine what Noelle was saying under her breath. She wanted to see their expressions, but fought the urge. They needed to talk a few minutes before she imposed.

"Oh, Montana," Noelle said in a singsong voice. "Patrick is here. Guess what? He didn't know I was going to be here either. Isn't that funny?"

"Oh, I'm sorry. I have been so busy, it must have slipped my mind." Montana said as she walked out of the kitchen to greet him.

"That's not the only thing that's going to slip," Noelle mumbled.

"Well, now that Patrick is here, everything should be ready soon. We can talk about business after we eat. Lord knows I can't think unless I've eaten."

"Must not have eaten in a long time," Noelle said under her breath.

"Excuse me?"

"You must be starving," Noelle said.

"I heard what you said, funny lady. Actually, it *has* been a while since I ate, but I'm going to take care of that right now. Would you like something while you're waiting?"

They shook their heads.

"Alright. I'll see you soon." Montana walked into the kitchen to give them some privacy.

Noelle looked at Patrick nervously. "I am so sorry. I don't believe her sometimes."

"Actually, no apology is necessary. I'm happy to see you, but if I had known you were coming, I wouldn't be here either."

Noelle looked confused. *Didn't Montana say he was interested in me?*

"I am, uh, shy around women I'm attracted to." Patrick continued, "I can't seem to get up the nerve to talk to them. The only reason I was able to talk to you the other day was because I treated meeting you as business."

"Oh, I see. Well, in that case, Montana told me you wanted to discuss some things concerning the business," Noelle said still puzzled.

"To be quite honest, I don't think you or Montana need me to explain any aspect of starting a business venture. You seem to be intelligent, assertive and determined women. I think she used that to get me over here. Frankly, I'm grateful she did."

"You are?"

"It would be a shame not to give it a chance since she went through so much trouble," Patrick said. He cleared his throat. "I have something to say, and I better get it all out at one time, otherwise I might never say it so here goes."

Noelle was apprehensive as she waited.

"I am thirty-six years old. I graduated from Vanderbilt University and I have an MBA from Harvard. I've never been married nor do I have any children. I've never been intimate with another man nor do I want to be, and I have never been in jail. I have used drugs, but I don't anymore. I adore my mother and respect my father. My mother gave me the strength to love and my father gave me the courage to use it. I believe you must become best friends to have a successful relationship. Do you believe in destiny?"

"Yes. Why?"

"I don't know if you're dating anyone and I don't even know if you're interested in me. But the first time I saw you, I instinctively felt that we were to be together. I know that sounds like a line, but I would like for us to talk and get to know each other slowly. Whatever happens is fine, but it will be without pressure. No expectations." Afraid of rejection, Patrick swiftly continued.

"I have never had a feeling like this and honestly, I don't know what to think of it. I know how to take calculated risks with money, but this . . . you . . . are out of my league.

"I am notably successful, but I'm not perfect. I have strengths *and* flaws. I know I've caught you off guard so I don't expect you to say anything. I will need to prove myself to you, but I can do that. Let's just start slow, if you're willing."

Noelle had only been speechless twice in her life. This made the third. They say the third time is the charm and she hoped this would be.

"Patrick, I, uh, I don't know what to say."

"Don't say anything." He lifted her hand and kissed it. "Just think about it. If you're interested, let me know. If not, I promise not to jump into the Chattahoochee." He smiled.

Tidal waves of emotion ran through her body. She felt lightheaded, giddy, and unexplainably happy. What was happening to her? She didn't remember praying for him, however, here he was in the flesh. It took every ounce of control she could muster to keep herself from jumping into his arms. He seemed too perfect, but there was one thing she was certain of—suddenly she knew Patrick would be her mate. She knew it instinctively.

They heard Montana walk into the room. "Well, I hate to interrupt this special moment, but brunch is served and food waits for no one." They sat motionless. "Please say you're hungry."

"I've sort of lost my appetite," Patrick said.

"Me, too."

"Well, guess what? Tough, you're still going to eat and you *will* enjoy it."

Montana led them into the dining room. She tried to get Noelle and Patrick to talk about business, but it was like peeling layers of an onion one at a time. They ate silently while Noelle and Patrick seemed to move closer without words.

Montana shook her head and sighed. "Okay, look you two. These are your assignments. Patrick, see if there's a place we can lease that doesn't cost a lot. I would prefer a historic home kind of like my house, but in a more diverse neighborhood. My preference is to buy, but if we can't, we'll lease." She took the papers off the sideboard.

"Noelle, here is the business plan. Please read it over and let me know your thoughts. I think everything is covered, but you'll need to check on the legalities, licenses, company name, business structure, insurance, permits, that sort of thing. You said you had some students lined up. I want to see their work. I'll interview them and we can review their sample designs. I'll also go to the Atlanta Design School and interview additional students. I will get stationery printed and look around for equipment. I'll also make arrangements for security and the open house. I'm sure I've forgotten something, but we can start there."

Six months later, Noelle and Patrick were engaged. Their relationship grew with great depth and intensity. Only God could have orchestrated something so beautiful between two people. Montana could not remember when she had seen Noelle so happy. They were natural and comfortable with each other, and the love they openly showed was formulated from the same cloth as great legendary romances.

Patrick had found a beautiful foreclosed home in Midtown. It did need substantial work, but it was well within their budget and an excellent investment.

Montana and Noelle hired three designers—Alexandra Farrow, Harrison Fordyce, and Cole Porter. Even though they were hired to design the clothes, they willingly volunteered to help paint, clean, and work on the interior of the house. The two owners hired a renovation company to paint the exterior and build out the space that they would give life. Three months later when the work was complete, both owners and designers went to see the shop. Noelle St. Claire was more gorgeous than any of them had imagined.

While Montana and Noelle were out shopping for Christmas, they decided to browse through a new art gallery. When they walked in, they saw a sculpture made of frosted glass entitled *Sisters*. The statue was of two women standing back to back each leaning against the other with intertwined arms as they used each other for support. It was a profoundly poignant piece. Without speaking a word they bought it even though it was a little expensive and placed the sculpture inside the arched niche in the wall. It commanded attention upon entering and became even more exquisite as the illumination brought it to life. It set the stage for the remainder of the shopping experience.

When the boutique was finally ready for its grand opening, Montana and Noelle were nervous.

"Everything looks really nice," Montana said, admiring the décor and food.

"It looks amazing," Noelle agreed, glancing from room to room.

"Who would have thought a year ago that we'd be here? I'm so glad we decided to step out on faith and start this business," Montana said.

"Me, too. And I can't think of anyone else I would rather go into business with."

They embraced tightly with a genuine respect and love for each other. Seeing a flash, they turned to see Patrick with his camera in hand shooting pictures of them. The women did not notice until later that the picture was taken as they stood beside *Sisters*, appearing to be a mirror reflection of the sculpture.

Chesne greeted the guests as they started to arrive and within what seemed like minutes the rooms were overflowing with people. When Anne Weitz, Garrett's secretary, walked in, Montana welcomed her.

"I didn't expect to see you here," Montana said, pleasantly surprised.

"Montana," someone called.

"I'm sorry, Anne. I'll talk to you later. No rest for the weary. Why don't you have a seat at one of the reserved tables outside?" Montana motioned to a host to seat Anne.

"Don't apologize. This is your big day. That dress looks amazing on you. It's good to see you happy."

After Montana spoke with the caterer, she was surprised again when she saw Stephanie walk in. Stephanie placed a package partially behind the counter and attempted to sneak out, but Montana caught up with her.

"Hi, Steph."

"Oh, hi."

"I'm glad to see you. I was disappointed when you didn't respond."

"I meant to. I just had to come and tell you how proud I am of you. I know this is the right business for you. You'll do great."

"How are things at Lafayette Drake?"

"They're going extremely well. Paul promoted me to a senior management position. After you left, things started falling apart. I stepped in to help in any way I could. Paul saw what a good job I was doing and created a position just for me. Can you believe it?"

"Yes, I can. I always knew you were going places. That is wonderful news! I am proud of you. This is only the beginning of great things to come. You'll see."

"Thanks."

"I can't wait for you to see the show. Let me walk you to your seat."

"I would stay, but Michael is outside waiting for me."

"You and Michael have worked things out?"

"Yeah. We're taking it one day at a time."

"That's the only way to take it."

"Have you talked to Garrett?"

"No. Some things just aren't meant to be."

"Or at least they don't seem to be until you change your perspective."

Montana digested what Stephanie said. She was right. "So what's with the package?"

"It's just something I got you as a thank-you."

"Thank you, Stephanie. But why?"

"For being my friend, for loving me no matter what, but mostly for not giving up on me. It means more than I can ever say."

"Ah, Stephanie you know you're my girl. Well, what is it? It's awfully big."

"You'll have to wait until you open it, but you can't open it until everyone leaves tonight."

"Thank you so much, Stephanie. I love you, you know." Montana hugged her.

"I know. I love you, too. Best of luck to you, Montana. I'll see you around."

"Okay. Thanks for coming by. It was good to see you. You've been on my mind, but I haven't had a chance to do much of anything else except this business. I'm sorry I haven't checked on you."

"No problem. I understand."

She looked at Montana and smiled exchanging a warm embrace.

Montana wandered over to the chef and was stopped in her tracks when she saw Garrett walk through the door. Her heart started beating frantically with love, then with anger. *I miss him so much. He looks even better. The nerve of him to show up here! What right does he think he has to share this moment with me?*

He worked his way toward her, but she managed to avoid him by staying unnecessarily busy. She did not know what she would say or do if he approached her.

An hour later, she saw Garrett and Anne seemingly engaged in pleasant conversation. She wondered if Anne had asked him to come.

Montana caught up with Noelle during the last half of the fashion show. "Did you know Garrett was here?"

"No. Where is he?"

"Sitting next to the lady with the silver hair." Montana pointed discreetly.

"Have you talked to him?"

"No, and I don't intend to."

"You can't be rude to our guests. You have to speak."

"Then you speak to him. I've got more important things to do." Montana turned and walked away.

"That girl can hold a grudge. Though I must admit part of me doesn't blame her," Noelle thought aloud.

Montana meandered around doing anything she could to keep from talking to Garrett. When she heard the audience's applause after the fashion show, she turned to see the guests' reaction, and looked directly into Garrett's eyes. They were so full of love and sincerity.

They stood staring at each other not sure what to say. "Good evening, Mr. Rivers."

"Montana, look we need to . . ."

"Say good-bye," Montana said as she walked away.

Montana saw Garrett place a note on the counter next to a bouquet of white flowers. Later when she went to retrieve it, the note was gone and the flowers had been moved to a small table in the corner. She could have kicked herself. Now she would wonder what he had written and there was no one to blame but herself. Sighing heavily, the remorse mixed with regret and filled her heart.

She walked over to Noelle and Patrick to tell them that she would close up. She locked the door and walked down the stairs. At the end of winter, she could smell life bursting forth waiting for the right moment in spring to break through. Turning to look at the store, she noticed how painfully beautiful it was. Immediately, she thought of her mother and felt the familiar sting in her eyes.

"I sure wish you were here to see this, Mama." She covered her face with tears.

CHAPTER TWENTY-NINE

"Love is a silent prayer."
Arabic Proverb

ontana arrived at the shop an hour before it opened to make sure everything was in place. She had done a thorough scan the previous night, but from experience, she knew something was always overlooked and this was no exception. In their excitement, she and Noelle neglected to notice there were no hours printed on the door. She made a note on her to-do list and added thank-you notes, music system, and cleaning service.

Montana and Noelle worked with a few local artisans to create tasteful, yet unique pieces of semi-precious jewelry. These items were displayed in two lighted antique curios. The ambience was warm and inviting, yet relaxed enough to entice people to spend money.

Visually browsing the shop, she saw the package Stephanie left. "I forgot all about this." Pulling back the paper, she gasped. Inside was a painting by John Biggers. Montana looked at it, but couldn't believe her eyes. It was *Jubilee* and she knew how much a signed and numbered edition cost. She wished Stephanie had not spent so much, but she would be kidding herself if she did not admit how happy she was to add this piece to her collection. Glancing around the store for the perfect place to hang it, she decided it would be better suited hanging in her home.

The chime rang softly as the door opened to the first visitor of the day. "Welcome to the world of Noelle St. Claire." Looking up, she saw Anne smiling. "Oh, my goodness, Anne, it is so wonderful to see you again."

"While I was here last night, I saw a few things that I wanted to look at again and possibly try on if I could."

"Of course you can. I'm sorry I was so busy, but there were so many people and things to tend to."

"And you enjoyed every bit of it. You were in your element. Besides, you had more important things to see about than an old lady like me."

"Nonsense. There is nothing more important than my friends. I just wished I could have spent more time with you. I would have loved to introduce you to my daughter, Chesne and my partner, Noelle."

"That's okay. I'm sure there'll be a next time."

"Not that it was a secret, but how did you know about the grand opening?"

"Well, besides it being in the paper, my niece created some of the jewelry you have on display."

"Really? Who is she?"

"Her name is Barbara Weinstein. Do you know her?"

"Are you kidding? She's a member of the Professional Women's Association and the Jewish Women's Club. She and I met years ago at a meeting. It was there that I discovered how genuinely talented and smart she is. Her fabulous designs are so timeless. Look, these are some of her pieces."

Anne was delighted as she glanced at the pieces Montana pointed out. There was an amethyst-and-pearl necklace with matching earrings; amber-and-moonstone earrings paired with a beautiful amber bracelet; and an intricate smoky quartz bracelet set in sterling silver.

"They are lovely. I always knew she was talented, but I didn't know she was *this* talented," Anne said.

"I'm glad to see you're doing well. I've thought of you often and wonder who is going to get after me for working so hard now," Montana said. "How are you doing?"

Anne started to say something, but decided against it. "I am doing fine. I've left Rivers & Associates."

Montana's eyes widened. "You left Garrett? But why?"

"Well among other things, I didn't want to waste any more of my life working when I have a chance to fully enjoy it. I don't want to have regrets about not doing the things I've always wanted. One of my childhood friends and I are going to travel around the world— one country at a time."

"Oh, I would love to be able to do that. You know Chesne would be in heaven if she could see all the places she reads about. To be surrounded by true friends, you are blessed. You and your girlfriend should have a wonderful time."

"Who said it was a girlfriend?"

"Uh, no one. I just assumed—"

"You know I loved my husband. We had some wonderful years together. I could mourn and grieve the rest of my life, but it wouldn't bring him back. He wouldn't want me moping around. Anyway, life is too short to be miserable, and too long if you are."

"You're right about that."

"By the way, how is Chesne? Is she enjoying school?"

"She's fine. Wait, let me show you a picture." She went to her purse and pulled out her wallet. "This is a picture of her when she went to D.C. with my best friend, Noelle, who is also my partner. This was taken last summer."

"Oh, that was the stunning young lady in the copper dress?"

"Yes, that's Noelle."

"Chesne is the most gorgeous child I have ever seen. There is something so special about her."

"It's in her eyes." Montana knew what Anne was trying to describe.

"Yes, you're right."

"I am so glad you came by to see me. I do miss talking to you."

"I'm happy to see you, too, but that's not the only reason I came by."

"It's not?" A lump rose sharply in Montana's throat.

"No. I came to buy some clothes. I cannot tell you the last time I splurged on myself. I've decided I deserve it. I worked for it and who better than me to enjoy it."

"Well, excuse me, Ms. Diva Extraordinaire."

Anne started laughing. "Now if you could show me what you have in a size ... well it used to be an eight, but it's probably a ten now."

"Right this way. Would you like some latte, cappuccino, or coffee?"

"I'll take coffee, please." Anne followed Montana to the coffee station filled with an array of condiments.

Anne prepared her coffee and Montana poured a cup of latte. After repeatedly pouring, stirring and tasting, they were finally ready to walk into the showroom. As they entered, Anne was once again impressed with the tasteful furnishings of the room. Montana invited Anne to have a seat as she pulled out some pieces to show her.

"With your hair and coloring, these would enhance your natural beauty more. Where are you traveling? Do you need any travel clothes?"

"We're going to France. I will probably need a few."

"When are you going?"

"In a month or so."

"France should be somewhat warm then and since most places don't have central air, you'll need lightweight, natural clothing that can transition easily into dinner clothes if need be." Montana chose several suitable dresses and pantsuits for traveling.

"You know, I think I'll take them all," Anne said, hours later.

"Anne, are you sure? I'm not trying to insult you, but these are expensive. Your total is about $4,800."

"I know. I'm tired of saving for a rainy day. I don't think anybody could have that many anyway. My husband and I grew up poor, so we have always been extremely frugal. I guess we could never learn to let go and relax when it came to money. Since his death, I've taken a hard look at my own life. Bert worked and never got to enjoy much of what he made because he wouldn't allow himself. I don't want to be that way anymore. I want to enjoy what I have while I can. Once I'm dead, it won't matter how much I didn't spend, only that I didn't spend it."

"I understand completely, Anne. You're right, you can't take it with you so you should enjoy what you can while you can."

"I'm really proud of you. You act as if you've done this your whole life. I guess in a way you have. I knew the first time I met you that you had a natural flair with clothes. You were so stylish and always looked so elegant. You are a phenomenal woman, and it shows in everything you do."

Montana was touched. "Thank you. So tell me about your 'friend.'"

"Actually, I came to ask about yours."

"Mine? I don't have one."

"You know who I mean."

"I haven't seen or spoken with Garrett since that day, and I'd really prefer not to speak of him now."

"Have it your way, but what you saw in that office was not the truth."

"What do you mean? That woman was all over him."

"Exactly. She was all over *him*."

"And what is that supposed to mean?"

"That woman tried to lure Garrett with everything she could from the moment they met. He told me how she boldly flirted with him and it made him uncomfortable. He continued to reiterate what their relationship was, but she was not listening. She even had the audacity to try to get close to me in the hope that I would influence Garrett on her behalf!"

"Then why continue the association? What difference does it make who was all over whom? The important thing is that he didn't tell me the whole truth." Montana felt the hurt rising to the surface.

"He didn't lie. Besides, he had a good reason."

"There is never a good reason to lie not even for me."

"There is if you're trying to surprise a certain person with an engagement ring." Anne watched her face.

"An engagement ring! He never said anything to me about proposing. We talked about marriage, but that's as far as it went."

"Is it customary for a man to discuss with his fiancée when he will propose to her? I've never seen a man so nervous about picking out stones. He showed them to me once he decided. I must say he did an excellent job. They are magnificent diamonds."

Regret clouded Montana's face settling in the furrows between her brows. The pain she denied from losing Garrett released itself into a torrential rainfall as her sobs rolled out like thunder on a hot summer night. Anne sat beside her and held her as a mother would a grieving child.

"I didn't know. I didn't trust him *again* and now I've lost him forever. How could I have been so insensitive? I am such a hypocrite! Here I was telling everyone else how to be a Christian, and I couldn't even love him as a Christian, much less as a mate."

"I wouldn't say you've lost him forever. If the love is true, it will never be denied. True love will always push its way to the top. Sometimes what you think you've lost is really something you've temporarily misplaced. You've just got to remember where you last had it."

"Thank you so much, Anne."

"We are only human. It's easy to jump to conclusions when the truth becomes distorted. Your desire to have a loyal and honest relationship is not a condition, but a requirement of true love. Don't be so hard on yourself. We are, after all, our own worst critics. You'll be just fine. I pray you find each other again, but if not, there is someone better out there for you."

Montana looked at Anne. "I've missed you."

"I've missed you, too." Anne walked to the door, hugging Montana before she left.

Michaela Beckford, one of the sales associates at Noelle St. Claire, walked in a few moments later and Montana decided to go to lunch. It was a beautiful spring day as she stepped outside and walked along the tree-lined streets to Colony Square. Her strength needed to be fueled by food, and since things were returning to some semblance of normalcy, she had to start doing a better job of taking care of herself. Today was one of the rare days in Atlanta when the humidity was low and the sun felt wonderful.

She walked to the food court and decided on a chicken Caesar salad and water with lime. Once she placed her order, she went to the newsstand next door to buy some fashion magazines.

Hearing someone call her name, she turned to see Garrett standing there in his handsome glory. They walked toward each other, neither saying a word. When they were close enough to speak, Garrett said, "Hi, Montana. How have you been?"

"I've been better. And you?" Montana's heart began pounding like a drum and she could barely stand.

"I really need to talk to you. Can I join you for lunch?"

"Sure. I need to talk with you, too."

Garrett bought a bottle of water and they headed outside. "Is this okay?" he asked finding a table in the corner, but visible from every angle.

"This is fine."

"Montana, I am so sorry about what you saw in my office, but—"

"I'm the one who should apologize. I was rude to you at the grand opening. I never gave you a chance. I thought I trusted you, but I guess deep down I didn't. When I saw women look at you, I didn't want to accept the jealousy that twisted my stomach. I was unfair to you.

"Anne stopped by the boutique and told me what really happened. This could have been avoided if I had loved you enough to let you explain. It's too late now. I don't know if you can do it today, or even tomorrow, but I pray at some point in your life you are able to forgive me."

"I can't say I blame you. I would have probably jumped to the same conclusion. There is nothing to forgive. I wouldn't exactly say it was too late." He unbuttoned his collar and pulled out a chain with a ring on it. "I've worn this since that dreadful day. I guess I always hoped this time would come."

He unhooked the necklace and the ring fell easily into his hand. Garrett pushed back his chair, walked toward her and knelt. As he did, people turned around and pointed.

"Baby, in everyone's life there is only one true love, one soul that is destined to be with another. I cannot live this life without you by my side, and I ask that you not let me. Montana, I have loved you from the first day I saw you and though we have had our challenges, our love has simply grown sweeter over time. Will you please marry me and honor me by agreeing to be my wife?"

He opened his hand and inside was a flawless three-carat oval-cut diamond set in an antique platinum setting. Two one-and-a-half carat diamonds flanked each side.

Montana gasped when she saw it. It was the most beautiful ring she had ever seen. Oblivious to the attention they were getting, she cried with great joy as she looked into eyes, which invited her in.

A simple yes required too much effort to utter. Her only answer was to look at him and seal their fate with a kiss. She was ecstatic as Garrett slipped the ring onto her finger.

The lunch crowd in the courtyard had now directed their undivided attention to the two lovers as they clapped and cheered bringing Montana and Garrett back to reality. Montana blushed as everyone's attention focused on her. Garrett hugged her tightly as their love took them on a flight toward heaven where two hearts rejoiced and upon returning became one as they landed softly on Earth.

CHAPTER THIRTY

"Walking in two is medicine for the soul."
Macua Proverb

*G*arrett and Montana attended premarital counseling with Pastor Brooks who spoke to them about marriage and the roles they were to fill. He stressed that the endeavor they were undertaking was a serious one and should not be entered into lightly for it was a commitment for life. "Marriage," he said, "requires hard work and there are no shortcuts."

"This marriage will consist of joy and sadness, pleasure and pain, but the test will be in loving each other enough to work through the problems. You need to become best friends as well as lovers. If your marriage is to be successful, God must be the head of it, and Garrett must be the head of you," he said to Montana. "You must submit yourselves to God and to each other," Pastor Brooks continued.

Montana had difficulty with submission until Pastor Brooks said, "Submitting does not mean that you are less than Garrett or weaker. In reality, it means the opposite. It takes a strong person to submit to another even though you are equal. Submission means humility not weakness. Montana, you will have much more responsibility because it will be up to you to make this marriage work. It is by your direction that this marriage will become a cohesive unit. Garrett is the head and as such, he is expected to bring the wool home, but it is you who will weave the fabric that makes your marriage beautiful. God breathed life into Adam, but he fashioned Eve. He put his best work into designing you. After creating woman, there was nothing else for God to create. If you read Proverbs 31 you will understand that you are already a virtuous woman," he added.

"Garrett, Montana was created to receive your respect, love, and honor. During intimacy, you are to give her pleasure, if she wishes to reciprocate that is her choice, but not her responsibility. You are to protect her and ensure that she is comfortable. You are in the role of provider, but since Montana works, too, you are expected to also perform half of the duties within the home. She will be your wife, not a slave and no significant decision is made without consulting the other. Montana is your crowning glory and represents you and the life you have provided. Her appearance, wants, dreams, and desires are your most important concerns after your submission to God.

"Each of you brings to this marriage weaknesses and strengths. They can bring you closer together or tear you apart. That decision is up to you."

Montana had many apprehensions that she did not voice. She had not had sex with any man since Garrett, but that was ten years ago, and she was not sure if she could still please him. Had the lack of it made her not want sex anymore, or would the love that she felt for Garrett make it even more special? She was certain that whatever the outcome, they would work through it.

They left Pastor Brooks confident and assured that they would love each other until death separated them.

The future bride and groom ran around planning their wedding, happier than they had ever been. Unlike most couples, they wanted to decide on everything together except the wedding dress. Though Montana had never been married, she did not want to wear white. It was not that it was hypocritical because as far as she was concerned if God forgave her of her sins, it did not matter what anyone else thought. It was simply a matter of preference; white was not a color she liked to wear. Cole Porter, one of the designers, created a striking soft ivory dress that made Montana look even more exquisite. Garrett chose an ivory tuxedo, shirt, and bow tie for himself and they agreed that the bridal party would wear purple.

Montana heard jazz playing softly in the background. It helped to soothe her nerves, which had become raw by the people bustling around in her dressing room.

"I don't mean to be rude, but I need some breathing room for a minute. Please excuse me." Montana moved to the other room with Trenice Jenkins, her makeup artist and stylist, following her. She closed the door.

Once seated, Trenice worked meticulously on Montana's hair and makeup. Montana rarely wore makeup because it felt so heavy on her face. Twice, she tried to touch her face, but Trenice pulled her hand away.

"Look, I have a masterpiece in the making. I am working too hard for you to ruin it. Don't you mess with me," Trenice teased.

"I'm not used to all this."

"But you are absolutely glowing."

"Thanks, but I don't feel that way."

"It's just butterflies. They'll go away. You'll . . ." She was interrupted by a knock on the door.

As it opened, Chesne entered wearing the beautiful dress Garrett bought her during his trip to Chicago. It was a perfect fit now as if it was made specifically for this moment. The slight makeup she wore created a sophisticated look, but her eyes maintained her innocence.

"You look amazing," Montana said, beaming as her daughter held her gaze.

"Thanks, Mama. You are beautiful, the most beautiful I've ever seen. I am so happy for you, for us. I can see how much you love each other."

A few moments later, Noelle and Olivia peeped in. "Is it okay if we come in," Noelle said.

"I should have known I couldn't keep you two out," Montana said.

"Oh, my goodness! Chesne is that you? I hardly recognized you. You look fabulous," Olivia said.

Chesne smiled, broadly. Thanks, Grand Livi."

Noelle turned her attention to Chesne. "You clean up pretty good, kid. Remarkable is actually the word."

"Thanks."

"We just came to check on you," Olivia said.

"And to see what miracles Trenice was performing on such raw material," Noelle teased.

Montana started laughing. "I'm fine, just a little nervous."

"This is the day you've waited for. You better *work* it, sis," Noelle said.

"Okay, so what do you think?" Trenice asked as she turned Montana around to look at herself. Montana stared blankly in the mirror not recognizing the woman she saw.

The person who stared back was truly beautiful and it was the first time she had ever seen herself this way. It was not vanity she experienced, but more appreciation of a great masterpiece that was given birth through the artistic Creator's hands. She was like a queen in a fairytale whose lifelong dream had finally come true. The magnitude hit her and a tear slid down her cheek.

"Girl, don't you mess up my perfection," Trenice teased lightly.

Noelle looked at her watch. "I don't mean to break this up, but you've got fifteen minutes to get your butt to the lobby of the church."

"Noelle, could you help me with this?" Montana asked. The dress glided on easily and came to life as it yielded to Montana's form.

"I have never seen you look this gorgeous. You take my breath away."

"Well, I guess it's show time. Can't put it off any longer," Montana said.

Noelle handed Montana her bouquet and smiled. "Heavenly, positively heavenly."

They walked to the lobby and noticed that the church had filled quickly. The wedding party heard their cue and walked into the church. Chesne scattered the white and lavender rose petals along the way. Just before the doors closed, she turned and smiled at her mother.

Lord, thank You for allowing this day to happen. Please don't let me fall flat on my face. Montana prayed quietly.

Garrett's father, Albert, walked up and stood beside Montana. "You are breathtaking. How are you holding up?" He kissed her hand lightly.

"Barely."

"I can't think of anyone I would rather have as my daughter-in-love."

Montana smiled nervously. Her mouth quivered, but Albert quickly told a joke to ease her mind. They heard the introduction as the doors of the church were opened and Montana started her journey down the aisle. The crowd stood and whispers floated around the room like whiffs of jasmine.

The warmness of the church was intensified by the glow of candles scattered strategically bathing the room in golden light. Lilies, roses, and spider mums were placed on the aisle end of the pews with iridescent purple ribbons edged in tiny ivory pearls. Heavy purple brocade covered the entire width of the stage behind the altar. Satin ivory rosettes anchored the strings of pearls that were scalloped along the width of the brocade and made a magnificent backdrop for the ceremony. Ivory tulle and purple ribbons topped the table that held the Unity candle.

"I'm not going to be able to do this," she whispered.

"You are doing fine. You are a stunning bride. Lean on me if you need to. If it makes it easier, imagine everyone naked. That should make you straighten up looking at some of the people here," Albert said.

Montana smiled. "Now I see where Garrett gets his sense of humor."

Garrett knew Montana was beautiful, but never had he seen her more radiant, more exquisite than the moment he saw her glide along the aisle.

"My bride belongs to another. I can't interfere. He wouldn't let me anyway," Satan said sadly then smiled brightly. *"But what he doesn't know won't hurt him."*

"Who gives this woman?" Pastor Brooks asked. "I do," Albert said then walked over to stand near his wife, Tracy.

Garrett held Montana's arm as he assisted her to his side. He looked at her and was overcome. He bent down and kissed her gently.

"I think you're a little ahead of the script," Pastor Brooks teased. The guests laughed lightly. Pastor Brooks spoke of how blessed marriage is and then said, "They will now read their own vows."

Montana spoke first. "I, Montana, take thee Garrett as my lawful and spiritual husband, to love and cherish all the days of my life. I promise to care for you when you are sick, warm you when the world is cold and be your constant companion. I promise to be faithful to this pledge and our love. I promise to respect you, support you and give you all that I am. I will build our home with love and make our bed with sheets of passion. My life was like a song with only lyrics until you came and gave it music. You have brought days of joy and sunshine into my life. I will collect each of these and keep them in a secret place so that when we are surrounded by storms, I can retrieve them and we can see the rainbows we have created with our love. I proudly stand beside you as we begin our journey of life together. I will honor you as the head of our family and God as the head of our lives. May His love be reflected in our eyes and in our hearts when we look upon each other."

"I, Garrett, take thee Montana as my lawful and spiritual wife, to love, protect, and cherish all the days of my life. I promise to care for you when you are sick, protect you from harm, warm you with my love, and be your devoted companion. I promise to be faithful to this pledge, our love, and you. I promise to respect you and give you all that I am. I will adorn you with riches untold and passion unsurpassed. My life was like a bird that had no song to sing until you came and reminded me of the music that lay hidden inside. You have brought meaning and substance into my life. I cannot imagine living a day without you by my side nor would I want to. You have painted my world with love and when we are old and gray, I shall look at you standing by my side and remember the love that has made us, we. I proudly stand beside you now as we begin our journey of life together. May our love be a beacon of hope of all that is possible with God's love."

Sobs and soft voices filtered throughout the church. "The rings please," Pastor Brooks said. Corbin, Garrett's brother, gave him the rings.

Pastor Brooks handed each ring to its respective owner. "Please repeat after me. With this ring, I give you my heart for it is the most precious gift I have to give. You are the better part of me and I promise to warm your days with my love from this day forward."

They exchanged rings and repeated the words of Pastor Brooks. Tears moistened Montana's face and made it as soft as dew.

"May you literally find the kingdom of heaven in each other's arms. Let your love become the stars that fill your nights and days with heated passion and lasting love. May you both be like cool water that quenches your thirst and refreshes your soul," Pastor Brooks said.

"You may *now* kiss the bride," Pastor Brooks teased.

Montana and Garrett gazed into each other's eyes. The world seemed to stand still for them as if this moment was etched in their memories and the Earth forever.

Pastor Brooks hugged Montana and shook Garrett's hand. "Ladies and gentlemen, I present to you Mr. and Mrs. Garrett Rivers."

Garrett and Montana turned around to face their guests. He kissed Montana longingly. They looked ardently at each other seeing the future reflected in the other's eyes. This union would be like a quilt blending their lives and creating memories that are sealed with the threads of love.

CHAPTER THIRTY-ONE

"No matter how full the river is, it wants to swell further."
Congolese proverb

The newlyweds flew to Victoria, a private island in the British Isles that was owned by one of Garrett's close clients for their honeymoon. It was a spectacular piece of paradise. There was no other place or time except here and now and they wanted to be secluded from everyone to enjoy the privacy that two anxious lovers crave.

They decided to stroll along the beach. The day was like one of God's majestic paintings as the sun shone brightly and the brilliance from the aquamarine water shimmered against the light. The clouds were as fluffy as cotton candy strategically placed on the most surreal blue canvas. The sands were made of the finest sugar cane and warmed their feet as they walked into the painting and became an integral part of it.

They were well hidden in this part of the beach as the rocks formed a natural fence around them. Garrett placed the blanket on the sand and they were grateful to share this moment. The sun glistened against her skin making it appear luminescent. He looked at her with eyes that were filled with absolute love.

She held his face in her hands and kissed him tenderly. His mouth, gentle at first, increased with intensity seeking to fill himself with her love.

Garrett was becoming aroused and Montana became aware that his arousal awakened desire in her that had been hibernating, ready and waiting for the time to resurface. Her breathing became quiet as a whisper as he slowly unbuttoned her shirt and began to remove her clothes. This was their first time together in years and he knew he needed to be gentle.

"You are so beautiful it hurts." Garrett bent forward gently kissing her navel. She shuddered as his tongue began making delectable swirls across her stomach. Soft, mellow moaning escaped from the back of her throat.

Garrett nibbled gently, moving slowly toward the feast that awaited him. Montana's body arched, asking for more in a language all its own. This was the moment she had prayed for, and it surpassed her most exaggerated imagination.

Garrett's desire was becoming unbearable. His swollen maleness developed its own heartbeat as it throbbed with aching anticipation. Not wanting to rush her, he took his time to give her the pleasure she needed and in that giving, he received the same. "Please, baby," she said as she reached her limit.

They were drunk with the wine of passion as their rapture lifted them higher. The ecstasy became so intense, it was almost unbearable as she was swept into an erotic storm. They composed a beautiful symphony and moved in rhythm and time creating perfect harmony.

Each cried out, desperately holding onto the other as moans of delight grew from the recesses of their souls. Montana felt his contraction against her own as they found each other again and again in the private paradise they shared.

The lovers returned to their retreat hungry having expended the repressed energy that previously filled them.

Satan was furious. *"I can't believe he was inside her. He doesn't deserve her. That was supposed to be me. I've got to find a way to get her. It's not too late. It can't be."*

"Flora, would you mind preparing dinner?" Montana asked the cook.

"Oh no, madam, I'm preparing it now. The lobster is almost done, and I'm tossing a salad. I wasn't sure if you wanted potatoes, but I cooked them anyway. The rolls will be out of the oven promptly," Flora added as an afterthought. Montana had told her how much she loved bread.

Garrett walked up behind Montana, hugging her. "I'm going to put something else in the oven soon," Garrett teased, patting Montana on her stomach.

"Garrett, we've got company," Montana said, looking at Flora.

Flora smiled as the passion between the two lovers reminded her of her own.

After dinner, Montana and Garrett went upstairs to the bedroom. She asked him to get some wine so she could plan how she was going to seduce him.

Montana undressed and showered with the almond and sandalwood gel, leaving her skin soft and wonderfully fragrant.

When Garrett returned, he saw the back of Montana as shapely as an hourglass that held the power of his life in its grains of sand. He slipped into the shower and put his arms around her, caressing her breasts skillfully as his fingers joined the shower gel for a slippery ride. He gently kissed her neck and licked the water that ran down her back. She pressed against him as waves ran through her reigniting the fire he had started earlier.

Montana tried to turn around to hold him, but he held her too close. His fingers played with her petals until they opened like an exotic night-blooming flower. Feeling herself swaying, she was swept away by the waves of ecstasy that coursed through her body. She needed an anchor to prevent her from being pulled into this intricate ocean of bliss and yet she wanted to get lost.

He pushed her over slightly as his hands massaged her back. She enveloped him with her love. Garrett tried to control the tempo, but she opened up more, allowing him access to an intensely secret place.

Gentle ripples surged through her. They cried out as they welcomed the release of passion and the quiet surrender that it brings. She was unaware of everything except Garrett and the intense joy he gave her. Montana never thought that each time they made love would be an experience filled with new pleasure that constantly recreated itself to become endless. "Oh, how I love you," she said, wrapping her arms around him.

The next morning, Garrett was energized. While Montana slept, he crept downstairs to make coffee. He walked outside to cut flowers for her. The bouquet was as exotic as the ecstasy they were experiencing on this island and upon their return, they would relive these memories again and again.

He heard Montana come downstairs. "Good morning, handsome. I love you, but you have done a terrible thing," she said.

"What have I done?" Garrett asked worried.

"You have filled me with joy and nourished my spirit with a love that surpasses anything I have ever experienced."

"That is just the beginning of things to come." He embraced her and placed both hands on her hips, bringing her to him. He kissed her gently on the mouth and moved to nibble on her neck.

"You're going to start something."

"Then it's working because that's exactly what I'm trying to do. Anyway, I'm trying to put a little honeybee into the honeycomb."

Montana glanced out the window and saw the water glistening against the sun. She took Garrett's hand and led him onto the veranda. "This is so beautiful. I will miss this place," she said.

"So will I, but we've created some wonderful memories here."

Garrett held her, his arms wrapped protectively around her. "I love you," he whispered.

"I love you more."

They held each other in silence inhaling the scenery and the gentle breeze. Birds sang melodious ballads, as the waves of the ocean became the drumbeats of their hearts. They spent the rest of their honeymoon wrapped in the glow of each other's love.

CHAPTER THIRTY-TWO

"Strong souls have willpower, weak ones only desires."
Chinese Proverb

"Hello," Chesne said in a smile that was the width of her face.

"Hi, baby," Montana replied.

"Mama! Where are you and Daddy?"

"We're about to leave the island, and I just wanted to make sure you knew what time we would be there so we could see you before you went to sleep. Our flight arrives at eight so we should be there around 10:30. I know it'll be late for you, so if you're asleep, we won't wake you."

"I'll be up. Is Daddy there? I want to talk to him."

"Yes, he is. Hold on, baby," Montana said, handing the phone to Garrett.

"Hi, princess."

"Hi, Daddy. I sure missed you."

"I missed you, too."

"Did you bring anything back for me?"

Garrett laughed. "No, not this time, but we'll take you on the next trip. This time was just for Mama and Daddy. Do you understand?"

"Yes," Chesne said resignedly.

"Our flight is boarding. I love you. We'll see you soon. Here's Mommy."

"We'll be there soon okay? I love you."

"I love you, too."

✤ ✤ ✤ ✤ ✤

The flight landed a few hours later. When they pressed the doorbell, Olivia and Chesne ran to the door.

"I'm so glad you're home," Chesne said. She asked lots of questions about their trip, but before she could finish, she drifted off to sleep.

Garrett took her upstairs to bed and kissed her gently on the forehead. "Good night, princess," he said. He looked down at her and wished with all his heart that she were his natural daughter.

"Olivia, thank you so much for everything," Montana said.

"You're more than welcome. I know you guys are tired so I'll talk to you in the morning."

"Thanks for understanding."

"I know what it's like to be married and in love. I also know what it's like to have your house thoroughly cleaned," she said, smiling.

Montana shook her head and smiled. "I'll see you tomorrow, but not too early."

"I know that's right!" Olivia winked. Montana slowly closed the door behind her.

"Where's Olivia?" Garrett asked as he returned.

"She went home. She said she knew we were tired."

"Olivia is so thoughtful and she loves you very much."

"She loves you, too."

"Well, she's getting there, but once she realizes how irresistible I am, she'll be hooked. No one can resist my charisma."

"Please spare me," Montana said.

"Come over here. You look ripe enough to pluck. I'm feeling a little hungry."

Montana smiled slightly.

"What's wrong, babe?"

"Garrett, there is something I should have told you years ago. Actually, I tried, but . . ."

"Whatever it is, we'll work through it, okay?" Garrett said concerned.

"I see how much you and Chesne love each other and there is a strong bond between you."

Garrett opened his mouth to say something, but let her continue uninterrupted.

"Do you remember when we were together the first time?"

Garrett nodded.

"Well, after we broke up, do you remember when you came over and we ended up making love?"

"Yes."

"A few weeks after that, I found out I was pregnant. I was happy and upset at the same time. I wanted to have your child and then I didn't. I was no longer with you, and the child would always be a reminder to me of us."

"Why didn't you tell me?" He held her hands as he watched her face struggle with the burden her heart had known too long.

"I tried to. I wrote a letter to you at your parents' address since I wasn't sure where you were. I knew your parents would give it to you. I also left messages on the answering machine."

"I never got the letter. Baby, I'm sorry, but as God is my witness, I never knew you sent a letter and I never got it. I don't know what happened with the messages. My sister Gwen was evicted and ended up moving back in with my parents. If she was there and saw the letter or heard your messages, she would have never told me."

"Well I didn't know what happened. I just knew I wrote to you and you never bothered to respond. So as far as I was concerned, you didn't care about your baby or me. I didn't have any choice in the matter and I had to make the decision that was best for me. I didn't hate you, but that doesn't mean, I understood. I needed to move on with my life and I could only do that if I forgave you."

"I'm sorry I wasn't there for you. I wish I had known. Maybe our child would be here now. But I thought you didn't believe in abortion."

"I don't. The child I was pregnant with, your child is . . . Chesne."

"It's who?" he asked as shock registered on his face, then a broad smile.

"It's Chesne."

"Thank you, God! Oh, my sweet and precious, Montana. Please forgive me and thank you. Thank you for who you are. If you had terminated our child, we both would have been robbed. Who would have ever guessed that years later, we would be married? I can't tell you how grateful, happy, elated, overjoyed . . . I have a daughter! We have a daughter!" Garrett hugged Montana tightly as if she held his destiny in her hands.

"I hope you aren't angry with me for waiting so long to tell you."

"I can't be angry with you. You saved our child's life. After everything that has happened since we got back together, I would be hesitant to tell you, too. Does Chesne know?"

"Not yet, I wanted to tell you first."

"Besides marrying me, this is the most precious gift you could have given me. I love you."

"I love you, too. Thanks for understanding. I was so scared. I didn't know how you would react once I told you."

"None of that matters. We are a family . . . and nothing has the power to destroy us. We are all that matters—Chesne, you, and me."

Later that night, Montana slipped off her amethyst robe pulling back the sheets. A few moments later, Garrett walked in and looked at her with longing, ingesting her whole. As she gazed back, his eyes were full of emotion that accepted and loved her unconditionally. She could have drowned in them. His eyes devoured her with the lustful appetite of a hungry man.

Their blood boiled hot as they plunged into a vortex that spun wildly. Excitement flowed through Montana's veins like liquid mercury that heats and rises, but does not burn. They were pulled into a sea of reckless abandon where their passion shook them fiercely. He kissed her stomach and knew a little honeybee was forming its own honeycomb. They drifted off to sleep in each other's arms—spent and pleasantly content.

Garrett awoke early the next morning. He shook Montana gently. She rolled over draping her arms around him.

"I'm a daddy," he said, smiling.

"Yes, you are," she said drowsily.

"Don't you think we should let one more person know that I'm her daddy?"

"Of course, I do."

"Then let's go, old girl."

Garrett and Montana walked to Chesne's room. He opened the door and walked in, looking down at her, his heart melted. Sniffing softly, he touched her cheek. Montana walked up behind him, hugging him like an anchor secures a boat.

"Thank you so much, baby," he said.

Chesne started to move. She looked up and saw her parents standing over her.

"What's going on?"

Garrett sat down on her bed. "Hi, princess."

She noticed he had been crying. "What's wrong, Daddy? Why are you crying?"

He looked at Montana who nodded. She knew he wanted to tell her, and she hoped she had not made a mistake by letting him. She prayed Chesne would forgive her for this secret she had hidden far too long.

"Well, I'm crying because this is the happiest I've ever been since I married your mom. I'm crying because I just found out I'm your daddy."

"You're my what?"

"I'm your daddy."

"I know that."

"No, I'm your *real* daddy."

"No, you can't be! Why are you being so mean?"

"It's the truth."

Chesne's eyes searched for her mother's in the dim light. "Mama, is it true?"

"Yes. Remember when I told you that Mr. Rivers and I were in love before?"

"Yes."

"Well, the last time we saw each other, we were intimate. I didn't find out until after we'd broken up that I was pregnant. I wrote telling him that I was pregnant with you. For many years, I was angry with him because I thought he got my letter, but he didn't. I know I should have told you long ago. I should have never kept anything like this from you. I was wrong. It didn't matter if I thought I would see him again or not, I should have told you. You had a right to know. I guess I thought I was protecting you in a way. I'm sorry, baby," Montana said shakily.

Chesne was quiet. She looked from her mother to her father.

"Chesne, I promise you, if I had received the letter, no matter what was going on with your mother and me, I would have been a part of your life. Since I met you, I've secretly wished that you were my real daughter, and I am so glad to know it's true. I don't know how you feel about me being your real daddy, but I'm asking that you not be angry and think about it. I hope you find you are as happy about being my daughter as I am about being your father." Garrett reached out to embrace her.

Chesne reluctantly held him lightly, but before she knew it, she was squeezing him with all her might. "I'm so glad you're my daddy. I knew we felt like a family and now I know why."

Unashamed, Garrett wept like a baby in her arms. "It's okay, Daddy. Now, we have everything we ever wanted." Chesne looked at her mother and saw her step back feeling her uncertainty. Chesne broke the embrace.

"Oh, please spare me. Can I put down my violin now?" Satan asked.

"Mama, I know you did what you thought was best. I don't hate you for looking out for me. Everything you did was because you love me. And to think, of all the daddies I could have, I ended up with the one I wanted and who really is my daddy."

Chesne held out her right arm to Montana who knelt beside the bed and joined them in a loving embrace.

Montana and Garrett had been home for a week, but it felt they were still on their honeymoon. Since they had told Chesne about Garrett being her father, the love they shared grew and became so warm and rich it provided nourishment to their spirits and hearts.

They frequently talked to Chesne to make sure she was adjusting to the dramatic, albeit welcome change. Chesne moved from a single parent household to two without skipping a beat.

Montana reluctantly arranged to move her things out of her beloved West End home into Garrett's. It broke her heart to put the house that had become her home on the market. She had invested so much of herself into it. It was as comfortable as an old friend.

She was sad to leave Olivia, but she knew they would do everything they could to remain as close as they had been. Montana had said her good-byes to Olivia the day before. It felt like she had lost a mother a second time. She had not expected leaving would be so emotional and hoped that the next occupant would be as happy as she was here. The next morning as she left, she looked around the house knowing she could not bear to see it again. She cried as she closed the door for the last time.

Montana drove to her new home. It was a beautiful house and she knew that love would make it a magnificent home. She walked into the house and saw Garrett and Chesne sitting on the stairs talking.

"Hey, you guys. You look tired."

"Hey," they said, smiling.

"We are," Garrett said.

"We were arranging my room, Mommy."

"Didn't the movers do that?"

"Yes, but *our* daughter, didn't feel it captured her essence."

"She's too young to know what essence is."

"No, I'm not. I know what makes me happy and what expresses my inner being."

"Oh, you do? Well, excuse me," Montana said, laughing. "I'm too tired to cook. You guys want to order pizza?"

"Are you buying?" Garrett asked.

"Yes."

"Then yeah, we want pizza," he said.

Montana shook her head. "Do I have to order it, too?"

"No, I'll order it," Chesne said.

"You can't. You're too young. I'll order it in a minute," Garrett said.

Chesne sighed. "One day, I'll be old enough to do everything." She walked into the kitchen.

As Montana watched Chesne walk away, Garrett scooped her up in his arms. "How ya doing, gorgeous? Are you okay? How was Olivia?"

"I'm okay. I didn't think it would be this hard leaving. I couldn't bear to see her today. It was too upsetting for both of us. I know she understands, but she's sad."

"We all are," Garrett said. He hugged her gently. "It'll be okay. We'll see her often, I promise."

"Okay."

Garrett stood and stretched. Grabbing the phone he placed the pizza order.

As they ate, they watched a family movie on Showtime and Chesne fell asleep. Garrett lifted her and took her to bed with Montana walking behind him. Chesne awoke momentarily, but did not let them know. Garrett tucked her in and bent over to kiss her on the forehead. "Good night, sweetie."

"Sleep with the God's angels," Montana said.

"Good-night, Mommy. Good-night, Daddy."

"I thought you were sleep," Montana said.

"I was, but you looked like you were enjoying yourselves so much carrying me, I didn't want to interrupt you."

"Good night, Chesne," Montana said, trying not to laugh.

"Night." Chesne drifted off to sleep again and started to dream.

✦ ✦ ✦ ✦ ✦

Satan looked up and saw her tossing in her sleep. "I wonder what she's dreaming about. There's only one way to know for sure." Without permission, he entered into her dream and became a part of it.

CHAPTER THIRTY-THREE

"Only a mother can understand the suffering of her child."
Arab Proverb

*A*s Chesne dreamt, she saw herself in the dream, but she was also removed from it as though she were making a film. Being the director, she was aware of the thoughts and feelings of all the members of the cast. This was her directorial debut and she had memorized the nuances of every character as she skillfully arranged the cast in actions and lines.

As Satan entered, there was an interruption in the picture and immediately everything went black. When he was able to see again, the scene had changed, but he was unaware and watched absorbing it all.

The alarm clock sounded. Montana and Garrett awoke finding themselves in each other's arms. "This is what you call living," Montana said sleepily as she stretched.

"No, it's what you call loving," he said. He turned and supported himself on his elbow as he kissed her. There was a knock on the door.

"Yes, Chesne," Montana said a little out of breath.

"It's time to get up. I want Daddy to take me to school. I want to show him off." A long silence occurred.

"What is it, baby?" Montana said, regaining her composure.

"How'd you know I was still here?"

"Let's just say, I've lived with you long enough."

"Can I come in?"

Montana looked at Garrett and he nodded. Montana exhaled heavily. "Yes, come on."

The door opened slowly. Chesne ran to the bed and jumped in. "This is great! I can sleep with my Mommy *and* Daddy now."

"No, you can sleep by yourself," Montana said.

"Is there *ever* going to be a time when I can sleep with you?"

Montana saw Garrett's heart melt and knew she was in trouble.

"Sure, baby. As often as . . . well sometimes."

Montana shot Garrett a look and climbed out of bed. "Guess the chance for a roll in the hay is over," she said under her breath.

In the shower, she was quickly awakened by the coolness of the water. "Something else could have awakened me just as well." Montana pouted.

Montana wrapped her robe around her. "Since you got me up, I think you better get ready for school, young lady, and you, Mr. Rivers need to go to work." Chesne and Garrett sat there smiling as if they were cohorts.

"Yes, ma'am," they said.

Montana started laughing. "You two are so amusing. I'm going downstairs to make coffee and start breakfast if anyone is interested. Well, let's snap to it, shall we?"

"Yes, sir," Garrett said.

"Yes, sir," Chesne said, laughing.

As they were finishing breakfast, Montana glanced at the clock. "Time to get going, baby."

Walking them to the door, Montana kissed Garrett. "I love you."

"I love you, too."

Bending down to kiss Chesne, she whispered the same.

"I'm ready, Daddy." Chesne looked at him, beaming like a bright ray of sunshine and grabbed his hand.

"Alright, baby. Let's go." He glanced back at Montana and smiled.

Montana felt a tug at her throat. *Finally*, Montana thought, as she thanked God.

After Garrett and Chesne left, Montana reflected on the power that Garrett had to ignite every aspect of her being. If she did not receive anything else in life, God had already blessed her richly.

She poured herself another cup of coffee and grabbed swatches of material, tucking them into her briefcase before heading out the door.

Montana suddenly missed Chesne and felt compelled to drive to school to see her. She didn't understand why she needed to, but she had learned not to question these things.

Fishing for her cell phone, she called the boutique to tell Michaela Beckford, her sales associate, that she would be late. When she got to Woodlawn it was ten o'clock. She walked into the school's office and asked to speak with the principal.

"Go on in," an assistant said.

"Hello, Joan," Montana said as she walked into her office.

"Good morning, Montana. Is there something wrong? Not that I'm not happy to see you."

"Nothing is wrong. I had to see Chesne. I don't mean to seem like an overprotective, paranoid parent."

"No need to apologize. I understand completely. Sometimes when that feeling hits me, it's so strong I can't fight it. Nothing's ever wrong. I guess it's just the plight of being a mother."

Montana nodded knowingly.

"I'll call her classroom."

Within a few minutes, Chesne came skipping into the principal's office. Montana was so relieved to see her.

"I'll leave you two alone," Joan said, walking out.

"Why did you come to see me? Is something wrong?" Chesne asked.

"No, nothing's wrong. I was thinking about how much I love you and I just wanted to see you."

"I love you too, Mama. I know what you mean. The same thing happens to me, but even more since we got Daddy."

"Well, do you think I could get a hug and kiss before I go?"

"Only if I get one back."

"Um, I'll see what I can do about that."

She and Chesne embraced, and the love they felt for each other sent shivers through them. Montana kissed Chesne. "Remember, how much I love you," Montana said.

"I will." Chesne looked at her mom knowing that she would always cherish the one thing they had between them—love in its purest form.

Joan Abernathy walked back into her office. "Are you guys okay, now?" They nodded.

Satisfied that Chesne was okay, Montana left Woodlawn relieved. Now it was time to get to work even though she knew everything was in order and under control at the boutique. Noelle had briefed her on what had happened since her honeymoon. They still had phenomenal sales, so much in fact, that Alexandra, Cole, and

Harrison had to create more clothes since they never recreated a design.

At Montana's urging, the three designers formed a subsidiary of Noelle St. Claire called C.H.A. Designs. They were inspired by the challenge of bringing something new and different to each project and being the creator who gave it life.

She drove to the store excited to get back to work and thrilled to return as a married woman. Her life was finally coming together. "Thank You so much, Father."

Her cell phone rang. "Hello, baby," she said, thinking it was Garrett.

"Hey, Montana. This is Patrick. I was wondering if we could meet today."

"Sorry I thought you were Garrett. Sure, we can meet today. It might be a little later since I haven't been in the store for a while, but I'm happy to do whatever I can for Noelle. I can't wait to see her face. She will not even see it coming."

"She will probably kill us when everyone shouts 'Happy Birthday.' "

"Yeah. She'll threaten to, but in all my years, she's never made good on one single threat she's made." Montana laughed.

She was driving on Piedmont and had pulled up to where it intersects with Peachtree when Howard Hewitt's "Say Amen" came on the radio. The light turned green. "Oh, I love this song!" She turned up the volume. The driver in the car behind her saw her on the phone and blew his horn, but she did not hear it.

"What did you say?" Patrick asked.

She started to drive through the intersection. "I said I love . . ."

Just then, the driver of a navy Land Cruiser sped through the light on Peachtree and slammed into the side of Montana's car. The impact was so forceful that her car was hurled into the air making a 360-degree turn once it landed.

The man behind Montana jumped out of the car. He got his cell phone and quickly dialed 911. Seeing a cell phone on Montana's dashboard, he tried to reach into the open window, but could not and quickly dialed the number displayed on it. He told Patrick that the person he had just spoken with had been in a serious accident.

"Where are you?" Patrick asked.

"We are at the intersection of Peachtree and Piedmont. Get here as soon as you can, sir, I don't know if she's . . ." Feeling his throat constrict, the man quickly hung up.

The steering wheel was pushed against her rib cage. There was blood on her face and a large gash across her forehead.

The man was obviously nervous. "Ma'am, can you hear me?"

"Yes," she whispered.

"Can you hang on?" he asked with a look of genuine concern.

She nodded, floating in and out of consciousness. She whispered, "Thank You God for the life You have given me. I hope You've found me worthy to be with You in Heaven. Thank You for Your mercy, please take me quickly. Don't let me suffer. Forgive me and take care of my family. If this is Your will Heavenly Father, so be it."

She tried to say something to the man, but stopped.

"You need to rest. I'll do the talking," he said.

Montana needed to tell him something and prayed for strength. "I don't have time for rest right now. I'll have plenty of time for that later, but I need to tell you what God has pressed upon my heart. When God blesses us, He gives us the best. He knows you're going through some things. Things you don't understand. All He wants is for you to trust and believe in Him as you did when you were a child. He loves you and waits for you."

He looked at her. "You need to save your strength, ma'am."

She smiled weakly. "Always follow your heart. It will lead you to God." Then she blacked out.

The emergency vehicles finally arrived and started working frantically to cut Montana out of the car.

Patrick sat there in shock trying to put together something that defied definition. He had pulled over when he heard Montana's screams through the phone. He was unable to react for a few minutes. When his mind caught up, he called Noelle.

"Hey, baby."

"What's wrong?"

"It's Montana. There's been an accident," Patrick said as his voice trailed off.

Noelle asked where she was and hung up without telling him good-bye. Her mind raced as she rushed to the scene.

Garrett was uneasy all morning. He had not slept well the night before. He kept having dreams that he was falling, which disturbed him. He called Montana on her cell. "Come on, baby, be there. I need to hear your voice." She was not at home and he was told she had not arrived at the shop. The uneasy feeling snaked deeper into the center of his being. The smell of roses surrounded him, and his heart started beating erratically.

Garrett needed to see Montana; he yearned for her touch. The sight of her would calm him. He decided to go to the boutique and surprise her.

It seemed every light in Atlanta caught him and he realized he had been anxious since he dropped Chesne off. He tried to ward off the feelings that had him on edge, but he could not shake them. Reaching an intersection at Peachtree, he noticed the commotion and flashing lights. "There *would* be an accident now. Lord, please let me find her." Garrett looked over to his left and almost drove through the light when he noticed someone on a stretcher. The chill of death went through him as he put the car in park and jumped out, leaving it running not caring about the cars behind him. He looked a little farther and saw Montana's car. He pushed his way through the crowd. "It can't be. Lord, please no!"

When Garrett finally got through the barricades of police and onlookers, he stopped dead in his tracks. He didn't know if he could go any closer. "Oh, God, why? Why, did this happen? You blessed me with her and then . . ."

He tried to walk to her side to let her know he was there, that he wouldn't leave her, but the EMT personnel wouldn't let him get close. "She's my wife," he said simply, and was let through. "Hey, baby. It's me. I'm right here. I just want you to know that I love you. I will never stop loving you. You are the center of my heart. I'm coming with you." But he couldn't walk—his legs were not obeying his mind.

The emergency personnel closed its doors once they helped him to his seat and all life was drained from him. He was numb. Looking at Montana, he saw the end of his life. Garrett tried to be strong, but the agony was too intense and he released an empty, hurtful cry. He dropped to his knees beside her, placing his face in his hands and cried. His body was tormented with anguish, sorrow, and indescribable pain.

✛ ✛ ✛ ✛ ✛

The man, who called 911 turned away, unable to witness the pain he heard. Tears threatened to fall from his eyes as Garrett's potential loss affected him as well. Uninvited tears came without warning and filled a once empty well. The driver prayed, "I am so sorry, God. Please forgive me. I know You love me and all I have done most of my life was to blame You and turn away. I'm ready now. Please help the woman who led me back to You. Let her live."

Chesne suddenly jumped when she smelled the faint scent of roses. It took her back to a time not too long ago when she smelled roses the moment her grandmother died from an aneurysm. She shuddered. As she tried to block out the emotions, she was overwhelmed. It was more than her heart could bear. An angel was with her and reached out to touch Chesne's shoulder, but she was too entrenched with her own grief to feel the angel's presence and see the sadness reflected in the angel's eyes.

The kind stranger heard a car drive up behind him and a woman jumped out of the car. He turned around and saw Noelle running up to him.

"Did you see an accident here a few minutes ago? Do you know where they took her?"

"They rushed her to Grady."

Noelle drove at the speed of light as she rushed to the hospital. When she got to the nurses' station, she was told to go to the waiting area and someone would be with her soon. Walking in, she saw

Garrett and hugged him. She tried to force the words from her throat, but they would not come.

Both Garrett and Noelle looked up when they saw the doctor walking toward them and their hearts jumped out of their chests.

"Excuse me, who is the next of kin for Ms. Rivers?" the doctor asked.

"We both are. I'm her husband and this is her sister," Garrett said. Noelle squeezed his hand in gratitude.

"She's asking to see her husband. Come with me, please." Garrett sighed heavily and put on the most cheerful smile he could muster before he entered the room.

"Hi, gorgeous."

Montana looked at him and blinked. There was a mask over her mouth and her breathing was ragged from the pressure on her lungs.

She lifted the mask. "Hi, baby. It's good to see your face. I think I got a little beat up."

Garrett looked at Montana and all the love he felt rushed from his heart to his eyes. His body racked with pain and he could only cry.

"Baby, there's no need to cry for me. I'm going to be just fine. You're not going to lose me. We will always be together."

"I love you so much, baby. I don't know what I would do without you."

"Well, lucky for you, you won't have to find out. You know you'll need to tell Chesne?"

"Yeah, I know. I don't know what to tell her."

"Just tell her I love her. They gave me some pain pills and I'm starting to get sleepy."

"Okay, I'll be right here. I love you." Garrett kissed her gently.

"I love you, too." Montana drifted off to sleep.

Garrett walked out of the room slowly. He was lost. His world had turned upside down in the blink of an eye. All he could think was why.

He saw Noelle anxiously waiting, pacing up and down the aisle. A chill ran through him as he walked down the hall. *I'll be able to talk to her when she wakes up. She'll be better then,* he thought.

Garrett walked up to Noelle hugging her with all his might. He glanced out the window absentmindedly and saw the sky darken as the sun hid behind the clouds. Noelle and Garrett shivered as a chill coursed through their veins causing their spirits to weaken. They knew Montana was dead. They could almost hear the angels mourning.

CHAPTER THIRTY-FOUR

"Death is like a robe, that, at some point, everyone has to wear."
Mandingo Proverb

Neither Garrett nor Chesne wanted to attend the funeral, but they knew it would look strange if the two people closest to Montana were not there. Montana would have understood, but sometimes people were not as understanding or as forgiving.

Garrett asked Olivia if she would come over and stay with them for a few days to help out. She gladly accepted Garrett's invitation. Olivia wasn't going to the funeral, but she didn't want to be alone. Being with them made her feel close to Montana. Olivia had said her good-byes in private. *A funeral is for the living. Only Montana's shell is in that box, not her spirit or her heart. Funerals pull out what little life is left in you,* Olivia thought.

Garrett had not been able to cry, though he valiantly tried, nothing came. The degree of loss he felt was so vast that it was unfathomable. He was going through the motions of living without the benefit of the life that helped him to live. God created his life, but Montana gave it purpose and direction.

Garrett knocked on Chesne's door. "Are you dressed yet, baby?"

"Yes. I'm coming."

Garrett was extremely concerned about Chesne. She had not spoken to anyone since Montana's death. It was obvious from outward signs that Chesne was reaching the end of her mental rope and he was determined not to lose her, too.

They rode to the church in silence each trying to evaluate their lives without the love of a wife and the care of a mother. As the driver of the hearse parked the car, they saw Noelle and Patrick. Chesne ran up to Noelle hugging her tightly as if by clinging to her, she could draw out the part in Noelle that Montana touched and bring her mother back.

They walked in and sat on the front pew. Garrett placed his arm around Chesne and hummed softly until her sobs became silent tears. Chesne's body heaved sporadically then she heard her mother whisper, "It's not time for tears now. Celebrate my life through yours."

The church became quiet as if death had made its rounds and killed them all a little at a time. Everyone who was touched by Montana's life was there even those that had met her only once. Grief and pain hung in the air like fog clinging to the sharp sides of a mountain—thick and suffocating.

Pastor Brooks began the eulogy. "Brothers and sisters, we are gathered here to remember the wonderful life of Montana Rivers, a compassionate, loving woman who knew no strangers. In order to honor her life, we should celebrate how she touched each of us. She left with us an invaluable gift, a piece of herself and that is what we should hold on to. Montana has seen the face of God and is in the presence of His angels. She is home.

"Now it is only natural that we will miss her physical presence but the memories she leaves behind will warm our hearts for years to come. Warm memories of her laughter that melted our hearts and her words that uplifted our spirits will be with us forever. She had the ability to turn the ordinary into the extraordinary. Somehow when you were in her presence, you didn't need homemade chicken soup to keep you warm on a cold, winter day. She did that simply by a smile or an unselfish deed."

Garrett heard Pastor Brooks giving the eulogy, but he couldn't listen, couldn't comprehend the words that were coming from his mouth. He sat on the pew feeling cold and distant. His heart was as black and empty as a bottomless pit. Unsuccessfully, he tried to reach the reservoir that lay hidden deep inside him but he could not, he had grown numb from death's cruel coldness. There was no joy, no sadness, and no breath.

He moved his leg and though his eyes recognized the movement, his mind did not. It was as if it was someone else's leg. His movements were unconscious, automatic responses. Garrett was jolted from his thoughts when Noelle pointed to Chesne who appeared to be sleeping. Garrett looked at Chesne bewildered, wondering how she could fall asleep at a time like this. Garrett gently nudged her, but when he did, he realized she was not sleep, but crying as tears stained both sides of her dress. Her face betrayed her youth and looked like that of a weary old woman. She did not seem to recognize where she was or why. Then a flicker of life showed in her eyes and she remembered . . . her Mama died.

Chesne looked at the casket in front of her, but could not believe her mother was in there. It was too still, too lifeless. She wanted to run up, open it, and shout out to everyone, "See, my Mama's not dead. She has too much life inside her."

It was hard to believe that the woman who gave birth to her, mended her skirts, tended her wounds, or listened to her concerns as if they were large enough to change the world, could be dead. This woman who told her about God and His mercy was the same woman who was at His mercy.

He did not save her, but He could have. God could do anything, Mama said. I've believed in Him all my life. He has always been my strength and help. Why didn't He help her? Who can I talk to? Who will tell me stories about life over a cup of hot chocolate? Who will know just the right words to say to ease the pain when I have trouble finding the words to explain it? Who will tell me that if I always do my best and what was right, good things would follow?

I did do good things, Mama. I did do what was right, but your dying was not a good thing. Tears filled her eyes like raindrops falling into a river, first one drop, then another until it became an ocean and burst through the gates that contained them. Unable to harness the hurt that destroyed her heart and shattered her soul, Chesne jumped up and ran to the coffin, clutching it tightly, clawing desperately to get to the life that had given up everything for her.

Out of breath and drained, she simply clung to it and cried miserably. "I never had a chance to tell you I love you, Mama! I wasn't able to say good-bye. Why didn't I know? How could I not know? Why didn't God tell me? I've done nothing, but love you and Him. Is this the cost of love? What am I supposed to do without you? You weren't supposed to die. Please tell me everything will be okay! I miss you! Please come back! Ask God to send you back. Mama, can you hear me? I love you, Mama! I love you!"

EPILOGUE

"Who builds the drum knows best what is inside."
Borandian Proverb

Chesne awoke from her sleep crying. Her dream was surreal and disturbed her spirit with its cutting-edge reality. She wondered if she was awake now. Satan, still under the influence of her dream, quietly stepped out. He knew he wasn't supposed to invade the privacy of dreams, but a little peek could not hurt anything. If he could not have Montana, at least no one else could since she was dead, and he was satisfied with that.

Garrett heard Chesne moving around. He knocked on the door and walked into the room to check on her. "How are you doing this morning, princess?" Garrett asked gently as he kissed her on the forehead.

"I'm okay, Daddy. I had a bad dream. It was about Mama."

"You've been having them lately. Do you want to talk to someone about it?"

"You mean like a shrink?"

"Yeah or a counselor."

"No, I'll work through it."

"Let me know if you change your mind, okay?"

"Okay."

"Guess who's here?"

Chesne shrugged.

"Olivia. She's downstairs waiting for you. I cooked breakfast already. Why don't you get dressed and come downstairs."

"I'm not hungry."

"But you need to eat something, even a little something. I'll wait for you downstairs. We'll eat together."

Satan watched as Chesne dressed. "She's got a lot of potential, just like her mother, but she's even more beautiful. Maybe, I should have been after her all along. Children are so much easier to persuade."

Satan heard his name and started to tremble. He recognized the voice and hated it when God called him. It normally meant there was going to be some kind of order that he would have to accept. He hated to follow orders from God because it was always about the greater good, not his good, but he knew he could not refuse.

"Yes?" Satan answered.

"Why are you still watching them? I told you that you were not to touch them. It is time to release your hold permanently. I am not allowing you in their lives anymore. You have tried for generations to defeat them and every time you have failed. It is time to let them go."

"I can't let them go. I won't."

"You don't have much choice. You can do it voluntarily or if you wish, I can . . ."

"No, not that. Why do You even ask me? You know I cannot refuse what You have commanded. I hate this."

"You should have thought about that long ago."

Satan sighed heavily. "I promise to relinquish any interest, or hold on Chesne. I promise not to pursue her or touch her life for the rest of eternity."

"You aren't through."

"What do you mean? Chesne is the only one still living."

"Have you peeped into anyone's dream lately?"

"No, I wouldn't do that. It is forbidden." Satan smiled nervously.

God was quiet. "You must release Chesne's entire family, including Montana. I am taking them all back."

"Yeah, yeah. I release my hold on Chesne, Montana, Garrett, and all the generations before them and after them. I promise."

"You know Montana is not really dead?"

"Yeah, I know because she accepts, Jes . . . uh, you know, Your son, she shall never die, but have eternal life."

"Do you know what happens if you break your covenant with me?"

"Yes, I know. I submit them to You and release any desire to possess them. You sure are going through a lot of trouble for these humans. They aren't worth it, but if You want them, they are Yours. I will not break this covenant between You and me for all time." Satan hung his head in defeat. This was the story of his life, but in all honesty, he drew the sword—God only used self-defense.

"Thank you. That's all I wanted to hear. I'm sure I'll see you around again."

"You can bet on it," Satan said, smiling as he scouted out his next victim, but something was bothering him. It was something important. He knew that God knew he had lied, but why hadn't He said anything. Satan slapped the palm of his hand against his forehead. He suddenly remembered. When he peeped in on Chesne's dream without permission, it caused her dream to become real only for him, which is why he believed Montana was dead even though she wasn't. "Damn, I could have had her, but now I've lost her forever! I can't believe I didn't remember. God blotted it from my memory. He knew she was not dead all along. He tricked me." Satan was furious. He stomped his foot on the ground and the earth rumbled. God shook his head and laughed heartily, causing the clouds to part and reveal the sun's magnificence through an array of rainbows.

Chesne finished getting dressed and slowly descended the steps to the kitchen.

"She had another one of those dreams," Garrett said. He heard Chesne on the steps and turned around. "Hey, you made it."

"Yeah," Chesne said slowly.

"Well, Good morning! What's with the gloomy face?"

Chesne turned around. "Good morning." She ran into her mother's open arms. "I love you, Mama. I love you."